iTLSBOK®
iTLS Body Of Knowledge
The Practitioner and Specialist Guide

Third Edition

Profitability with No Boundaries

iTLSBOK®
iTLS Body Of Knowledge
The Practitioner and Specialist Guide

Third Edition

Optimizing Theory Of Constraint, Lean, and Six Sigma Results

Focus
Reduce Waste
Contain Variability

Reza (Russ) M. Pirasteh

Robert E. Fox

14 13 12 11 10 5 4 3 2 1

Library of Congress Cataloging-in-Publication Data

Pirasteh, Reza M., 1956–
Profi tability with no boundaries : optimizing toc and lean-six sigma / Reza M. Pirasteh.
  p.cm.
Includes bibliographical references and index.
ISBN- 978-1-954000-26-1 (alk. paper)
1. Theory of constraints (Management) 2. Six sigma (Quality control standard) 3. Industrial productivity. I. Title.
HD69.T46.P572010 658.4_013—
dc22

2010021466

ISBN-978-1-954000-26-1

Publishers: Reza M. Pirasteh & Robert E. Fox

Production Administrator: Reza M. Pirasteh

Our Mission: To promote operations excellence, and organizational profitability with no boundaries, ethically, in a sustainable manner through learning, quality improvement, and transfer of critical knowledge, promoting individual advancements, organizational, and community excellence worldwide.

Published by Publish Authority
Newport Beach, CA and Roswell, GA
PublishAuthority.com

Printed in the United States of America

Contents

Figures and Tables

Preface

This book is a result of a serendipitous meeting in 2007. Despite different career paths and experiences, we had each arrived at the conclusion that American industry was encountering a continuing, but unnecessary, decline in competitiveness. Over several decades many efforts to improve productivity had come and gone, both because they were ineffective and because in some cases they were counterproductive. We also believed that the situation was worsening because practitioners of the continuous productivity improvement (CPI) methodologies of choice—Lean, Six Sigma, and the Theory of Constraints (TOC)—often operated in a divisive rather than collaborative fashion. Each group seemed convinced that their methodology was the true religion. While they battled over who had the best solution, the competitiveness of many American industries continued to decline.

We believe we know the core problem that caused previous improvement approaches to fail and are concerned that this obstacle will impair current efforts. We also know that when TOC, Lean, and Six Sigma (iTLS) are combined in a unique fashion results improve dramatically. A scientifically conducted study in the United States showed that iTLS projects produced more than four times the benefits of either Lean or Six Sigma projects. Subsequent experiences in other countries have produced even greater benefits. We have had an opportunity to implement iTLS in 15 countries in a variety of operations, including discrete and transactional environments, with phenomenal success. The resulting benefits include significant improvements in quality, productivity, and profitability. We also have developed an understanding of how these internal improvements can be further leveraged to increase sales, market share, and profits.

The book deals with the details of "how" and "why" and is directed at those responsible for implementing iTLS.

Throughout the book we often use both "we" and "I" in describing our views and experiences. "I" is used when describing an experience unique to one of us, although we don't normally distinguish which one. "We" is used when referring to our collective beliefs.

If your intention is to learn how to systematically improve quality, process reliability, and throughput while creating a waste-less enterprise, then you should

1
Productivity Growth and Prosperity

FORD

Henry Ford was an extraordinarily strong-willed man. He believed he knew better than anyone else on almost any subject. His single-mindedness enabled him to achieve many accomplishments, but his drive was also responsible for the decline of the company he built. Ford grew up on a farm near Detroit and showed an early mechanical penchant. In his spare time he tinkered with engines. In 1899 he formed the Detroit Automobile Company, which later became the Henry Ford Company. He built several automobiles but left in exasperation in 1902. The stockholders wanted him to begin selling cars, but Ford was not convinced that his models were good enough and wanted to continue development.

In 1903 he formed the Ford Motor Company with $28,000 raised from investors. By 1908 he had developed eight models and was producing 100 cars a day. The stockholders were ecstatic, but Ford was not. He wanted to discontinue the existing models and focus solely on the Model T. The shareholders sued Ford in an attempt to prevent this change. After a lengthy court battle, Ford bought out the minority shareholders.

The Model T was an instant success. Between 1908 and 1927, when the Model T was replaced by the Model A, Ford produced and sold nearly 17 million cars, nearly half the world's sales. Production increased and the price of a Model T declined almost year after year. The Model T was priced at $970 when it was introduced and at only $290 in 1927.

The rigor that was built into Ford's system has often gone unnoticed. It was probably the first real "just-in-time" system. When an ore boat arrived at the River Rouge Plant from the Mesabi Range, it was immediately unloaded, and within 28 hours the ore had been turned into steel components that were part of a Model T rolling off the assembly line. Even before the super-efficient River Rouge Plant was constructed, Ford was producing cars from iron ore in less than five days, which included the 48 hours it took for the ore boats to transit the Great Lakes.

The River Rouge Plant was Ford's ultimate effort at creating an integrated, self-sufficient river system. In the process, he purchased a railroad, 16 coal mines, 700,000 acres of timberland, a sawmill, a glassworks, and a fleet of ore boat freighters. He accomplished all this without borrowing a single penny.

His river system was so tightly integrated that Ford claimed he didn't own or use a single warehouse. Almost all his inventory of raw materials, component parts, and finished cars were in transit. The only exception was iron ore, which needed to be stockpiled before winter because the Great Lakes froze over, preventing shipments.

Initially, Detroit was the center of the production and assembly of all Model Ts. As sales and demand grew, Ford built branches (assembly plants) in other areas of the country. The production of components remained in the Detroit area, and a tightly controlled system was devised to distribute components to the branches.

In order to make Ford's river system flow quickly and smoothly, 14 standard boxes were designed to hold a specific number of parts. He took it a step further by developing 25 standard rail car loadings, making it unnecessary to count the number of parts in transit—one only needed to count either the number of boxes or rail cars. The average in-process time of rail cars was 6.18 days, which they referred to as the "float." The amount of inventory in the float was known hourly. In order to ensure that there was no glitch in the flow of parts, employees monitored switching at rail yards to prevent disruption.

The same attention to fast, smooth flow was given to production operations. Single-purpose equipment was used to avoid losing time in change-overs. The idea was to keep everything flowing—work was to move to the worker rather than vice versa. The work needed each day was not to exceed what a capable worker could repetitively produce. Tightly linking production plans to expected sales was critical to avoiding inventory building up or falling behind on orders. Production planning and sales met monthly to ensure a smooth flow of work.

The impact of Ford's system was almost immediate and widespread. In 1879 two in eight citizens in America lived in cities, but by the time of Ford's death in 1946 five in eight did. Wealth and prosperity became much more widely spread, and the standard of living increased dramatically. Opportunities for travel and work other than farming increased dramatically. An often-ignored effect was the creation of an agricultural revolution and the near disappearance of the plow horse. Because Ford also applied his approach to the production of tractors, farmers shifted from producing hay to more profitable crops.

Ford's single-mindedness had its downside. In 1914 he more than doubled the daily wage ($2.34 to $5.00) while reducing the workday from nine to eight hours. His motivation was twofold—he wanted to get the very best workers and to create more buyers for the Model T. However, his basic attitude toward workers was that their contribution was primarily physical—they were to do the proscribed work, not contribute to how it could be done better. In 1932, in the depths, of the Great Depression, he lowered the daily rate to $4 (it had climbed to $7 in 1919). When the workforce attempted to unionize, he employed an array of underhanded efforts to thwart it. It wasn't until 1941 that he finally, with great reluctance, became the last of the Big Three automotive companies to sign a labor agreement with the United Auto Workers (UAW).

Ford was totally convinced that he knew more about the market than anyone else. Despite important improvements in the automobiles of his competitors, he held firmly to the basic design of the Model T. For instance, he continued to use planetary gear transmissions rather than conventional gear shifts, mechanical brakes rather than hydraulic ones, a four-cylinder engine instead of those with six or eight cylinders, and black paint rather than many colors. This reluctance to change caused the eventual decline of Ford Motor Company. Within a few years after the Model T was discontinued, Ford fell from the unquestioned industry leader to third place.

SLOAN

On the surface it may not be immediately apparent how cost-accounting procedures and thinking transitioned from enabling sound economic decisions to causing destructive ones. We've tried to illustrate what happened when the majority of costs involved in these procedures changed from mostly variable to mostly fixed. We've used the ratios for material, labor, and overhead costs that were prevalent at GM early in Sloan's era and those that were more common to GM's cost structure near the turn of the century. These percentages will not necessarily represent those that exist in the reader's company, but we believe they are representative of the shift that occurred since cost-accounting management become the dominant way of making many economic decisions.

Product Pricing

One of the early applications of cost accounting was as an aid in pricing products. At the start, when the majority of a product's cost varied directly with volume, the cost of product could have been represented as shown in Table 1.1.

Because 90% of the costs in this example vary directly with volume, it is a good representation of the product's cost regardless of volume. A selling price of greater than $1000 would both cover the variable costs and contribute to overhead and profit—the higher the price, the greater the profit for that product. However, if the product commands only a price of $800, it should be discontinued because the out-of-pocket variable costs are $900.

Table 1.1 Product costs when most costs are variable.

Cost category	% of product cost	Cost	Cost variable?
Material	55%	$550	Yes
Labor	35%	$350	Yes
Overhead	10%	$100	No
Total	100%	$1000	

However, when the percentage of the three cost components changed and became less variable, the use of fully burdened product costs often resulted in uneconomic decisions, even though the total product cost remained the same. Now, even at an $800 selling price, it would make sense to retain the product since the total variable costs that would disappear are now between $350 and $450. Even a product with a negative margin contributes to the absorption of overhead costs. If the product is dropped, this contribution disappears and the overhead allocated to the remaining products increases. We have seen many examples where companies "rationalized" product lines only to find that profits declined rather than increased (Table 1.2).

Investment Decisions

When the majority of a product's cost varies directly with volume, sound equipment investment decisions are a straightforward proposition. In the following example, approximately 90% of the costs vary directly with volume (Table 1.3). If an equipment investment opportunity reduced these costs in half, the product cost would be reduced to $500, with about $50 associated with the allocation of overhead, a questionable savings. If the overhead cost didn't change, the real savings would be $450, a very small difference. If the volume of production were known, the total savings could be compared to the required investment and a return on the

Table 1.2 Product costs when most costs are not variable.

Cost category	% of product cost	Cost	Cost variable?
Material	35%	$350	Yes
Labor	10%	$100	????
Overhead	55%	$550	No
Total	100%	$1000	

Table 1.3 Investment decisions when most costs are variable.

Cost category	% of product cost	Cost	Cost variable?
Material	55%	$550	Yes
Labor	35%	$350	Yes
Overhead	10%	$100	No
Total	100%	$1000	

investment could be calculated. If the return met the company's investment criteria and sufficient capital were available, it would be a good investment.

The use of the same procedure that produced sound economic decisions when most of the costs were variable now results in an unsound economic decision when a much smaller portion of a product's cost vary with volume.

In the cost structure at the end of the last century, the only real savings are probably $350 for materials, which would result in savings on only $175/part, not $500. Such a difference would have a huge impact on the return on investment (ROI) and be the demise of many proposed investments. Yet the same procedure in calculating savings and ROI continues to be used today, which assumes that the product cost is reduced by $500 (Table 1.4).

It may seem difficult to believe that his procedure could have been widely misused. However, even a cursory review of the ROI of manufacturing companies suggests that this misuse is widespread. Over the years, manufacturing companies have made large investments in new equipment and facilities. Typically at least a three-year payback is required, a 33% minimum return. Since the ROI of such companies was approximately half that rate before these investments, we should expect that the company's ROI should rise over time. The sad fact is that for the most part they have remained flat or declined.

Table 1.4 Investment decisions when most costs are not variable.

Cost Category	% of product cost	Cost	Cost variable?
Material	35%	$350	Yes
Labor	10%	$100	????
Overhead	55%	$550	No
Total	100%	$1000	

Table 1.5 Make vs. buy decisions when most costs are variable.

Cost Category	% of product cost	Cost	Cost variable?
Material	55%	$550	Yes
Labor	35%	$350	Yes
Overhead	10%	$100	No
Total	100%	$1000	

Make vs. Buy

In this example, $900 of the $1000 product cost is totally variable. If the product could be purchased for $800, the company probably should do so since at least $900 of costs would disappear (Table 1.5).

Using exactly the same procedure but with a different cost structure, the answer would be to continue making the product until the purchase price dropped to at least $450 (Table 1.6).

I experienced a real-life example of how cost-accounting principles resulted in a bad decision at a major automobile company. The company had an opportunity to produce a small clutch for a Japanese competitor. It had all of the necessary equipment, manpower, and know-how to make the product. A small expenditure was needed for some specialized tooling. The Japanese company had told the automobile company that it needed 50,000 clutches the first year, but that the volume would grow substantially in future years. The automotive company also received strong indication that if its price were between $5 and $6 it would win the contract. A standard cost analysis is shown in Table 1.7.

The reality of the situation was that the only out-of-pocket costs to produce the clutch were for materials and tooling. The labor to make the product was available at no cost—they were currently in training and make-work programs because the union agreement prevented layoffs. The management, equipment, and space were also available at no additional cost. When the manufacturer presented its case to the financial group, it was informed that it could not bid one

Table 1.6 Make vs. buy decisions when most costs are not variable.

Cost category	% of product cost	Cost	Cost variable?
Material	35%	$350	Yes
Labor	10%	$100	??????
Overhead	55%	$550	No
Total	100%	$1000	

Table 1.7   Standard costs of clutches.

	STD cost	Out of pocket cost	Profit/unit @ $5.00
Material	$1.26	$1.26	
Labor	$0.82		
Tooling	$0.12	$0.12	
Overhead	$4.21		
Total	$6.41	$1.38	$5.03

penny below the standard cost. As a result, the company missed an opportunity to earn over $250,000 in just the first year.

If this were an isolated example, it would be one thing; unfortunately we have seen thousands of such decisions that made no economic sense but were made because the manner in which the cost of a product was calculated.

The final and most devastating impact of cost-accounting thinking is how it values inventories. It employs a value-added concept that assumes that as raw materials are processed, the labor and overhead associated with the processing should be added to the raw material cost in determining the standard cost of the product and associated inventories. This means that as the level of finished goods increases, a portion of the increase occurs because of the labor and overhead included in the product cost. When these costs are included in inventory (capitalized), they are excluded from the calculation of profit for that period. When these inventories increase, the reported profit for that period also increases. The opposite happens when the inventory is reduced. The labor and overhead that had previously been capitalized are included as additional expense in the calculation of net profit. When managers are rewarded based on net profits, the temptation to inflate profits by increasing inventories is often unavoidable.

The following example illustrates how a 10% increase and decrease in inventories affects the bottom line.

	Year 1	Year 2	Year 3
	FGI $10,000,000	$11,000,000	$10,000,000
Std. cost of FGI		$1,000,000 increase	$1,000,000 decrease
Material	35%	$350,000	($350,000)
Labor	10%	$100,000	($100,000)
Overhead	55%	$550,000	($550,000)
Amount Capitalized		$650,000	($650,000)

In year 2, profits are artificially increased by \$650,000 because the labor and overhead expenses that were actually incurred are excluded from the calculation of the net profit—they were capitalized. In year 3, profits artificially fell by \$650,000 because the expenses that were capitalized in year 2 were added to those in year 3. If you were the manager whose bonus was based on net profit, would you want to increase or decrease inventory? When the "system" drives misguided behavior, we should fix the system, not criticize the managers.

Cost-accounting management made an enormous contribution to growth, wealth, and prosperity in its early years. It also caused changes that eventually led to destructive rather than constructive decisions. The most devastating example we are aware of occurred as the result of a highly successful experiment. An automobile company experimented with a different way of providing its cars to dealers. In one state, it shipped a portion of the cars that dealers ordered to a central distribution point rather than directly to the dealers, although the dealers continued to own the inventory. The dealers maintained smaller inventories on their lots, but with enough variety that consumers could see and drive all models. If the consumer wanted to purchase a car with features not available on the lot, the dealer could check the central distribution point to see whether the desired car could be available in a day or two. If it were available, it would be shipped and a sale made. The distribution center also had some capability to modify its cars to fit the buyer's specific needs, such as changing the seats, audio systems, and the like, making it even more likely that the exact car the buyer wanted could be made available.

The experiment was a great success; inventories and shipping costs were significantly reduced. Most important, sales rose because more consumers could quickly get the exact car they wanted. So why didn't the car company make it standard practice for all its models? The simple reason was that such a system would significantly reduce the amount of cars held by dealers, which meant a one-time drop in sales to dealers, even though sales to consumers would increase. Such an inventory reduction would have temporarily reduced the car company's profits when it was implemented. Fearful of Wall Street's reaction, it decided not to implement this system company wide.

The decline of U.S. automobile industry has been well chronicled and a variety of reasons suggested for this erosion. Unfortunately, little attention has been given to the role of cost accounting, which makes it difficult for other companies to avoid repeating the same mistakes.

OHNO

At one point in our journey, Eli Goldratt and I met with Taiichi Ohno in a Chicago hotel room. When you are communicating through a translator, the initial exchanges are somewhat slow, but it quickly became clear that the atmosphere was one of mutual respect and that there was a desire for an exchange of ideas. We had some insight into Ohno's thinking since we had read a dog-eared bootleg translation of a manuscript, he had written describing his approach. Several years later, a refined version was published in the United States.

At that time a variety of reasons for Japan's success were being bandied about. At a macro level, the reasons ran the gamut from low wages to favorable exchange rates to a highly dedicated workforce. While there was some truth to these reasons, the Japanese continued to increase their leadership in the automotive and a number of other industries even as these factors became less and less important.

At a micro level there were other perceptions. Consultants who visited Japan in the early days reported that the Japanese were using practices that differed from those widely used in the Western world. These practices encompassed a wide range of disparate activities, from fast changeover of equipment, to allowing workers to stop production lines when there was a problem, to an intense focus on quality and eliminating waste, to the use of just-in-time and kanban techniques to manage the flow of production. Even when they became well documented, there didn't seem to be any overarching philosophy to the Toyota Production System.

However, Ohno's paper hinted at an overall approach. It was notable that it barely mentioned those specific micro techniques and didn't even refer to the macro reasons ascribed for their success. He emphasized at great length the measurements needed to make his system work, a factor not widely reported on by our Japanese experts. Consequently, we were looking forward to gaining a much better understanding of why his system worked so well.

Early on in the conversation we asked Ohno, "Why does your system work so well?" He surprised us by replying, "I don't know. I have asked some economists the same question, but they have never given me a good answer. I just kept trying different things. Those that worked I kept, those that didn't I discarded."

He did indicate a willingness to share what had worked. He said that several years ago this conversation would not have possible, but today he felt his company and other companies in Japan were now strong enough to compete globally even if some of the secrets for their success became widely known.

Ohno expanded on this thought by providing some history. He said, "I had this idea of a fast, even-flowing river in which there were no dams that slowed the flow or rapids that sped it up. After the end of World War II, I began developing my system. It was to be a river system where ideally the only materials flowing were those needed for cars that customers were now buying. There would be no unneeded parts, yet we would always have the parts that were needed.

"I started first in our assembly plant. It is here that we assemble both the major components and the final automobile. It was not an easy task since we were forced to figure out how to make different models on the same assembly line. We simply could not afford to build plants that were super-efficient at producing a single model like our Western competitors. We also could not afford to build cars that customers were not buying. We were forced to develop a very flexible mixed-model assembly process, one that was closely synchronized to customer purchases.

"We were deathly afraid of building an inventory of unsold cars since that could cause a deep cutback in our production schedules and employment. Ever since our bloody strike in the 1950s we had committed ourselves to avoiding layoffs. The assembly plant had to be flexible and responsive and produce only the models that customers were buying. This restriction caused us to limit the options available on our cars. Too many options would have introduced additional complexity into my river system. You Americans did the opposite and offered more and more options, which made me happy because I knew it would make your production system more costly and inefficient. It took us many years, but eventually we made a mixed-model system work in the assembly plants.

"We then moved to our machine shop, which proved to be even more difficult. The parts needed for the various models were often quite different, which meant the machines making these parts needed to be very flexible. Unfortunately they were not. The machines were designed to work like yours. They could produce a single part at a time in a highly efficiently manner. As an example, a big press uses a die to make a specific part, like a fender. But since the fenders on all cars are not the same, you need many different dies. We had to devise ways to change these dies very quickly in order to be synchronized with the mixed-model assembly schedule. When we started it took more than an eight-hour shift for a skilled setup person to reset a press to make a different part. Today we can do it in minutes, and the people do not have to be so highly skilled.

"We needed to make such improvements on many types of machines. The biggest obstacle was not in finding ways to change over the machines quickly. It was in convincing our managers and workers that they should operate in this fashion. Once someone finished setting up a machine, they wanted to produce as many parts as possible—that was the efficient way. I had many struggles to persuade people that it may be efficient for that machine, but it was very inefficient for my river system. In the end it would create a lot of waste—wasted material, time, and effort in making parts that might never be used. Our people always looked at efficiency from their narrow viewpoint. I was looking at it from the viewpoint of the company. It was a long struggle, but we eventually made the river system work in the machine shop.

"We then called our vendors and showed them what we had done. We asked them to build similar river systems that synchronized with ours. We did not impose it on them; instead we offered to assist them in their efforts. It took time for them to adapt, but eventually many became very proficient at synchronizing their production with ours.

"Making my river system flow smoothly and rapidly took nearly 40 years of continued, incremental improvement. I knew that waste both slowed down and interrupted the flow. We identified seven types of waste, which we call muda. One of the most important and difficult wastes to eliminate was the waste of producing more than we needed. The idea of producing efficiently continually caused us to produce more than necessary. This was a tremendous waste of materials, manpower, equipment, and space. It also blocked us from producing what was needed.

"The biggest source of this waste was the belief we could accurately predict or forecast what was going to be needed. I did not believe this was possible. Customer tastes change, and if we tried to produce cars based on these predictions, we would both produce products that they didn't want and fail to produce the ones that they did. It seemed to me that it would be better to have a system that reacted quickly to what people were buying rather than try to forecast what they might buy in the future.

"In 1973 when the first oil crisis occurred, many Japanese companies were badly hurt. At Toyota it only caused a small pause in our continued improvement. Other Japanese companies, in particular our competitors, asked how we accomplished this miracle. We invited them to visit our company and showed them what we had done. Several of them decided to copy our approach, and we were happy to assist them.

"In 1978 a second, but less severe, oil crisis occurred. This time it didn't have any impact on our continued improvement. As a result, more Japanese companies wanted to know about our system. Again, we were very open in explaining it and assisting them in copying our process."

Ohno paused, as if to consider his next words, and then said, "I'm proud to be Japanese and I wanted my country to succeed. I believed my system was a way that could help us become a modern industrial nation. That is why I had no problem with sharing it with other Japanese companies, even my biggest competitors. But I was very, very concerned that you Americans and the Europeans would understand what we were doing, copy it, and defeat us in the marketplace."

He went on to say that when Americans and Europeans came to visit Toyota that he did his best to confuse them as to why Toyota was so successful. He said, "I explained it by talking about techniques, like quicker machine setups, reduction of the seven wastes (muda), and other techniques with Japanese names like kanban and kaizen. I did my best to prevent the visitors from fully grasping our overall approach. Today I am ready to be open and explain fully what we did. We are now strong enough to deal with any competition."

He elaborated on why his river system was a much more efficient way to make automobiles and many other products. "We have tried to tie all activities and improvement efforts directly to the sales of our cars. That way all the materials we purchase and all the activities we do to convert those materials are expended on cars that get sold. It is impossible to predict exactly what models our customers will purchase so we tie our river system as closely as possible to what they are buying. In that way very little material and effort is wasted.

"The opposite happens when you try to predict or forecast how many of each model you should produce. You Americans schedule your assembly plants based on a forecast that you know will be incorrect. You and your vendors order materials, produce parts, and assemble cars based on this forecast. If you produce too many of one model then you have to reduce the price at the end of the model year in order to sell it. At the same time you lose sales of cars that customers want to buy because you cannot produce enough of them. These are enormous wastes. Why does it occur? You have superefficient assembly plants, but a very inefficient, wasteful system.

"The problem is even worse for your component plants and their vendors. Since your supply chain is long and not as closely linked as ours, there is a great tendency to overreact and underreact. First you order materials and make products based on the cars you are producing, not those that are selling. When you discover that sales are less than predicted, the car companies and their vendors have already purchased materials and produced parts that will never get used, a huge waste. At the same time they have to continually expedite other parts and materials at great cost. I think this helps make the airlines and trucking industries profitable by causing your suppliers to regularly ship materials at premium rates."

We absorbed and agreed with Ohno's philosophy of closely tying customer demand to all the supply chain activities, since we were espousing a similar approach. We did marvel at the incredible persistence he displayed in achieving it. However, we were curious as to whether or not he encountered the same obstacle we constantly faced in trying to achieve similar results. We asked him, "How do cost accountants in Japan think? Do they believe strongly in local efficiencies, making big batches in order to save changing over equipment and the like?"

When the question was translated, the mood in the room changed dramatically. Ohno became very agitated and waved his arms and pounded the table during his response. While he was not completely bald, his hairline had receded considerably. When he began his response, he began to get red around the collar and by the time he had finished it the top of his head was red.

We were aghast at the change in his attitude and feared that our question had been mistranslated and had somehow deeply offended him. However, once his reply was translated, we realized it was not the case. He said, "You have touched my rawest nerve. The cost accountants in Japan think just like they do in the Western world. They believe in all those things you mentioned and many more that are at odds with my river system. These beliefs were the biggest obstacle I had to overcome."

Having routinely faced the same obstacle, we were intrigued and asked, "How did you manage to do it? How did you overcome this huge obstacle?" His reply was most interesting and helped dispel some other myths we had heard about Japan. He said, "First I kept the cost accountants out of my plants, but I found that was not a solution. I needed to keep these ideas out of the minds of my people. It wasn't the cost accountants that were the problem, but all of these ideas about the efficiency of an operation. They were contrary to my desire to create an efficient system. I spent many years trying to persuade people to think differently, but without much success."

Having tried many approaches to educate and convince managers to replace such local measures with more global ones, we were eager to understand how Oho had done it. We asked, "So how did you do it?" He replied with a sly smile, "I used a gun! I literally would shoot people if they didn't follow my direction. It was brutal, but eventually it worked." We smiled to ourselves recalling the difficulties we had faced in similar efforts. We also realized the Japanese approach to "consensus decision making" didn't always work.

We told Ohno that we were in complete agreement with his approach of closely connecting customer desires with a short, responsive supply chain. We also related several stories of our own encounters with cost-accounting obstacles and how they inhibited this process.

We did say that few in America believed that this was the reason for Japan's success and that most believed it was because of the quality of your products. We indicated that this belief was reinforced by a widely viewed two-hour Sunday night TV special, "Why Japan Works." The essence of the program was Japan's commitment to improving quality by adhering to the principles of Dr. W. Edwards Deming. We told him that this TV program helped inspire the Total Quality Movement (TQM), slogans like "Quality is Job One" and the spending of untold amounts of money to improve the quality of products.

We asked Ohno if he viewed quality as the most important factor and whether it was "Job One" at Toyota. I remember him smiling and saying, "There are two reasons we try to improve quality. If our product is better more people will buy it. Also, bad quality causes big disruptions in my river system. If a car must be returned to the dealer for repair, it disrupts the flow of my river system. The river system is supposed to flow only forward, not loop backward.

"When something in our assembly plants or machine shops needs to be scrapped or reworked it disrupts and slows the flow, it is a big waste. Eliminating these disruptions reduces the cost of making a car and assures that we have a better product. Improving quality wasn't our primary focus. We tried to remove everything that disrupted achieving a fast-flowing river system. Machines that break down and workers that are absent also disrupt the flow. We had to reduce all types of disruptions to make our river flow quickly and smoothly.

"When the experts from your country visited, they noticed that our machines were very dependable, our quality was high, and that we had few people absent. I understand that many went back to your country and suggested you implement preventative maintenance programs, quality circles, and other programs in order to copy our results. I do not think that they understood why we did these things, which might explain why these changes often weren't very helpful. I tried to prevent them from understanding why we wanted a river system, and I think I was successful."

After Ohno had finished his explanation of the Toyota Production System, he asked, "Do you agree with what I wanted to do and how I went about it?" We conferred for a brief moment, since we had such enormous respect for Ohno and what he had accomplished. His system changed the economics of the world and those changes continue to this day. Finally, we responded, "We couldn't agree more with what you were trying to do, but respectfully we would like to suggest that there may have been a faster way to get there. Let us use a small diagram to illustrate."

On a sheet a paper I drew a picture (Figure 1.1):

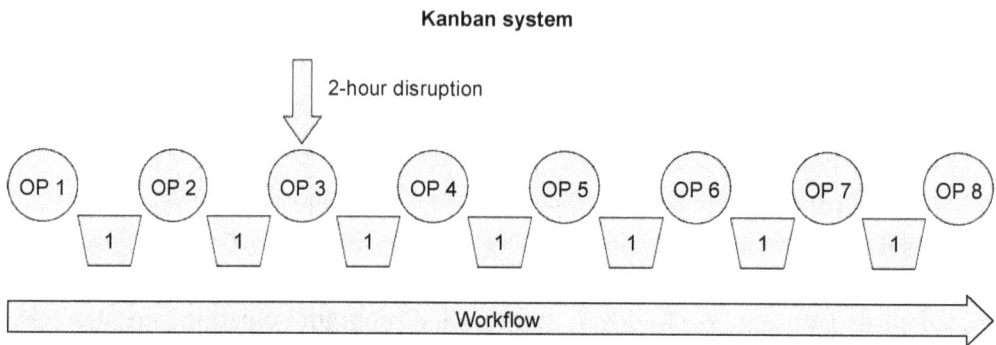

Figure 1.1 Kanban system.

We explained the diagram: "The circles represent different operations in making a product. The small piles between the circles represent inventories. In your kanban system the size of these piles may vary. For ease of illustration we're suggesting that each pile represents one unit of time; it could be one hour, one shift, or one day depending on how far you have refined your system. As we understand your kanban technique, which is how you control your river system, these piles are not allowed to exceed a predetermined size.

"In this example, we'll assume that their size is one hour. When the inventory pile following an operation has one hour of work, the preceding operation is supposed to stop producing. Let's assume the last operation directly feeds the marketplace. Whenever it processes material, the preceding inventory pile drops below one hour, causing the feeding operation to replenish it, which, in turn, causes all prior operations do the same thing in a delayed lock step. The status of the inventory piles is the signal for the preceding operation to either produce more products or stop producing.

"Now, as you well know, there are always disruptions in the flow of materials. Despite your 40 years of effort to reduce them, they still happen even today. Machines do break down, parts are not always within specifications, and people make mistakes. If we have a two-hour disruption at operation 3, then the following operation will be starved and must stop producing. Eventually all the following operations may shut down. Because of this disruption, the inventory pile in front of the disrupted operation will be full and soon all preceding operations, again in lock step, will stop producing.

"The good news is that a great deal of attention is then focused on the source of the disruption, and actions are likely to be taken to temporarily, and hopefully permanently, eliminate the problem. The bad news is that during this time throughput is lost. Since throughput is very valuable, the damage is not small. Now this is not just a one-time loss. It is an ongoing problem because once there are very few disruptions that interrupt the flow, you deliberately reduce the sizes of the inventory piles so that disruptions once again interrupt the flow and cause throughput to be lost.

"As we understand it, you spent many years reducing the inherent disruptions in the flow before you dared to introduce kanban to control the flow of your river system. If you had introduced it earlier, there would have been chaos. There would have been so many disruptions that you would have lost a great deal of throughput and the system would not have worked.

"Machine changeovers are big disruptions to flow. A kanban system could not have functioned if it took eight hours to change press dies. Initially, poor quality, unreliable machines, and undependable workers all caused large disruptions. You had to dramatically reduce these disruptions before you dared implement the kanban approach to manage flow."

Ohno interrupted and said, "You are absolutely correct. The kanban system was one of the last things we implemented, not the first. I agree with what you are saying, but I don't yet see how we could have implemented it more quickly."

We asked, "What if you had focused the inventory in the system rather than spreading it across many operations?" Ohno got a puzzled look and asked, "Focus? I'm not sure what you mean."

"In any flow, there is always one operation that has less capacity than the others, the weakest link in a chain, if you wish. Let's assume it is here," and we drew an X across operation 5 (Figure 1.2). "Now instead of spreading the seven days of inventory evenly across the system, let's both reduce the amount of inventory in the system to four days and concentrate most of it in front of the weakest link, operation 5. We will allow both the preceding and following operations to process whatever material is available to them. However, we will only release new material into the system at the rate that the weakest link processes it."

"I see what you are suggesting, but I still don't see how it would be better," Ohno commented.

"Suppose that operation 3 again has a two-hour disruption. How much throughput would now be lost?" we asked.

Ohno took a long time to reply and hesitantly said, "I don't think any would be lost because the weakest link could continue to work, although the inventory in front of it would be reduced."

Drum buffer rope system

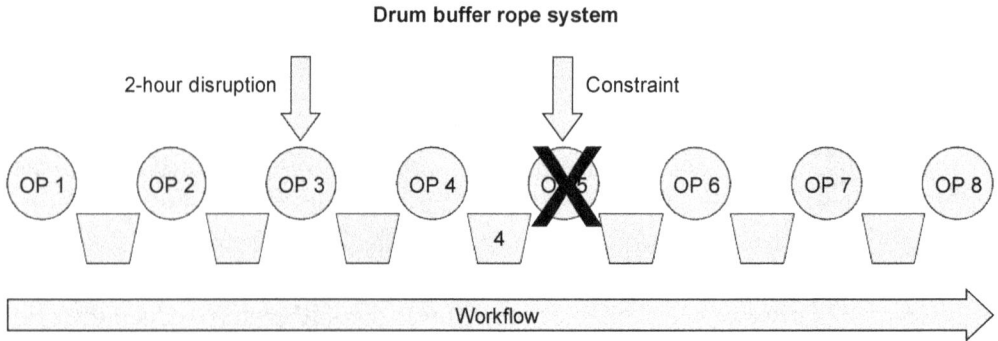

Figure 1.2 Drum buffer rope system.

We nodded and said, "So in some ways, focusing the inventory is better than spreading it across the system. By doing it in this fashion even though you have less inventory in the system, it is better protected against losing throughput." Ohno pondered these ideas for what seemed like the longest time and finally said, "I see. Please go on."

"Let's take it a step further. If we monitored the operations that caused the inventory at the weakest link to decline, wouldn't those operations be the best candidates for improvement since they are causing the worst disruptions? Once the source of these disruptions is eliminated, you can safely reduce the inventory in the system, still keeping the majority of it in front of the weakest link, so that throughput is seldom lost. In this fashion, you may be able to better prioritize the causes of disruptions to your flow and work on the worst first. It also would have allowed you to begin controlling your river system earlier since the impact of even large disruptions to the overall flow would have been buffered by the pile in front of the weakest link."

Ohno studied the diagrams at great length, saying nothing. Finally, he raised his head and said, "If I had seen this possibility I believe I could have developed my system in less than half the time. I didn't know which disruptions were most important, so I treated them all equally. We probably wasted a lot of time removing small ones when we should have been working on the big ones. It was like being in a jungle where many animals might attack me. I used the same big gun to kill each one regardless of how dangerous it was. That was probably not the best way, but it was the only way I could see to do it at the time." I thought to myself: "Thank heavens you didn't. My country would have suffered even more if you had. At least we've had some time to respond and change our ways."

As we departed, we bowed and thanked him for his time and insights. In return he bowed slightly and graciously said, "Thank you. I think I now better understand why my system works so well."

The meeting with Ohno provided us with a wealth of new insights and also validated some old ones. The most important validation was that the same cost-accounting culture that hampered the performance of Western industries was also prevalent in Japan. However, it was a surprise to learn that the tenacity of a single individual, Taiichi Ohno, had blunted their negative impact on a major Japanese industry. That a single individual could have such impact was an inspiring "blue-light" insight. For us it was the Good Housekeeping Seal of Approval for our view that the world had changed and Western industry had not yet sufficiently adapted to the change.

The power of moving from a focus on reducing costs to generating more throughput is probably our most important insight. We believe it is the biggest shift that has occurred in the last century. The companies and countries that are adopting this perspective are winning. Those that are not are slipping backward in the race to thrive and survive.

The fact that many Western companies have retained a major focus on cost has had two major negative repercussions. First, it has caused them to waste large amounts of money. Some of the results of a local approach to efficiencies are bloated inventories, excessive operating costs, lower quality, longer lead times, and poor delivery performance. The drive for local efficiencies is particularly obvious at the operation level where the "cost" of setting up a machine causes companies to produce more products than are needed by the market, a considerable waste. In the U.S. automotive industry, this mind-set was taken to a new level when assembly plants were designed to very efficiently produce a limited variety of models. These plants were so inflexible that the "costs" to change them over to produce other models was often prohibitive.

The inflexibility of converting machines and even entire plants is a huge albatross for companies. It means that they have to accurately forecast demand for products, which as we have seen can be a fool's errand. The result is always that they almost always produce too much of some products and too little of others.

The manner in which these costs and revenue losses are reflected on a company's financial statements often obscures what is happening. Inventory write-offs occur only periodically, usually around year end. The timing and magnitude of these write offs are usually driven more by tax considerations rather than reporting how effectively their management system has functioned. They are usually treated as one-time events that are not likely to recur. In fact, they occur day in and day out and result from how factories are managed. Moreover, these costs do not show up on the reports that measure how efficiently they have managed production. On the contrary, the creation of unneeded inventory makes their performance reports look even better.

There is another, sometimes more deleterious, aspect to producing more than customers want. Inventory write-offs typically occur when it is deemed that the item can no longer be used and it is simply thrown away or sold for scrap value. A more subtle loss occurs when it is necessary to mark down the price of a product in order to sell it. The U.S. automobile industry is notorious for marking down prices at the end of each model year in order to move unsold cars. The same phenomenon occurs regularly in many other industries, in particular those that are attuned to fashion and style. A large retail industry has arisen just to market discontinued or overstocked products.

Do these costs show up on the reports by which we judge the performance of production operations? The answer is almost never. They are instead reflected in lower margins, a responsibility of sales and marketing, not operations.

The second repercussion can be even more important. It is the failure to capitalize on market opportunities. The inflexibility of a cost culture causes companies to waste material, capacity, and labor by building unneeded products. This culture also results in a shortage of *needed* products. This failure can cause a loss of both short- and long-term sales. Where is the lost revenue and lost profit recorded on our financial statements? The answer is nowhere. It only shows up much later when a company slips behind its competitors. At such times the cost culture is used as an excuse on why we cannot compete. It's because the wages in other countries are very low. While there is truth in this fact, it's too often used to mask the lost profit from managing our companies from a cost perspective.

The overriding insight that has occurred repeatedly on our journey is that companies need to link their activities much more closely to their markets and synchronize the links in their networks accordingly. Making decisions based on forecasts guarantees that we will always be wrong. The closer a company's supply system is to actual market demand, the more likely it will be successful.

We believe that a key reason for Toyota's success was its focus on continually generating more throughput. Henry Ford had that focus until his constraint shifted from production to the market. General Motors found a way to do it in a much more complex environment, at least when most of the cost of a product directly varied with volume.

A FOURTH WAVE—iTLS

For over 40 years I had been learning, practicing, teaching, and researching on continuous improvement methodologies. I had successfully used Lean, TOC, and Six Sigma individually in various environments, industries, and organizations and had realized considerable results for the enterprises involved. As my learning grew deeper in practical applications, the real-world strengths and weaknesses of these improvement systems became more pronounced and apparent to me. I noticed visible gaps in each approach when used individually. This initially caused me some disappointment, and I felt that my beloved process improvement philosophy was incomplete. I rapidly realized that I needed to recalibrate my expectations and ego. It was time to learn what was needed next in order to overcome the shortcomings. I erroneously expected that since I had invested my passion, interest, time, and resources in learning a methodology that had appeared as an intellectual and technical breakthrough in achieving process improvement, it would be the only answer to systematic organizational growth and improvement. Of course, this whim had been my ego's desire, and the reality was different. I had neglected to consider that learning itself is endless. It is a continuous evolutionary phenomenon; it is a *process* and not a *single event*!

When I was a novice practitioner in martial arts at the age of 14, I recall how enthusiastic and passionate I was to learn this art through a particular school. I naïvely wanted to believe what I was so passionately learning was the only way of martial arts. So initially I had hesitation in learning and applying approaches and techniques from what had seemed to me at that time to be competing schools. My older brother, Nasser, who was a creative sculptor, asked to talk to me one day. He had seen how passionately I had been practicing martial arts and also had noticed that I had been in heated discussions with my cousins who were also practicing martial arts but in different styles. Nasser apparently had noticed that when my cousins and I talked about our martial arts and schools, each of us profusely defended our style and claimed that it was the most effective and complete style and that we were not willing to even consider other styles. My brother explained to me that the most successful artists were the ones who learned and practiced in more than one style of an art form. He also explained that it is the social responsibility of an artist to learn as many dimensions and styles as possible in order to be able to create something new and innovative for the community. He further explained that this behavior was certainly not an act of disloyalty to a school or teacher or a circle of associates and friends. He said, "Look, you are putting so much effort into martial arts and are doing well now, but I am concerned that you may be looking at only one dimension and may be limiting your learning, physical, and intellectual growth by not expanding your knowledge and experience with the other potential styles."

It took me awhile for my brother's advice to sink in; however, I realized that my behavior was not in the best interest of my physical and intellectual growth in the realm of martial arts and life in general. So, I reached out and participated in other martial arts schools, seminars, and instruction; I read numerous books about their philosophies; and I became friends instead of foes with the other passionate practitioners, particularly with my cousins. My accepting behavior impacted my cousins as well, and we all became simple students. I shared what I knew and learned and applied their ways, tools, and techniques to enhance the capabilities and practicality of my knowledge. It was an amazing transformation; the speed, depth, and breadth and enjoyment of our knowledge in conjunction with our physical changes were much more in natural harmony. The results were eye opening, encouraging, and mind opening; we became more effective, yet we were wasting less energy and efforts. I competed comfortably with competitors in different styles and various levels of experience, which was very gratifying. My lessons learned included realizing that the martial arts systems and philosophies are interdependent and that there is always at least one better way to do anything; that better way, however, may appear to me only if I am aware and open minded enough to see it! I also learned that that the better way has always been there! I just needed to mindfully see it.

Years later, in the midst of real-world challenges as a serious practitioner of continuous improvement systems, I faced a similar situation and needed to take a similar approach. I learned and used various tools and approaches to enhance the capabilities and practicality of what I was trying to accomplish through continuous improvement systems.

The results, as expected, were extremely encouraging and mind opening. Our implementation teams were experiencing faster and smoother implementations. The users better understood the reasons for the changes and became more involved in the process. The inherent benefits included a more sustainable implementation, further satisfying the client customers, implementation managers, and application users. I was determined to learn the available knowledge and take the best of the best and transfer that knowledge to my clients, students, and the interested communities worldwide.

The organic effect of these efforts guided me to apply practical combinations integrating TOC, Lean, and Lean–Six Sigma during the mid-1990s. Years later, I noticed that there were also other practitioners from various industries and environments experimenting with combinations of Lean and Six Sigma. When I combined Lean, TOC, and Six Sigma approaches and tools for arrays of continuous productivity improvement (CPI) activities, the flow of the river system, their speed, length, and dam heights were significantly affected. The total cycle time required to resolve problems improved dramatically.

I carefully studied the strengths and weaknesses of each methodology and noticed that these systems actually complemented one another and, contrary to some opinions, were not in conflict at all. This was like a déjà vu, like when I was learning martial arts and found different focuses on strengthening different parts of the human form. The martial arts philosophy itself consisted of teaching flexibility, adaptability, and conformance with change in mind as well as the body, which came with deeper understanding of this marvelous teaching.

The idea of continuously improving river systems added to the experiences and lessons I had learned from operations drove me to understand and explore the shortcomings of my predecessors. I was fortunate to have had the experience with marital arts, which shaped my thinking. Having a static and rigid mind-set, particularly in approaching continuous improvement, is not only a conflict with the spirit of improvement, but also a harmful behavior that eventually causes stagnation and distinction as the negative inertia sits in.

Unfortunately, it is possible that some stagnant-minded individuals occupy management positions and are *not willing to listen to fresh ideas or any ideas that they did not create.* You probably have come across similar situations when managers were not willing to accept your better suggestions, methods, or approaches, despite their considerable merit, because of the "not-invented-here" syndrome. Furthermore, some managers are not willing to empower their employees to fully apply themselves and implement better practices because of an ego-driven and fear-based viewpoint.

As I was experimenting with combinations of Lean, Six Sigma, and TOC, I discovered that it does make a significant difference how you integrate these systems and their components to compress the project cycle time, improve return on investments, and sustain improvements. Imagine that you intend to make a refreshing tonic and you have all the ingredients; however, there typically is a particular recipe or formula that best satisfies your taste, thirst, and sense of pleasure. Using the same ingredients in a different proportion could result in a not-so-pleasant tonic. I view the iTLS system and its components in a similar way and believe that their right combination can produce a potent CPI tonic that is effective, sustainable and could bring a feeling of ecstasy to an organization.

How effective is an iTLS system? In 2002, I took the challenge of scientifically examining the effectiveness of iTLS applications. But how would I know how effective iTLS is if I did not have a reference point to measure iTLS's performance against it? The logical approach would have been some sort of a designed experiment to quantitatively compare iTLS with other popular improvement systems, like Lean and Six Sigma. Luckily, I finally discovered an excellent formula for applying these powerful approaches into a comprehensive and well-integrated system. There were many claims that one methodology was superior to the other and so on, but there had never been a comparative analysis scientifically performed that clearly quantified how effective each methodology was or what the "interaction effect" would be if they were combined.

Obviously, all of the top three improvement systems were useful and effective, but how effective? I was fortunate to have an opportunity to scientifically test my hypothesis with a large electronics firm. Coincidently, at that time I was completing my engineering doctoral work, and I proposed the idea of researching the effects of CPI methodologies to my dissertation advisor, Dr. Kim Farah. She welcomed the challenge and encouraged me to argue the topic with the dissertation committee. I prepared my topic defense paper and laid out the logic, need, and scientific approach for the research, which the dissertation committee fortunately approved. It took over two and half years of solid work, sweat, coaching, mentoring, traveling across the globe, data collection, analysis, and interviews to complete this experiment.

The good news was that iTLS not only worked, but that it yielded great results. On a project-to-project comparison the iTLS system yielded bottom-line results that were 400%+ greater than those obtained from either Lean or Six Sigma. What is even more encouraging is the fact that we are in the early stages of determining how to best use iTLS to manage flow in network systems. My recent work in refining this process strongly suggests that future results will far exceed what has been demonstrated so far. It also appears that this is a new wave following Ford, Sloan, and Ohno's approaches. More important, iTLS is not limited to high-volume discrete A river systems but is applicable to all four network shapes and a wide variety of environments. The other encouraging aspect is that it doesn't take very long to implement a iTLS and obtain significant results.

We will explore in a future chapter how iTLS focuses more sharply on areas that increase throughput, as opposed to just saving costs, resulting in making even greater gains. Obviously, throughput is what generates revenue and facilitates profitability and growth in an enterprise. What bring growth and prosperity to an organization is more sales, revenue, and profits, now and in the future. Cost savings have only a limited impact on growth and prosperity. Cost cutting often promotes a very short-range view in contrast to in-depth long-range planning for growth. In many instances, we have observed that this behavior has huge costs in terms of employees' loyalty and productivity. The way productivity is measured plays an important role in how organizations behave. Too often productivity measures are focused on efficiencies and local optimization instead of generating more throughput.

Through my continuous improvement journey I have had a wonderful opportunity to work with some of the world's CPI legends: Robert Fox, Eli Goldratt, Gerald Nadler, John Ballis, Joseph Campbell, and Gurmeet Naroola. These individuals have significantly influenced my views of continuous improvement philosophy and shaped my thought process in formulation of iTLS. I am sincerely grateful to all of their contributions, mentoring, and friendship.

This book is an attempt to speed the process of a new wave of CPI in order to greatly improve how our companies are managed and spread wealth and personal freedom.

2
The Productivity Improvement Dilemma

A parable is perhaps a fitting way to portray how some managements approach and attempt to implement continuous productivity improvement in their organizations.

"Once there was a wealthy but foolish man. When he saw the beautiful three-story house of another man, he envied it and made up his mind to have one built just like it, thinking he was just as wealthy. He called a carpenter and ordered him to build it. The carpenter immediately began to construct the foundation, the first story, the second story, and then the third story. The wealthy man noticed this with irritation and said: 'I do not want a foundation or first story or a second story; I just want the beautiful third story. . . . Build it quickly.'"

Many existing business models have failed to sustain profitability and continuous improvement, particularly in the United States. Manufacturing operations have been unable to implement sustainable continuous improvement strategies effectively and, as a result, our position in the global business environment has suffered. This suffering is evident in various forms of inefficiencies (operations are not cost-effective and are moved from the United States to Mexico, China, India, etc.), low or lack of continuous profitability, poor work cultures, unmotivated employees, job losses, business losses, and a significant slump in stock prices. Pew Research Center reported on April 14, 2021: "Workers in low-wage jobs experienced the greatest drop in employment. From February 2020 to February 2021, employment among low-wage workers fell by 11.7%, from 28.1 million to 24.8 million. This compares with a loss of 5.4% among middle-wage workers, whose employment fell by 5.5 million over the period" (Table 2.1).

The answer is not to continue doing the same old thing and expect different results—a definition of insanity. It is time to understand why historical approaches to implementing improvements have come up short of desirable and sustainable results. It is also clear that executives must recognize that they must apply continuous improvement methodologies to transform their organizations in order to achieve the desired throughput and profitability. There is, however, a serious dilemma over which continuous improvement methodology to use in order to obtain the maximum benefits from their investments.

Table 2.1   Job losses—

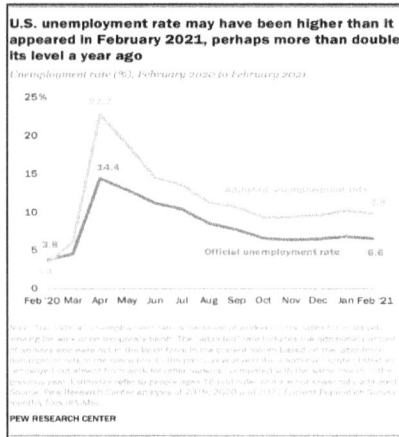

U.S. unemployment rate may have been higher than it appeared in February 2021, perhaps more than double its level a year ago

PEW RESEARCH CENTER

The improvement efforts of the last couple decades have a checkered history—some techniques have come and gone, awards for improvement have gone to companies that stumbled or failed, and certifications standards like ISO are not well correlated to company successes.

There is no consensus on which improvement techniques to use. Most improvement projects use Lean, Six Sigma, or TOC—very few combine two or more of these techniques in a logical and effective fashion. The bottom-line results of each of these approaches have been mixed, and critics are beginning to question their efficacy.

There also is a recurring issue that annoys organizations that use CPI techniques. Most organizations implement CPI efforts using projects. In many instances, improvement project teams claim either hard savings or cost avoidance only to find that operations management cannot substantiate the realized savings. In many cases, the improvement projects do not contribute to the bottom line. If profitability does not improve significantly, then maybe the project efforts were a waste! A typical CPI project team of 3–8 members may spend from 4 to 40 hours per week on the project for say four weeks. In this example, the team could be spending over 90 hours per week, or 360 hours for a four-week period. If there is no measurable benefit from the teams, these hours and efforts are a waste of valuable resources. Such experiences cause management to doubt the value of CPI efforts. Expectedly, these results do not increase employees' morale regarding CPI activities. Even worse, it may cause employees to react apathetically when it comes to efforts that claim to improve profitability, competitiveness, and quality.

As in the story about the foolish man building a house, thinking only of the results and being impatient with the work required to obtain, such results are likely to be a mirage.

It is essential to understand the attributes of the current popular CPI methodologies and how they might best be used to build a strong foundation for sustainable improvement systems. Dave Nave compared the three powerful continuous

Table 2.2 Comparison of improvement programs.

Program	Six Sigma	Lean thinking	Theory of constraints
Theory	Reduce variation	Remove waste	Manage constraints
Application guidelines	1. Define 2. Measure 3. Analyze 4. Improve 5. Control	1. Identify value 2. Identify value stream 3. Flow 4. Pull 5. Perfection	1. Identify constraints 2. Exploit constraint 3. Subordinate processes 4. Elevate constraint 5. Repeat cycle
Focus	Problem focused	Flow focused	System constraints
Assumptions	A problem exists Figures and numbers are valued System output improves if variation in all processes is reduced	Waste removal will improve business performance Many small improvements are better than systems analysis	Emphasis on speed and volume Use existing systems. Process interdependence
Primary effect	Uniform process output	Reduced flow time	Fast throughput
Secondary effects	Less waste. Fast throughput Less inventory Fluctuation—performance measures for managers Improved quality	Less variation Uniform output Less inventory New accounting system Flow—performance measure for managers Improved quality	Less inventory/waste Throughput cost accounting Throughput—performance measurement system Improved quality
Criticisms	System interaction not considered Processes improved independently	Statistical or system analysis not valued	Minimal worker input Data analysis not valued

Source: Dusharme (2004). "Got Six Sigma on the Brain?" *Quality Digest 24*(11), 25–32.

improvement methodologies—Six Sigma, Lean, and TOC—and summarized his findings in Table 2.2.

It is clear that despite the considerable strengths of each methodology, they each have shortcomings. Critics point out the following issues with TOC:

- Minimal worker input is considered. Human resources are not valued.

- Data analysis is not valued.

- Quality is not considered.

- Process variability and error management is not considered.

- Continuous improvement is not considered.

Regarding Lean:

- System interactions are not considered.

- Processes improved independently. The interdependency of the systems are not systematically considered.

- Process focus may be missing.

- Statistical or system analysis not valued.

Relating to Six Sigma:

- Does not address necessary process constraints. Can certainly improve and perfect non-value-added processes. Typically it is locally focused.

- Minimal worker input is considered.

A study published by Dusharme (2004) indicates that from 2001 to 2004 there was a trend of companies abandoning Six Sigma at a rate of three or four a year. "There are several reasons for this. The most likely is that Six Sigma, in practice, is really no different than other quality programs. If it shows tangible results, companies continue to use it until they reap the immediate benefits. At that point, the major cost savings due to reduced variability have been realized. If Six Sigma efforts haven't been expanded to include the product-design function, then companies most likely will abandon the program." Table 2.3 shows the distribution of time one company has been using Six Sigma.

Table 2.3 Distribution of time a company has been using Six Sigma.

No. of years	This year	Nov. 2003	Feb. 2003	Nov. 2001
< 1 year	22%	18%	21%	30%
1–2 years	23%	20%	28%	32%
2–3 years	18%	23%	23%	17%
3–4 years	15%	16%	11%	7%
4–5 years	10%	10%	6%	3%
5–10 years	10%	11%	7%	10%
10–15 years	2%	2%	1%	0%
> I5 years			2%	0%

Source: Dusharme (2004). "Got Six Sigma on the Brain?" *Quality Digest 24*(11), 25–32.

The survey notes that despite the potential of Six Sigma programs, respondents complained because of:

- Lack of management support
- Lack of resources
- Lack of management alignment and understanding
- Lack of resources
- Unreasonable expectations
- A misunderstanding of what Six Sigma actually is

Table 2.4 depicts the response statistics to the survey.

Ballis (1996) identifies six barriers as the top reasons for the failure of improvement efforts:

1. Lack of belief that change was necessary
2. Lack of leadership by upper management
3. Lack of adequate skills or experience
4. Turf wars
5. Lack of reward and recognition system
6. An inability or unwillingness to downsize

Motorola University (2004) offers its six reasons why Six Sigma efforts fail:

1. When leaders do not consistently demonstrate their sponsorship and commitment, Six Sigma can fall short of expectations.

   As with any critical organizational change effort, Six Sigma requires leaders to stay engaged in the effort. For Six Sigma initiatives to succeed, leaders must reinforce the importance of Six Sigma to their organization in their regular communications and in the ways that they manage their business and people.

2. Experience shows that Six Sigma is likely to fail if it is not directly linked to the organizational strategy.

   Using a balanced scorecard is a best practice associated with Six Sigma implementation. The scorecard helps identify and prioritize the Six Sigma improvement projects that will have the greatest impact on strategic objectives and desired business results.

   Organizations should avoid initiating a "collection of projects" that is disconnected from the organizational strategy.

Table 2.4   Support of Six Sigma implementation.

	This year	Nov. 2003	Feb. 2003
Management fully supports our Six Sigma program			
Agree	74%	79%	77%
Disagree	12%	18%	18%
Neither	12%	4%	5%
I would have used more training on Six Sigma prior to starting Six Sigma projects			
Agree	36%	41%	41%
Disagree	42%	45%	44%
Neither	22%	14%	15%
I understand the overall goal of Six Sigma projects prior to starting them			
Agree	84%	89%	86%
Disagree	9%	7%	9%
Neither	7%	4%	5%
We are always given enough time to properly implement Six Sigma projects			
Agree	44%	52%	45%
Disagree	34%	37%	44%
Neither	19%	11%	11%
We are always given enough resources to properly implement Six Sigma projects			
Agree	38%	45%	41%
Disagree	41%	43%	48%
Neither	19%	12%	10%

Source: Dusharme (2004). "Got Six Sigma on the Brain?" *Quality Digest 24*(11), 25–32.

3. Six Sigma efforts will fail if projects are not managed and tracked aggressively and if the people involved are not held accountable for results.

   Six Sigma is most successful when organizations implement a process for regular reviews of projects. These organizations maintain line of sight to the progress, track overall performance, and hold champions and teams accountable for timely execution.

4. Six Sigma is hailed for its bottom-line impact, so if Six Sigma projects are executed without clear financial results, leaders will be disappointed with the efforts.

   The secret to avoiding this problem is to quantify anticipated results before initiating projects, and to ensure they are tightly linked to business unit budgets and the bottom line. It's wise to involve a finance representative to establish rules and guidelines, and to stay involved in the quantification effort.

5. When organizations do not take a structured approach to how they allocate resources to support their Six Sigma efforts, Six Sigma will probably fail.

6. Six Sigma can fail if an organization places too much emphasis on the mechanics and technical aspects of the methodology.

   Six Sigma is a framework, not a recipe. Paying more attention to the steps than the desired outcome can result in too much bureaucracy and delayed impact.

   It's better to view the approach as a framework with a robust tool set, and then apply the relevant tools to the improvement opportunity!

Harrington (2005) suggests that using Six Sigma by itself is not appropriate in all cases: "Using six sigma as the operating standard isn't appropriate for all activities. For some it will cost too much to achieve, while for other it's too loose a standard." The goal of Six Sigma is reducing variation. Yet Harrington also suggests that very few Six Sigma projects result in decreased variation. Rather, they focus on improving the efficiency and effectiveness of the processes. In these cases, application of Lean tools may be more effective, because Lean focuses on process improvements.

Avery Point Group (2005) suggested in a study that Six Sigma dominates Lean by a wide margin as the more prominent and popular improvement methodology. Avery (2005) used three indicators leading to this conclusion:

1. Publications on both Six Sigma and Lean topics in the last five years indicate Six Sigma outpaced Lean by a wide margin.

2. Internet engine keyword search counts indicated Six Sigma is outpacing Lean by a two to one margin. Lean searches, however, have been increasing.

3. Based on Internet job postings, use of "Six Sigma" keywords outpaced "Lean" consistently by 50%.

Avery (2005) suggested that this difference may have been due to the fact that Six Sigma methodology has moved into non-manufacturing areas, but Lean has remained largely perceived as a technology for improving manufacturing processes.

The implementation of Six Sigma largely depends on top management support. About 50% of the Six Sigma implementations fail due to lack of management support. This puts the implementation of Six Sigma at a 68% failure rate. Success of Six Sigma or any continuous improvement effort large depends on the ability of the firm's culture to change and accept the new improvement approach. The implementation is where an organization typically faces problems (Arthur, 2005). Some of Arthur's findings:

- 60% of the companies implementing Six Sigma fail to consistently meet their objectives.

- 30% of the companies changed their CEO at least once in 2000 or 2001.

- 58% changed their CEOs at least once between 1998 and 2001.

"Florida Power and Light, for example, won the Deming Prize for Quality in 1989. A change in CEOs in mid-1990s, however, killed its quality program. Now another change in leadership is bringing it back" (Arthur, 2005, 36). It is important for the organization's management to supply the necessary resources for a successful continuous improvement methodology application. "Facing unprecedented pressure to improve performance across the board, organizations cannot afford to forgo the benefits of either Six Sigma or Lean" (Snee, 2005, p. 63). It is the expectation of any organization to improve its performance and key indicators, such as scrap, rework, defects, yields, on-time delivery, customer satisfaction, cost of quality, cost of goods sold, capacity, and productivity. These improvements must be translated to gains in market share and increased shareholder values. Therefore, it would be more effective for proponents of either Lean or Six Sigma to build a framework to create a holistic performance improvement methodology that applies improvement of all kinds (Snee, 2005).

IMPROVEMENT CHALLENGES

At the strategic level, operations and plants are expected be productive and efficient so that the company can compete in the marketplace and satisfy their customers and stakeholders. Operations that are not as efficient as their competition frequently find themselves resource-constrained due to their ineffectiveness. Therefore, despite the importance of improving productivity and quality, these operations often claim that they lack the resources for these efforts. Many of these plants and operations continue to generate scrap and rework. When asked why they do not fix these problems managers often claim that they do not have the time or resources to spare for making process improvements! The efforts they spend on rework consume all spare resources. This resources activation does not translate in to maximizing their throughput. However, it may make efficiencies look good at the local level. This is a common example of the local optimization phenomenon. Rework is a non-value-added activity, which means it is not paid for by the customer. In order to put in place a systematic approach to problem solving that minimizes rework and scrap, operations need to adopt a process improvement methodology. Therefore, we are back at the earlier point of deciding which CPI methodology should be adopted.

It is already well established that these three methodologies have delivered significant value over the past three decades. When it comes to choosing among these CPI approaches, however, it is almost like buying a new car. You know that most cars provide the same major features of being able to transport you from point A to B. However, each model has a series of features that, depending on your requirements and preferences, may be more attractive to you. Some of these features could be fuel economy, ownership costs, eco-friendliness, life, and maintenance complexities. Because data on these features are readily available, you should be able to choose a car relatively painlessly. However, with CPI methodologies, until recently there has not been much benchmarking data to objectively quantify the contributions generated by each methodology. Now that data are available, it is prudent to understand this information and make a more quantitative selection of the continuous improvement methodologies available. This approach should be particularly attractive to organizations with complex and diverse operations that intend to take the continuous improvement to the next level. Scientific data clearly point to iTLS as the new methodology for continuous improvement. Throughout the remainder of this book, we will use the terms iTLS and TLS interchangeably to describe this methodology. Each wave of continuous improvement approaches has helped to surface the hidden obstacles, that were impeding the performance of our river system. iTLS enables users to benefit from the previously hidden, but positive, interaction effects that result from integrating TOC, Lean, and Six Sigma. CPI techniques should continue to evolve, and iTLS is a natural and organic result that takes continuous improvement approaches to the next higher level of performance (Figure 2.1).

iTLS has proven to be solidly effective in tackling organizational issues at all levels and in synchronizing the efforts with what matters the most to the organization. The TLS approach needs to be taken deep into the culture of the organization making it as part of its natural DNA. It requires that the leadership commit to educate, train, coach, and mentor the organization with the knowledge that iTLS may bring about quick and exciting results. It is essential to continue propagating iTLS learning and practice across various organization levels. This

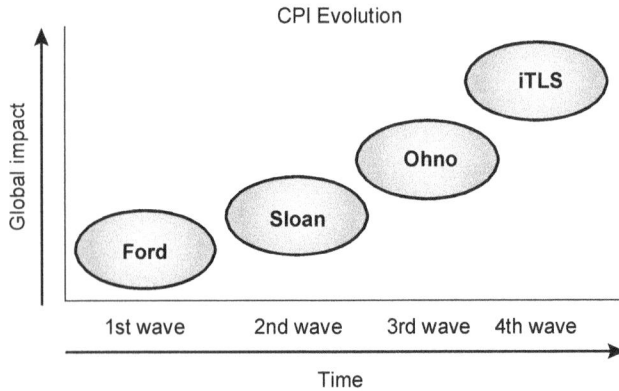

Figure 2.1 Four major waves—the evolution of continuous improvement.

learning and growth needs to be carefully managed to keep it aligned with the organization's objectives. The beauty of the iTLS approach is that because it is not tool biased, its nature allows for continuous fine-tuning and organic adjustments. When the iTLS model is introduced into an organization, it needs to be focused on generating bottom-line results. It will help the organization align and strengthen its framework and infrastructure, highlight the weak links and non-value-added elements, identify key contributing factors for error and variability, and "pull" the organization's strategy more directly toward its strategic objectives.

Improvement efforts have often fallen short of enterprise-wide expectations. Many Lean, Six Sigma, and TOC implementations by themselves have had questionable financial benefits. Frequent improvement projects have claimed significant victories, but the companies' bottom lines have remained unaffected. This effect has eroded and often damaged top management support; it has created doubts about the effectiveness and sustainability of improvement techniques. Obviously, leadership and top management support are key to the success of improvement initiatives. Unpredictable and unstable financial returns discourage practitioners from seeking the full support of top management. iTLS has been designed to optimize benefits gained from TOC, Lean, and Six Sigma tools and techniques in a synergetic arrangement. The application of iTLS can expedite regaining top management's confidence and support in investing resources in such improvement programs and efforts.

In the upcoming chapters, we will address the dilemma of improvement and a critical necessary condition, the presence of an appropriate measurement system. Having illustrated the limited results and lack of consensus about how to improve an organization's operations, the focus will shift to understanding the core problem. We will examine the affects of local optimization and their devastating adverse effect on the organizations as a whole. We will focus on the need for global measurements like throughput (T), inventory (I), and operating expenses (OE); the fact that all organizations can be depicted as chains or networks; and the fact that variability exists. The major implications are that real improvements can be measured only by their global impact, that T is the longest available lever, and that efforts should be focused heavily on bottlenecks or constraints and on reducing variability and dependencies. Additionally, we will discuss the world's favorite CPI methodologies so that as we progress throughout this book we can refer to familiar terminology and understandings.

In the next chapter, we briefly examine TOC, Lean, and Six Sigma, the three most popular CPI methodologies.

Notes

3
CPI Favorites: TOC, Lean, Six Sigma

THEORY OF CONSTRAINTS

The Theory of Constraints (TOC) is a management philosophy formulated by Eliyahu Goldratt. This method takes a systematic approach to optimization. It recognizes that outputs of a system are a function of the whole system, not just individual processes.

$$\text{System: } Y = f(x) \text{ or } Y = f(x_1, x_2, x_3 \ldots x_n) \tag{1}$$

Where:

Y is the process measurement, outcome, output, or response
$f(x)$ is the process containing various variables

$f(x)$ is referred to as system throughput (T). When a system is viewed as a whole, we realize that the output is a function of the weakest link. The weakest link of the systems is the constraint. A constraint is anything that limits the system's throughput (T). Constraints in systems usually take one of the five forms shown in Table 3.1.

TOC postulates that no production system can work faster than its slowest operation, which is the constraint.

Obviously, CPI is about causing some level of change to the existing way of improving operations. TOC questions the logic of change and puts it in perspective so that change agents, organizational leadership, and management have an in-depth understanding of why a change in their organization is necessary and, when change takes place, what sort of expectations should they have. TOC asks a few simple but powerful questions:

- Why change? (What is the purpose and need for change? It's important to ensure that a global system view is maintained to avoid the distraction of trying to improve an area that will not improve the overall system.)

- What to change? (What is the leverage point?)

Table 3.1 Types of constraints.

1. Resources

2. Material

3. Policy

4. Political

5. Market

- What to change to? (What are the simple, practical solutions?)

- How to cause the change? (Overcoming the inherent resistance to change.)

Clearly, change for the sake of change is a waste of effort and resources, so it is essential to fully understand why some level of change is necessary and what this change is going to bring when accomplished.

Assuming that the need for change is established, it is vital for an organization to focus on the key leverage points. Understanding and finding the leverage point in a process will optimize the results and minimize the efforts. As a simple analogy, assume that you are making a soup by using 10 ingredients. Unfortunately, after combining all your ingredients, the soup does not taste as you expected. Now you have two choices: restart from the beginning or change the proportion of the ten ingredients. The question is, which ingredient would you adjust to achieve the desired taste? You can begin by varying each ingredient individually and seeing how it affects the taste or you could vary a combination of ingredients. Certainly, each process involves money, time, and resources. Creating the desired taste for this simple product could take a considerable amount of time. If you can determine in advance which ingredient contributes most (significance) to the taste and then focus your efforts on fine-tuning that factor, you have minimized your non-value-added efforts. This significant factor is the leveraging element that, when adjusted, significantly changes overall process performance, in this case, taste. So the question of "What to change?" must be thoroughly examined to identify the leverage factor. This element is also called a key critical input variable (KCIV), key input variable (KIV), and so forth. In the following equation, where the process is a function of $X_1, X_2, X_3, X_4 \ldots X_n$, it is vital in our effort to achieve optimization to figure out which one of the Xs, or variables, are the KIVs.

$$f(x) = X_1, X_2, X_3, X_4 \ldots X_n \qquad (1)$$

This level of focus ensures that change process is at the system level or global level of optimization and prevents distractions that could erroneously concentrate on factors at the subsystem level, which may locally optimize but not contribute significantly to the overall system's performance.

The next question of "What to change to?" is another key element in process improvement. If it is not clear what the end will look like, then there is a tendency to tinker with the processes indefinitely. Looking back at our example of the soup, if it is not clear what your soup should taste like, then the process of tinkering can go on indefinitely and you would never know when you have achieved the desired taste. You would not know how to measure your process success, because there is no baseline to measure it against. Clarification of this vital question forces the process to fully understand the voice of the customer (VOC), voice of the process (VOP), process capabilities shortcomings, gaps, specifications, customer and market requirements, and so forth.

The last question asks how are we going to cause the changes that we identified so that it will be sustainable. It is natural to experience resistance to change, so it is prudent and a necessary condition to understand the culture and nature of the processes where the changes are going to take place. By understanding the processes, their underlying culture, norms, and so forth, we can develop practical and effective communication and transformation strategies. It is not uncommon for a brilliant idea to get a bad rap or be killed because it receives a high level of resistance from the implementation recipients. Stickiness of a process improvement has a lot to do with how well the implementation team understood the processes, cultures, people, and systems and how well they are able to involve process owners, get their full buy-in and trust, obtain top management support, and communicate cross-functionally. If this issue is not addressed up front, then it becomes visible only when implementation is facing a level of resistance that could endanger the implementation. The rework process at this phase is much more difficult, complex, and time and resource consuming than if it had been addressed initially as part of implementation planning.

If care is not exercised, the focus of the improvement effort might be on a sub-system which even if it is improved will not significantly impact the overall system output. TOC focuses attention on the orchestration of efforts so that overall optimization takes place in a system, not in individual pieces. Typically, organization charts lead to workflow by function, which can result in competing forces within the organization. With TOC, systems are viewed as a whole, and work activities are directed so that the performance measures of the whole system are improved. This approach reduces the risk of sub-optimizing, which is improving a non-critical factor, or improving a sub-system (factor) of the overall system. TOC views a system as a chain, or network, of interrelated activities.

The TOC system chain extends from market demand through the organization chain all the way to suppliers. The system rules (policies) drive the constraints which need to be examined. Consider an example of what happens when a high-level view of the overall system is not addressed. An organization works at improving internal process efficiencies. As a result of the improvement, capacity increases, which increases production levels. Excess inventory is then created because production is greater than demand. Only then is it discovered that the constraint is really the sales and marketing process, not production capacity.

Contrasting TOC with total quality management (TQM), a widely used management approach, highlights its advantage. TQM has often been implemented by dividing the system into processes and then optimizing the quality of each process. This approach is preferable to chasing symptoms, but new problems can be created if the individual process is not considered in concert with other processes that it affects. TOC focuses on reducing system bottlenecks as a means to continually improve the performance of the entire systems. According to Goldratt, the vast majority of constraints result from policies (e.g., rules, training, and other measures), while few constraints are physical (e.g., machines, facilities, people, and other tangible resources). For example, a large portion of highway road repair seems initially to be physically constrained by traffic flow, but the real constraint is government acquisition policy, which mandates the award of contract to the lowest bidder. This drives contractors to use low-quality materials to keep their costs down and remain competitive, which in turn results in more frequent highway repair.

TOC considers three metrics of system performance: throughput (T), inventory (I), and operating expenses (OE).

$$T = (Total\,sales\,revenues - Total\,variable\,costs\,for\,producing\,a \\ product\,or\,service) \tag{2}$$

$$I = All\,the\,money\,temporarily\,invested\,in\,items\,it\,sells \tag{3}$$

$$OE = Money\,a\,firm\,spends\,transforming\,inventory\,into\,throughput \tag{4}$$

Focusing on these dimensions can lead a firm to abandon traditional management cost accounting for internal decision making while at the same time improving its competitive price advantage. TOC believes that the traditional financial measures, such as return on investment (ROI), net profit, and cash flow, do not tell us what to do daily at the operational level. It is not easy for first- or second-line managers to decide how their actions might affect net profit, ROI, or cash flow. In contrast, TOC measures of T, I, and OE are more easily understood in relationship to operational decisions. Within the iTLS approach, we can view these as the system's metrics that drive project selection and measure improvement results. OE, which is the fixed expenses (overhead) of the system, is the money flowing out of the system. The relationship of TOC metrics are described as follows:

$$Return\,on\,investment\,(ROI) = \pm\ \Delta\,I/NP \tag{5}$$

$$\text{Net profit} = T - \text{OE} \tag{6}$$

$$\text{Cash flow } (CF) = T - \text{OE} \pm \Delta\text{I} \tag{7}$$

T is limited by the system constraints. OE is primarily generated by non-constraint resources. Using TOC, the focus is on creating overall system improvement by making changes to the constraint.

TOC uses five focusing steps to recognize and remove constraints (Table 3.2).

Step one begins when we identify the system's constraint. The test should be what element is limiting the system's performance. Using Table 3.1, determine which element is the bottleneck. Detect whether the constraint is internal (resource or policy) or external (market, suppliers). Then assess the degree of difficulty in breaking the constraint. If the constraint can be broken easily, break it and look for the next weakest link in the process chain. If the constraint is difficult to break, proceed to step two.

Step two is when we decide how to exploit the system constraint, which means how to get the most out of the existing constraint resource with little or no additional investment. For example, if the constraint is the capacity of a surface mount technology (SMT) assembly machine some of the ways to increase capacity would be:

- Staggering of shifts

- Making sure preventive maintenance is done on the machine so downtime is minimized

- Setting up the machine externally to reduce machine downtime

The idea is to maximize the contribution of the resource to profit.

In step three, after deciding how to exploit the constraint, we need to subordinate or synchronize everything else to that decision. This means that all non-constraint resources must be supporting the constraint, because if any of these

Table 3.2 Constraint management steps.

Steps	Definition
1	*Identify the constraint*
2	*Exploit the constraint*
3	*Subordinate other activities to the constraint*
4	*Elevate the constraint*
5	*Avoid negative inertia—go to step 1*

support elements feeding, following, or directly impacting the constraint impede its performance, then the constraint's throughput will be reduced. This reduces the total system's throughput and profitability. Any time or throughput lost on the constraint cannot be replaced without adding additional resources.

Step four is when the constraint is elevated to a nonconstraint by actions other than the subordination process. For example, if the constraint is internal, additional machines or shifts can elevate the capacity of the constraint. If the constraint is external, such as in the market, efforts like an advertising campaign might be appropriate for elevating the constraint.

In step five, after the constraint has been elevated and becomes a nonconstraint, another portion of the system will become the constraint, and will need to be addressed. After improving the constraint, we should not assume all system problems have been solved. To avoid this negative inertia, we should investigate the entire system to find the next potential constraint before it becomes a systemic issue.

A particular value of TOC is that it helps organizations avoid firefighting. TOC can be the guide as to exactly where improvement efforts should be focused. TOC metrics focuses on throughput, investment/inventory, and operating expenses.

In summary, TOC focuses the organization's attention on the constraint processes; breaking these constraints typically yields significant benefits.

One of the particular strengths that TOC offers is the idea of global optimization of the organization instead of local optimization of a particular operation or process. Let's review the significant difference between the two management approaches.

Global optimization is a process of making strategic and tactical decisions on policies, improvement efforts, expenditures, and so forth for the betterment of the entire organization, not one particular area, department, or division. The decisions are made based on the idea of improving the overall organization's performance. This management practice obviously is quite complex, because it requires management's awareness of how the strengths, weaknesses, opportunities, and threats (SWOT) of the various functional areas impact optimal decisions. This approach requires close communications among all of the organization's leadership, a culture of teamwork and gain-sharing, and a clear understanding of the organization's strategy. Under this approach, it is possible for an entity to appear inefficient; yet its contributions may be critical to the betterment of the entire organization's performance. In these situations, the management payouts and bonuses need to be based on the entire organization's performance, causing entities to cooperate with one another. In such organizations, entities are more willing to share resources with other internal entities. This atmosphere allows for better sharing of experiences and best practices and takes advantage of organizational synergies, which, in turn, reduces operating expenses and improves profitability. Typically, organizational metrics are not designed to promote this approach; instead they are mostly focused on each entity's efficiency or target achievement. We will discuss in a later chapter how creating a balanced scorecard can facilitate a global optimization strategy.

Local optimization, in contrast, is a management decision-making model that strives to maximize only its own function's benefits. It is driven by organizational metrics that focus on each entity's performance efficiencies. Management payouts and bonuses are calculated on such efficiencies. Focusing on an entity's performance forces the entity's management to consider only its internal performance metrics, often causing entities to become rivals and compete against one another for better efficiencies rather than collaborating as links in an overall chain. This behavior creates non-value-added and counterproductive activities and weakens the entire organization. As one can expect, under this management approach organizations are reluctant to share resources and best practices or take advantage of the internal synergies. It is typical to notice higher operating costs and lower profitability under this approach. Unfortunately, this approach is popular because it appears to be less complex to the organization's leadership.

We knew a subcontracting manufacturer with a global footprint. One of its customers required services from two of its plants in different geographic locations. Each plant was managed by its own local resources. The customer's business was split between two sites, 10% for plant A and 90% for plant B. Both plants were measured on their efficiencies, and plant management compensated accordingly. Both plants were required to maintain a significant supply chain infrastructure to support the customer's production process. Obviously, plant A, with 10% production volumes, was not as efficient as plant B. On a global basis, this customer was very profitable for the company. Plant A was continually pressured by company management for its inefficiency, which, in turn, had an adverse impact on bonuses. Plant B, in contrast, was praised for its efficiencies, because it was able to take advantage of economies of scale. In order to improve its efficiencies, plant A began cutting costs by reducing the supply chain staff supporting this customer, which improved plant A's overall performance. Unfortunately, the attention devoted to the customer declined and response times lengthened. The customer began complaining! Plant A's management perceived the small business volume as a burden to their internal efficiencies and failed to respond to the customer. The customer became further frustrated and eventually took its business to a competitor. The impact was that plant A's efficiencies improved some, because it reduced the resources allocated to support the low-volume business and received bigger bonuses. The company at the global level lost a profitable customer. Plant B also lost revenue and profitability. Clearly, misguided measurements promote wrong behavior, and in this case, they forced the plant to strive for local optimization regardless of its impact on other entities and the company as a whole.

LEAN

Lean is a systematic improvement process for removing waste and non-value-adding activities from every aspect of the business. The Lean methodology attempts to identify activities that do not add value to the profitability of a business and either eliminate them or transform them to activities that are profitable (Womack et al., 1991). Lean consists of discipline, daily practice, and tools. A Lean culture develops through these practices, and they become habits that change the organization's culture.

Six principals summarize Lean:

1. Specify the value.

2. Identify the value stream.

3. Make value flow without any interruptions.

4. Let the customer pull value from the producer.

5. Pursue perfection.

6. Implement with agility.

Principle 1: Specify the Value

Lean identifies value in three dimensions (Table 3.3):

1.1. Value-add (VA) is any activity that satisfies a customer requirement that the customer is willing to pay for. These are the activities that generate revenue and, when managed properly, bring profit to the organization. These activities, therefore, need to be the focal point and delivered with maximum efficiency. Since VA is the core contribution of business to its customers, customers expect VA to be safe, high quality, cheap, and available. Organizations that are able to deliver VA to their customers will succeed. Ballis (2001) defines

Table 3.3 Types of value.

1. Values Add
2. Business Value-Add
3. Non Value-Add

work cycle efficiency (WCE) as a metric to measure the efficiency of an organization in delivering VA:

$$WCE = \frac{Value\text{-}add\ Time}{Total\ Cycle\ Time} \qquad (8)$$

Imai Massaki (1997, 22–23) refers to this as the ability to repeatedly deliver only VA to customers. "There is too much muda (waste, often wasted time) between the value added moments. We should seek to realize a series of processes in which we can concentrate on value adding processes—Bang! Bang! Bang!—and eliminate intervening downtime." Standard and Davis (1999, 61) use golf as an example to illustrate this measurement. The golf club's head actually contacts the ball for about 0.02 second; this is Imai's "Bang!" or value-adding moment. Suppose a game takes four hours to complete with about 90 strokes. Only 1.8 seconds, or 0.0125 percent of the time, is actually spent on adding value. It is critical for businesses to fully understand their process value stream, customer requirement, and WCE in order to optimize profitability.

1.2. Business Value-Add (BVA) is a category of activities that a business does to sustain its infrastructure, such as buildings, government compliances, licenses, training, information systems, financial systems, and appraisals. These activities may not explicitly be identified and directly paid by the customer, but they are essential for the operations.

1.3. Non Value-Add (NVA). The Japanese define NVA as "muda" or friction, referring to the energy that gets lost without any benefit to the organization. Muda hides itself in various forms within the processes (Figure 3.1).

Many times muda is not easily recognized and removed. Therefore, it requires understanding of the process and customer requirements and process capabilities in order to properly identify muda and plan for its removal. Muda is typically not paid for by the customer, and its existence degrades the profitability of the firm (Ballis 2001). Figure 3.2 is useful in characterizing value in process.

Bakerjian (1993, 9-2) and Ohno (1988, 19–20) cite seven types of waste. These seven characteristics can be viewed as the "seven sins of production." See Table 3.4.

These seven forms of muda should be identified during the value-stream mapping and reduced, eliminated, or improved.

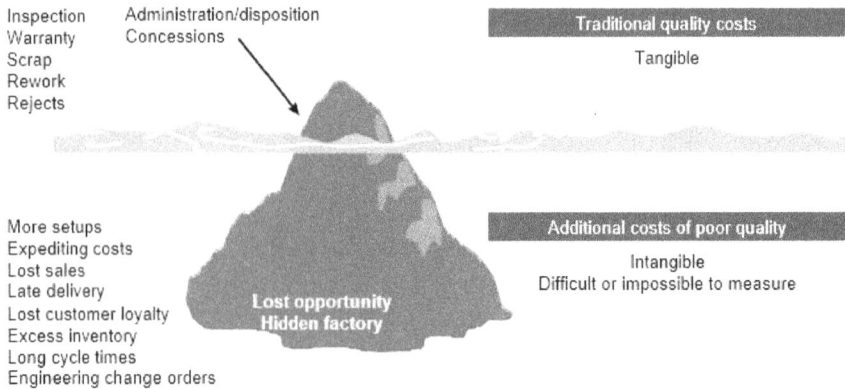

Figure 3.1   Hidden factory.

Principle 2: Define the Value Stream

The value stream is the map of the process that identifies every action required to design, order, and make a specific product. This map clearly shows how values flow throughout the organization. Using the three characterizations of value allows a business to investigate which activities are VA, BVA, and NVA.

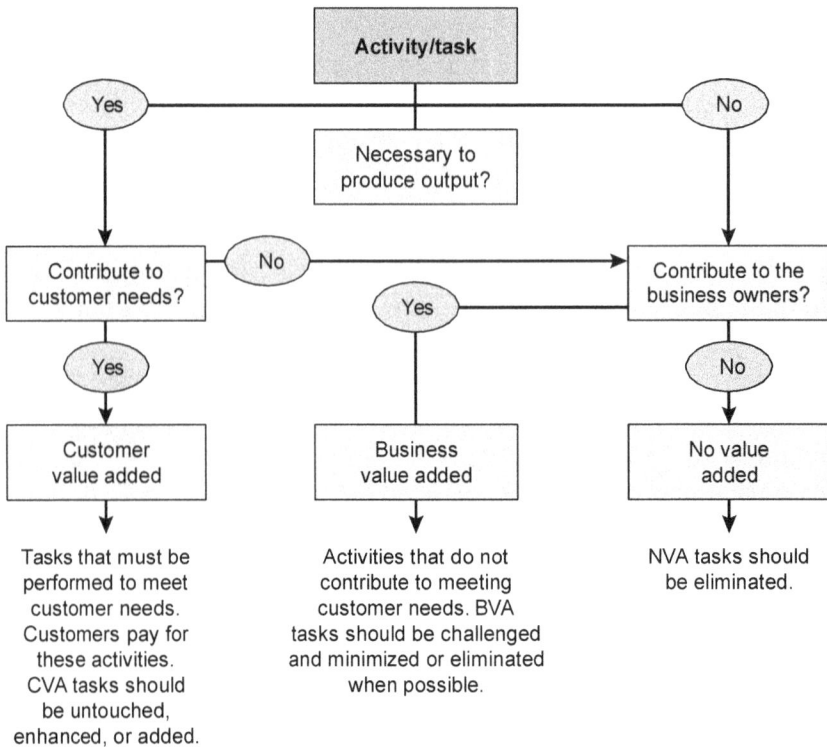

Figure 3.2   Value characterization decision flowchart.

Table 3.4 Seven sins of production.

The 7 wastes— "Muda"	Definition	Examples	Causes	Countermeasures
Overproduction	Producing more than the customer needs right now	Producing product to stock based on sales forecasts Producing more to avoid set-ups Batch process resulting in extra output	Forecasting Long set-ups "Just in case" for breakdowns	Pull system scheduling Heijunka–level loading Set-up reduction TPM
Transportation	Movement of product that does not add value	Moving parts in and out of storage Moving material from one workstation to another	Batch production Push production Storage Functional layout	Flow lines Pull system Value stream organizations Kanban
Motion	Movement of people that does not add value	Searching for parts, tools, prints, etc. Sorting through materials Reaching for tools Lifting boxes of parts	Workplace disorganization Missing items Poor workstation design Unsafe work area	5S Point of Use Storage Water Spider One-piece flow Workstation design
Waiting	Idle time created when material, information, people, or equipment is not ready	Waiting for parts Waiting for prints Waiting for inspection Waiting for machines Waiting for information Waiting for machine repair	Push production Work imbalance Centralized inspection Order entry delays Lack of priority Lack of communication	Downstream pull Takt time production In-process guaging Jidoka Office Kiazen TMP
Processing	Effort that adds no value from the customer's viewpoint	Multiple cleaning of parts Paperwork Over-tight tolerances Awkard tool or part design	Delay between processing Push system Customer voice not understood Designs "thrown over the wall"	Flaw lines One-piece pull Office Kaizen BP Lean Design
Inventory	More materials, parts or products on hand than the customer needs right now	Raw materials Work in process Finished goods Consumable supplies Purchased components	Supplier lead-times Lack of flow Long set-up times Paperwork in process Lack of ordering procedure	External kanban Supplier development One-piece lfaw lines Set-up reduction Internal kanban
Defects	Work that contains errors, rework, mistakes or lacks something necessary	Scrap Field failure Rework Variation Defects Missing parts Correction	Process failure Mis-loaded part Batch process Inspect-in quality Incapable machines	Gemba Sigma Poke-yoke One-piece pull Built-in quality PB Jidoka

This typically is the initial objective of defining the value stream of a process. The BVA and NVA activities are explored for elimination or optimization. A valid value stream should begin and end with the customer (internal or external). Figure 3.3 is an example of an order fulfillment value stream.

After the identification of value in business process and its stream, the flow of the value needs to be considered. VA is what the customer pays for, and hence it should get to the customer and out of the business process as quickly as possible in order to convert the VA to cash for the business. The VA should generate revenue without any interruptions or queues caused by either the process or quality.

Principle 3: Make Value Flow without Any Interruptions

Production systems and resources have to be organized in a manner to facilitate a smooth flow of product throughout the system. The following are considerations in creating a production flow that optimizes value added:

1. Scheduling system and level loading—In the Lean environment, sales and production scheduling are core members of the product team, in a position to plan the sales campaign as the product design is being developed and to sell with a clear eye to the capabilities of the production system so that both orders and the product can flow smoothly from sales to delivery. The key approach is the concept of takt time, which synchronizes the rate of production to the rate of sales to customers. Figure 3.4 depicts the relationship of takt time and balanced workload.

   It is desirable for the workstations to have capability of production in less than the takt time. This is to account for natural process variability and to prevent resources from becoming bottlenecked. Figure 3.5 illustrates a production takt time of 15 seconds, but the production resources have more capability and are able to produce at a rate of 11 seconds. The additional capacity would guard the entire system against unforeseen downtimes. The scheduling approach needs to balance the workload among the workstations and prevent overloading or underuse of the resources.

   When workstations are not balanced, there is a tendency for systems to accumulate inventories. As shown in Figure 3.5, the station with 6 seconds takt is able to produce at a rate of 2.8 times faster than required takt. This would result in building significant amount of inventories that will incur carrying costs. The next station with the takt time of 17 seconds would be incapable of processing

Top level value stream of order fulfillment

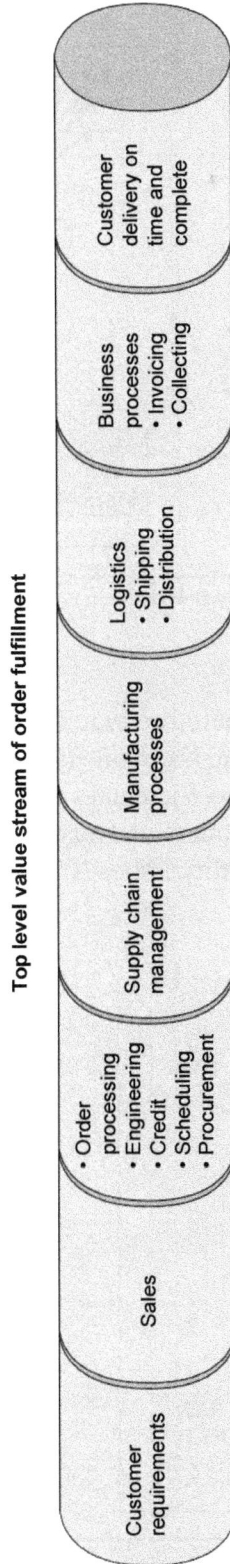

Figure 3.3 Order fulfillment value stream.

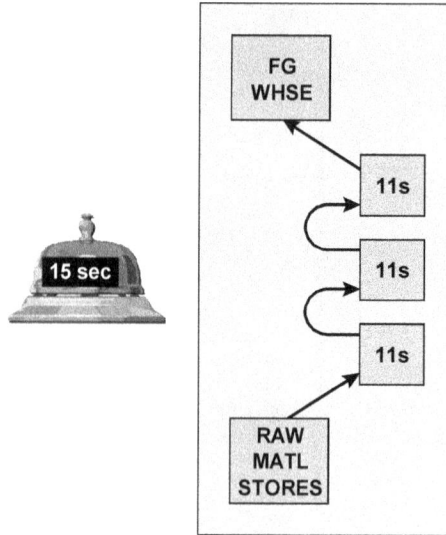

Figure 3.4 Takt time and balancing workload.

the required product and therefore would accumulate the inventory built by the first station. The last workstation would often be starved for work and have very low efficiencies (about 46%). Such a system would result in lack of organization; waste of materials, money, time, and space; and perhaps quality issues (Chase et al., 2004).

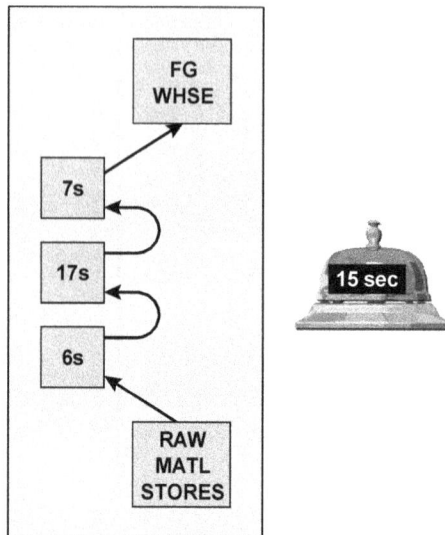

Figure 3.5 Takt time—unbalanced work.

2. Production layout—physical floor layout could facilitate smooth flow or inhibit it based on how it is designed. Typical production flows are as follows:

   1. Job shop

   2. Batch

   3. Assembly line

   4. Continuous

The matrix in Figure 3.6 describes the typical application for the four process flows identified here.

Traditionally, production layouts organize the facility by department or resource type. For example, in a bicycle production shop the layout would be by the type of activity: tube cutting, tube bending, mitering, welding, washing and painting for the frame and handlebars, and final assembly of the complete bike. Because the process produces a wide range of models using the same production equipment, some machines would be overused and some underused. This creates an unbalanced flow. Due to inefficiencies in interdepartmental transportation, the jobs tend to move in batches. This accumulates inventory on the floor and increases the investment locked inside the operation. The higher the inventory levels, the slower the production cycle time. In this type of layout, it is common

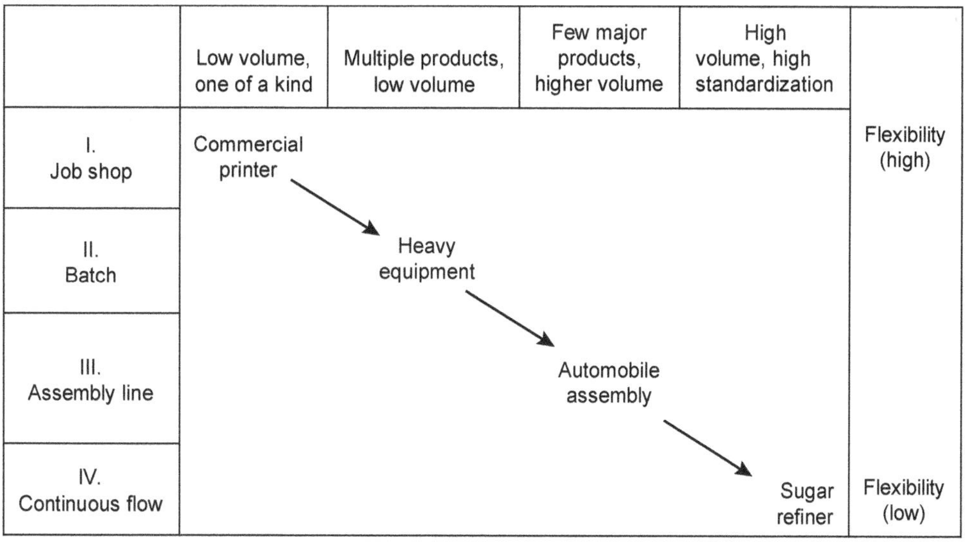

	Low volume, one of a kind	Multiple products, low volume	Few major products, higher volume	High volume, high standardization	
I. Job shop	Commercial printer				Flexibility (high)
II. Batch		Heavy equipment			
III. Assembly line			Automobile assembly		
IV. Continuous flow				Sugar refiner	Flexibility (low)

Source: Chase et al., 2004.

Figure 3.6 Process flow matrix.

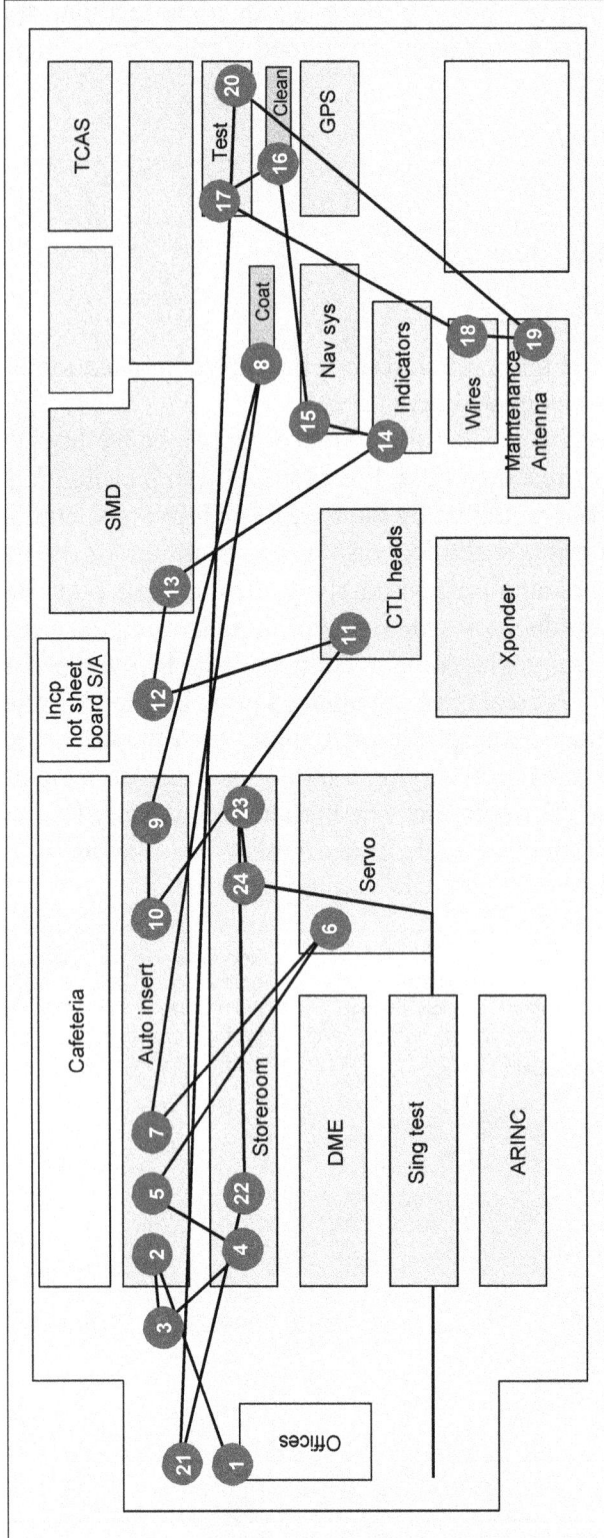

Figure 3.7 Workflow transportation logistics.

to observe transportation paths continually crossing and creating a spaghetti flow. Figure 3.7 is an example of an operation with overlapping and back-and-forth flow, or spaghetti flow.

An alternative to the traditional layout is the cellular layout, which Heizer and Render (1991) call a subset of process-oriented layout. Work cells are organized around part families and not around machine types. This is more characteristic of the product-oriented layout, and perhaps cellular production is best described as a combination of both. The work cell plays a critical role in Lean manufacturing environments, cutting transportation distances greatly and improving workflow. R. E. Flanders (1925) has been cited as the originator of the work cell, but the concept explicitly appears in Ford (1922). Figure 3.8 is an example of a traditional layout, and Figure 3.9 shows a work cell.

3. Statistical process control (SPC) at the source—By statistically monitoring and controlling the processes, companies can identify and solve product-quality issues at the source, reducing rework and scrap, which adversely impact cycle times and inventories. Implementation of SPC with involvement of the well-trained

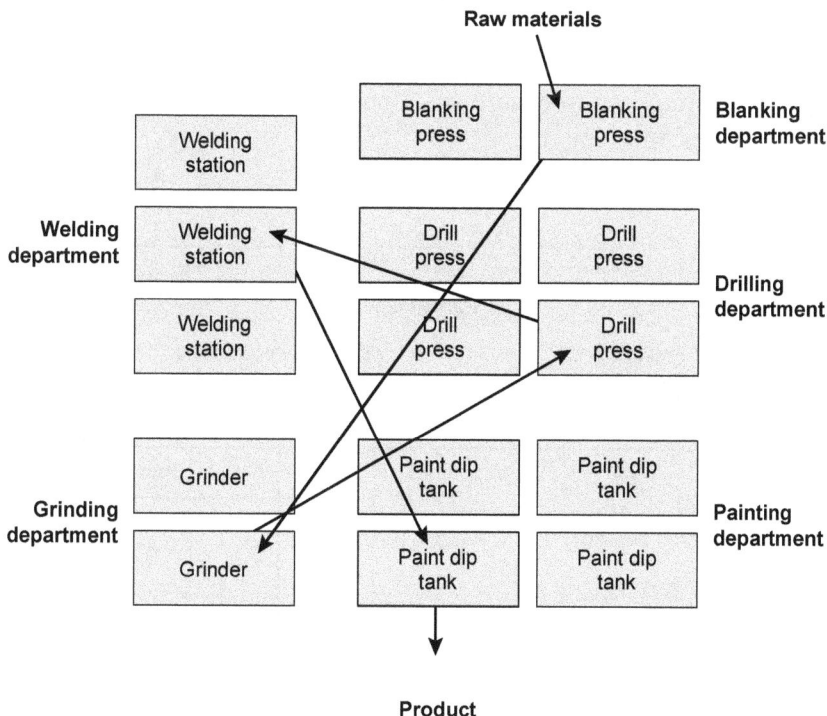

Source: Levinson & Rerick (2002).

Figure 3.8 Example of a traditional layout.

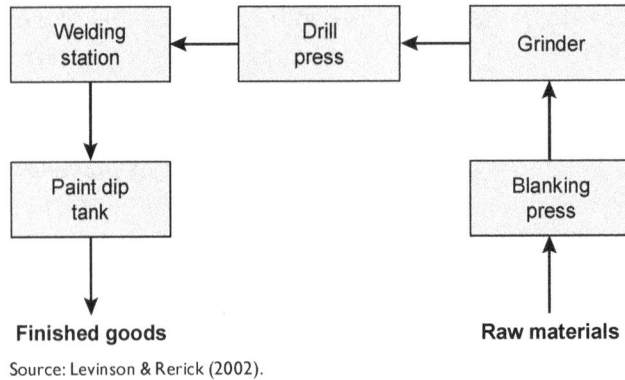

Source: Levinson & Rerick (2002).

Figure 3.9 Example of a work cell layout.

employees and empowering them to take action when necessary could substantially improve product reliability and process flow (Chase, Jacobs, & Aquilano, 2004).

4. 5S-CANDO (Can Do) 5S*CANDO a systematic technique for cleaning, organizing, and arranging a workplace. Implementation of 5S reduces the muda of searching for tools, as everything has a place (Figure 3.10).

    Removing clutter from the floor and bringing organization and standardization will assist in flow improvement. Institution of such a discipline creates a collaborative and caring attitude. Continuous training is required to ensure sustainability of the process. Table 3.5 summarizes 5S elements.

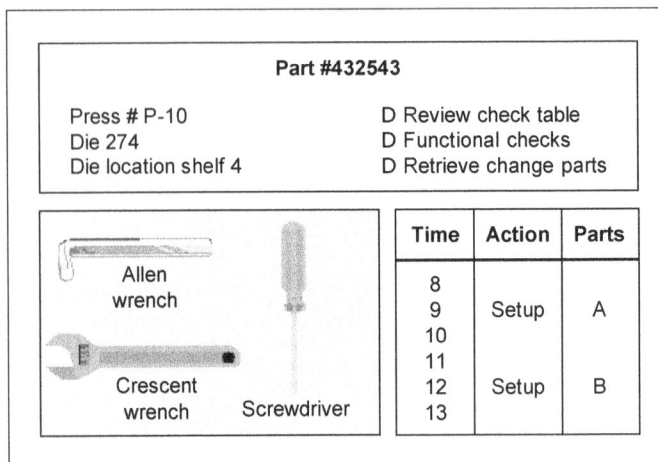

Figure 3.10 5S-CANDO.

Table 3.5   Components of 5S.

Translation	Description	S-Japanese
1. Sort	Get rid of clutter	Seiri
2. Set in order	Organize the work area	Seiton
3. Shine	Clean the work area	Seiso
4. Standardize	Use standard methods to keep sort	Seiketsu
5. Sustain	Maintain through empowerment	Shitsuke

Benefits:

• Improved safety

• Improved morale

• Ownership of workspace

• Improved productivity

• Improved maintenance

• Identifies muda

Continuous and ongoing improvement is a way of looking for even better ways to organize and clean the workplace and remove muda. Kaizen is a Japanese word (kai "take it apart" and Zen "think"). Kaizen means ongoing improvement. Kaizen strategy has been the most important concept in Japanese management—a key to Japanese competitive success. Within the context of kaizen are specific tools and techniques that an organization should deploy throughout the organization, from worker to management. Kaizen has been effective in Japan, but it cannot be implemented in its pure form in other environments, such as the United States, due to the drastic differences in the cultures.

In an interview conducted by *Quality Digest* (Smith, 2005) with Masaki Imai, this question was asked: "You've said that U.S. executives haven't used Kaizen and Just-In-Time techniques as effectively as other business leaders. Why do you think this?" Imai responded: "In my observations, there are two primary reasons for this. The first is that Western executives tend to believe that substantial improvement costs a lot of money. They seem to think that they must have the latest state-of-the-art technology and equipment to improve. I call this the innovative approach. Although innovation is indeed an important part of progress, it is only one component. Kaizen and standardization are equally important in sustaining a successful business. The West's slow adoption of Kaizen is also due to a focus on short-term results. Western managers are often looking for the next 'silver bullet' solution. Successful Kaizen ultimately requires culture change, and this is something that Western managers are not often trained for" (Smith, 2005, 54).

Four elements have been identified for sustaining kaizen:

- Management attention and commitment

- Workforce involvement

- Quantifying and communicating the benefits of kaizen to employees to help them see the need for sustaining the gains

- Standardization

5. Preventive maintenance (PM)—a continuous and smooth process flow can best be established when all equipment functions properly and breakdowns and downtimes are minimized. PM establishes ground rules for systematic machine maintenance and upkeep. Many successful PM programs have involved employees as process owners to check and perform simpler maintenance functions on the equipment they use.

6. Poka-yoke (error-proofing)—Error-proofing is a manufacturing technique that reduces human intervention and judgment to prevent mistakes. Dr. Shigeo Shingo introduced this technique to Japan as baka-yoke (fool-proofing). He changed it to poka-yoke because workers inferred from baka-yoke that management perceived them as stupid (Shingo, 1986, 45). Error-proofing and error reduction improve quality of the process and product, increase efficiency and speed by reducing scrap and rework. Figure 3.11 shows that the use of pear-shaped holes eliminates the need for bolts. The result is a process that is faster, less costly, and more repeatable because the bolts have been removed.

7. Visual Controls, such as 5-S system, and Takt boards—Visual controls describe workplace safety, production throughput, material flow, quality metrics, or other information. Visual controls supply the feedback to an area, much the same way that SPC can give process feedback to the operator running a particular operation.

A demand-driven system plays an important role in creation of a smooth production flow.

A cellular concept in a production environment would minimize process interruptions, accumulation of work-in-process and inventories, and improve

Old—18 min   New—1.6 min

8 bolts to be removed   0 bolts to be removed
                               8 half-turns to loosen

Eliminate lost nuts, bolts, different sizes nuts and bolts

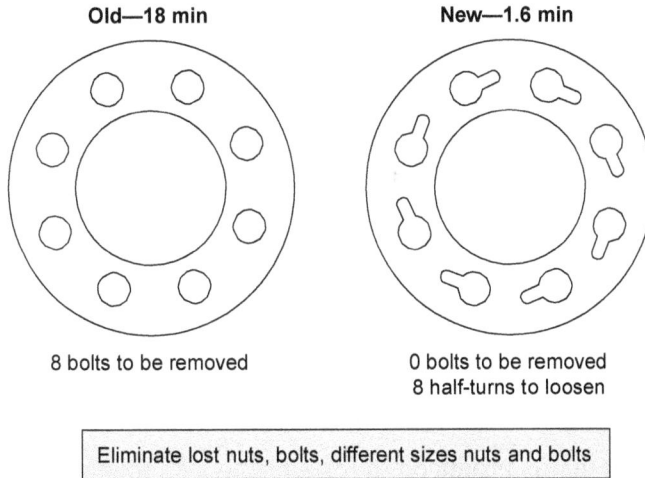

Figure 3.11   Poka-yoke, error-proofing.

product quality and cycle time. A smooth flow requires a demand-driven system instead of a push one (Sekine, 1998).

Principle 4: Make Customer Pull from Supplier

Lean systems work best when the process flow is demand driven. Toyota's production system formulated just-in-time as an integral component of the Lean process, which is a pull system. This means that the production instructions are demanded or pulled by the customer, instead of being pushed into the system at the first operation by the production control department downstream processes call for work as they complete the jobs they have. Resources will be activated only to produce what is demanded, or pulled, by the customer, no more, no less. The pull system at its ultimate form is one-piece flow in which each operation works only on one piece at a time and has no excess inventory in front of it. A Lean system with no inventory to hide problems and decouple processes will expose quality problems and improve communications. In the case of a system with inventory, a worker who gets a defective piece can simply discard it or throw it back in the pile and work on another. He or she need not notify the operation that produced the defect. This is not an option in an inventory-Lean factory.

Schonberger (1982) raises the point that if a workstation makes a defective part in a Lean factory, the downstream internal customer will complain immediately because there is no inventory buffer to conceal the defect. Schonberger also adds that the Japanese reduce the stocks and take workers out of the line to expose problems. Removal of the inventory reveals quality problems and unsteady production rates. The Japanese also reduce work-in-process (WIP) by removing kanbans, without which upstream stations cannot produce WIP. Removal of workers reveals inefficient methods and equipment that can hide when extra labor is available. Visible demand, a related concept, ties in with production control. The idea is that each workstation should be able to determine its downstream customer's needs. Kanban systems use various signals, such as manual card or computerized systems, for notification of what to build, how much to build, and when to build. Kanban rules provided by Ohno (1988, 40–41) are as follows:

1. A kanban is a withdrawal order, delivery order, and work order.

2. No one can make a part without a kanban. (Don't make anything that isn't needed.)

3. A kanban must be attached to each part or lot.

4. Everything that is produced in response to a kanban must be defect-free.

5. Reduction of the number of kanbans promotes operational improvement.

Kanban uses small batches, representing often only a few hours' worth of production. Because the batches or lots are small, machine setups are frequent. Frequent setups are a key objection to implementation of one-piece flow or small-lot processing.

Kanban

Setting up a kanban system requires determining the number of kanban cards (or containers) needed. Each container represents the minimum production lot size. An accurate estimate of the lead time required to produce a container is key to determining how many kanbans are required (Chase, 2004).

$$K = \frac{DL(1 + S)}{C} \tag{9}$$

$$K = \frac{(\textit{Expected demand during lead time} + \textit{Safety Stock})}{\textit{Size of the Container}}$$

K = Number of kanban card sets (a set is a card)

D = Average number of units demanded over some time period

L = Lead time to replenish an order (same units of time as demand)

S = Safety stock expressed as a percentage of demand during lead time

C = Container size

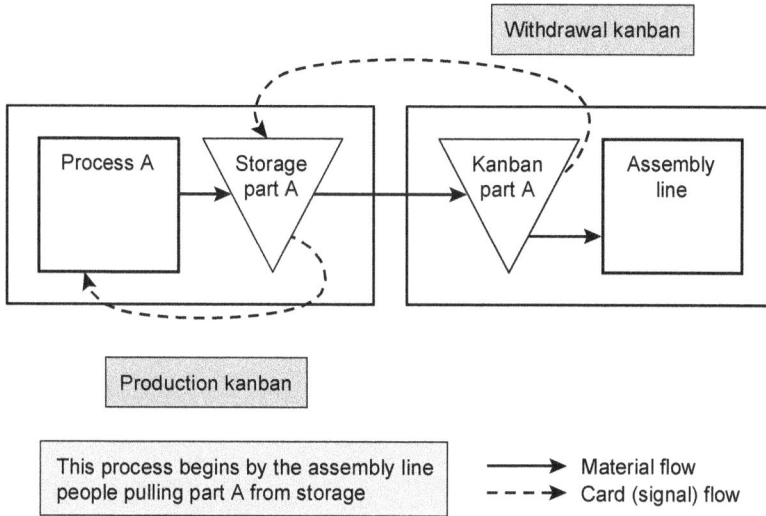

Figure 3.12   Kanban system mechanics.

Source: Chase, R. B., Jacobs, R. F., & Aquilano, N. J. (2004). *Operations Management for Competitive Advantage* (10th ed.). New York: McGraw-Hill.

The kanban cards are used as work instructions in a pull system, as shown in Figure 3.12. As an assembly line needs parts, it pulls from the kanban A that pulls from storage area A. As parts are pulled, the signal goes back farther to instruct process A to produce parts in the same quantity as was used in storage A and instructed by kanban A.

There are similarities between kanban and the TOC. In TOC, the constraint is the only operation that can request more production starts. Inventory is kept only in front of the constraint, which should never run out of work.

Suzaki (1997, 212–215) shows that small lots also improve communications. Inventory decouples workstations and operators from each other. People take work from the incoming inventory pile. When it is finished, they put it in the outgoing inventory pile. This reduces interaction and communication. As workers make products that are required by the next operation (their customer), communication between workers improves and quality problems are discovered much more quickly. Inventory hides problems, as shown in Figure 3.13.

The TPS has identified four key areas:

1. All work shall be highly specified as to content, sequence, timing, and outcome.

2. Every customer-supplier connection must be direct, and there must be an unambiguous yes-or-no way to send requests and receive responses.

3. The pathway for every product and service must be simple and direct.

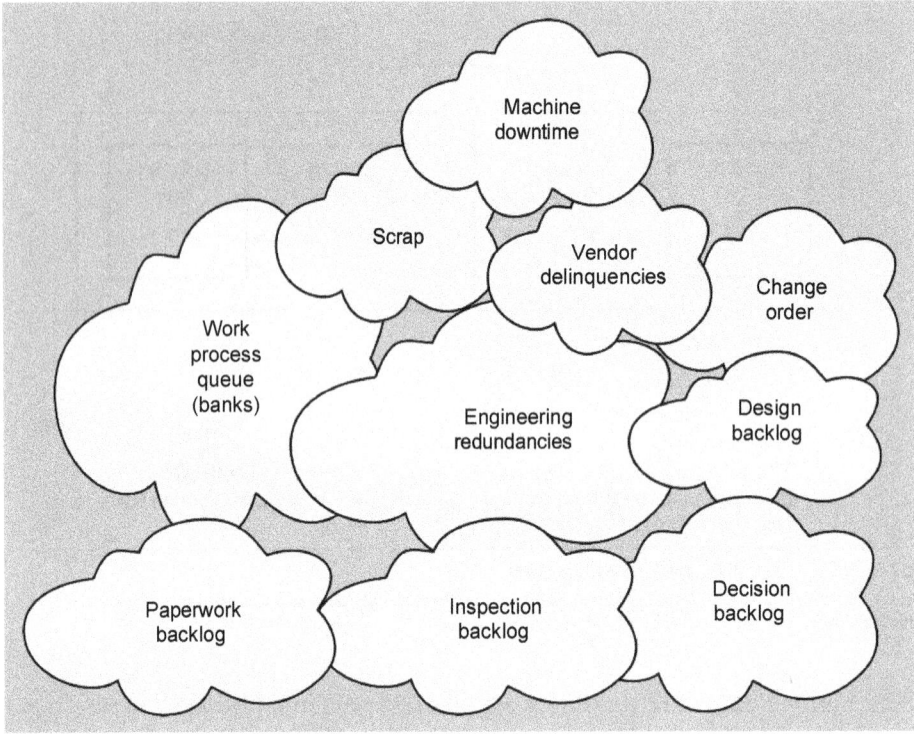

Figure 3.13 Inventory hides problems.
Source: Chase et al., 2004.

4. Any improvement must be made in accordance with the scientific method, under the guidance of a teacher, at the lowest possible level in the organization.

A successful pull system requires the following:

• Linked operations

• Balanced workstation capacities

• Redesigned layout for flow

• Emphasis on preventive maintenance

• Reduced lot sizes

• Reduced setup/changeover time

Quality assurance is an important element of the process, and a pull system will not function properly in its absence. Therefore, a pull system also requires:

• Worker responsibility—Workers must perceive themselves as process owners and accept accountability for their work area and quality.

- Measure SPC—SPC would allow employees in real time to attend to quality issues and constantly monitor their process quality performance.

- Enforced compliance—All rules and standard operating procedures must be followed at all times to ensure process consistency.

- Fail-safe methods.

- Automatic inspection—It has been proven that human visual inspection is at best 80% reliable. Therefore, this role should be transferred to more reliable systems where fatigue, boredom, job repetitiveness, and emotions do not affect performance. Automatic inspection systems have the capability of being more repeatable with fewer errors and variability.

Pull systems also demand a reliable schedule with some frozen horizon for production. Therefore, it is required for customers and suppliers to have a much closer relationship and deeper understanding of demands, expectations, and schedules. Pull systems attempt to pull value in pursuit of perfection.

Principle 5: Perfection

At this phase of the Lean process, the improved processes need to be fine-tuned by removing variations. Reducing variability results in process predictability and precision. At this stage of the process most of the muda has been discovered and eliminated; all VA and BVA are precisely identified for specific processes. After removing NVA, the process value stream should contain only VA. This VA needs to flow like a smooth river, while being pulled by the ultimate customer. This would depict a demand-driven system that is free of waste and flows from the source to the customer without major turbulences and interruptions. A demand-driven system minimizes cycle times and inventories and improves quality. It is the right stage to develop standard operating procedures and put in place tools to control process accuracy and repeatability. Tools used would range from SPC, gage R&R, checklists, control charts (IMR, X bar & R, etc.), and poka-yoke systems. Implementing perfection prior to this stage may be a waste of resources and effort, because processes may not be at their optimal settings. Instituting perfection prior to this stage would only create perfect non-value-added components. The Japanese take the route to perfection in two ways. One approach is kaizen, or incremental continuous improvement efforts, and the second is kaikaku, or quantum leap, which is the radical path to perfection. In fact, every enterprise needs both these approaches when pursuing perfection. Every step in a value stream can be improved in isolation to good effect, and there is rarely any ground for concern about investing to improve an activity that will soon be replaced altogether. Most value streams can be radically improved as a whole if the right mechanism for analysis can be put in place.

In order to effectively pursue both radical and incremental improvements, two final Lean techniques are needed. First, in order to form a view in their minds of what perfection would be, value-stream managers need to apply the four Lean principles: value specification, value-stream identification, flow, and pull. Then, value-stream managers need to decide which forms of muda to attack first through the deployment of what the Japanese refer to as Hoshin Kanri. The idea of Hoshin is for top management to agree on a few simple goals for transitioning from mass to Lean, to select a few projects to achieve these goals, to designate the people and resources for getting the projects done, and finally to establish numeric improvement targets to be achieved by a given point in time.

Principle 6: Agility

The entire Lean process is focused to eliminate waste and introduce profitability and competitiveness into the business. Therefore, speed of implementation plays a critical role in positioning the firm to take advantage of its Lean performance. Slow implementation warns competition and takes away the element of surprise. The competition will respond to suppress the firm's efforts if it is signaled by slow implementation. The Lean implementation, when followed properly, is a quick method of process improvement, because it activates all resources involved in the process at hand and takes their input into consideration (Womack & Jones, 2005).

Despite the fact that many businesses are adopting Lean methodology, few businesses have succeeded in achieving the level of performance improvements expected. Countermeasures to be addressed include:

- Initial implementation kick off and planning

- Establishing urgency

- Vision

- Training requirements and approach

- Goal setting

- Selection of the right metrics

- Identification of enablers and roadblocks in key Lean tools, including value-stream mapping, teamwork, empowerment, and kaizen

- Setting up an effective project management methodology and approach

Often the desire to improve the bottom line is vague during the initial implementation kickoff. Often there is a failure to clearly understand and articulate the desired three critical elements:

- Customer satisfaction

- Human factors

- Financial key factors

"The focus on customer satisfaction gets a lot of lip service, but usually it is second fiddle to the financial needs of the owners and stockholders" wrote Crabtree (2005, p. 18).

Project management should focus on desired results by identifying the key projects that must be completed. Team engagement and adequate resources and timing are keys to successful project completion. Even with careful planning the lack of the proper resources may result in unsuccessful project completion. It is also important to have constant feedback among project management, team members, and project sponsors to assure deployment of resources and the necessary adjustments during the project.

Imai suggests that 99% of the kaizen failures are due to the factors that top management either does not understand kaizen or is not fully committed to its implementation (Smith, 2005).

The MPI Group suggests:

Not surprisingly, many of these Lean discrete manufacturers report better operations and financial performances than their non-Lean peers. For example, sales per employee among discrete manufacturers using Lean and/or TPS is $176,000 (median). Among discrete manufacturers not using Lean and/or TPS, sales per employee is $54,000, and among discrete manufacturers without any improvement methodology, sales per employee is just $37,125. Similarly, on-time delivery is 95.6% (median) among Lean and/or TPS users, vs. 90% among non-Lean discrete manufacturers and 85% among firms without an improvement methodology. Two-thirds of Lean discrete manufacturers (66%) report increases in inventory turns over the last three years vs. 36% of non-Lean discrete manufacturers and manufacturers without improvement methodologies.

In some ways, then, discrete manufacturers who go Lean are becoming more Toyota-like. And yet, good as some of these results are, other metrics are comparable to—or even worse than—non-Lean organizations. For example, median gross margins are 10% lower (median) among Lean discrete manufacturers than non-Lean discrete manufacturers. This is not exactly Toyota-like performance, but Toyota has been at Lean for more than 50 years. Sustaining Lean improvement among discrete manufacturers with more recent adoptions may take time. Why haven't current Lean adopters differentiated their companies as much as Toyota and others? One reason is that many firms now applying Lean often choose the simplest, easiest-to-use tactics—with correspondingly low-level results. Stories abound, for example, of discrete manufacturers falling in love with 5S—basic Lean organization practices—and turning their plants into showrooms, with each tool in its place and well-marked walkways differentiated from work areas. Yet, while 5S is a necessary concept within Lean's mandates to stabilize, standardize, and improve, merely rearranging tools provides little bottom-line impact.

Even more advanced Lean methods such as *quick changeovers, poka-yoke, or single-piece flow* are too often wielded as hammers looking for obvious nails, perhaps generating local improvement, but not providing organization-wide results. This is especially true among discrete manufacturers. While the vast majority of Lean discrete manufacturers (97%) report using Lean in their production areas, far fewer take Lean outside of production: 23% use Lean in finance and accounting, 26% in customer relations, and 29% in administration. In fact, Lean discrete manufacturers report that only 60% (median) of their organizations' overall processes have been addressed with Lean Manufacturing (John R. Brandt & George Taninecz, 2009).

SIXSIGMA

Six Sigma is a rigorous and disciplined methodology that uses data and statistical analysis to measure and improve a firm's operational performance by identifying and eliminating "defects" in manufacturing and service-related processes. Commonly defined as 3.4 defects per million opportunities, Six Sigma can be defined and understood at three distinct levels: metric, methodology, and philosophy (Chase et al., 2004).

Many measurement standards (C_{pk}, zero defects, etc.) came on the scene later, but credit for coining the term *Six Sigma* goes to a Motorola engineer named Bill Smith. Six Sigma is a federally registered trademark of Motorola.

In the early and mid-1980s with Chairman Bob Galvin at the helm, Motorola engineers decided that the traditional quality levels—measuring defects in thousands of opportunities—didn't provide enough granularity. Instead, they wanted to measure the defects per million opportunities. Motorola developed this new standard and created the methodology and needed cultural change associated with it. Six Sigma helped Motorola realize powerful bottom-line results; in fact, the corporation has documented more than $16 billion in savings as a result of Six Sigma efforts.

Hundreds of companies around the world have adopted Six Sigma as a way of doing business. This is a direct result of many of America's leaders openly praising the benefits of Six Sigma. Two of these industry leaders are Larry Bossidy of Allied Signal (now Honeywell) and Jack Welch of General Electric.

Six Sigma has evolved. It's more than just a quality system like TQM or ISO. It's a way of doing business. Six Sigma can be seen as a vision, a philosophy, a symbol, a metric, a goal, or a methodology (Figure 3.14).

Six Sigma—A Metric

The roots of Six Sigma as a measurement standard can be traced back to Carl Frederick Gauss (1777–1855), who introduced the concept of the normal curve. Six Sigma as a measurement standard in product variation can be traced back to the 1920s when Walter Shewhart showed that three sigma (standard deviations) from the mean (μ) is the point where a process requires correction.

$$\text{Standard deviation} \qquad \sigma = \sum \frac{(\bar{x} - \mu)^2}{n - 1} \qquad (10)$$

The +/- three standard deviations was defined as natural tolerance or variability of the process due to randomness (Juran, 1993) (see Figure 3.15).

$$\text{Process natural variability: } \mu \pm 3\,\sigma \qquad (11)$$

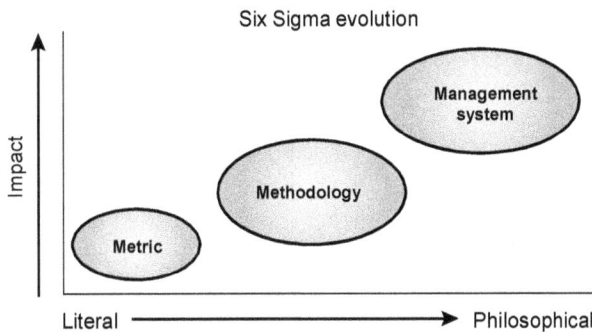

Figure 3.14   Six Sigma evolution.

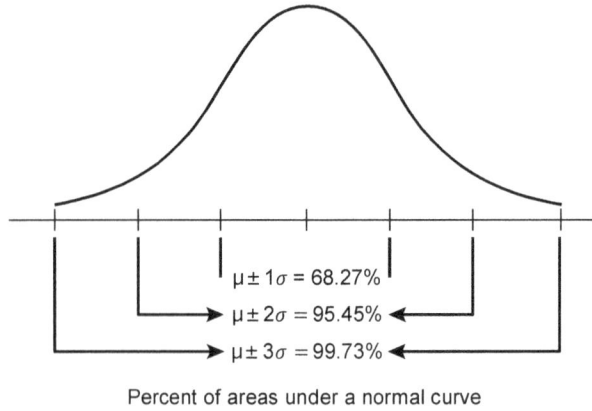

$$\mu \pm 1\sigma = 68.27\%$$
$$\mu \pm 2\sigma = 95.45\%$$
$$\mu \pm 3\sigma = 99.73\%$$

Percent of areas under a normal curve

Figure 3.15 Normal distribution.

Any events taking place outside this range are considered rare events. If a process is set with its natural variability equal to the customer specifications, then the slightest drift in the process μ will mean that a portion of the process will be outside of customer specifications. This is referred to as a process that is not capable (Figure 3.16). Process capability is identified as C_{pk}:

$$Process\ Capability\ Index: C_{pk} = min\ \left[\frac{(USL - \bar{x})}{3\sigma}\ or\ \frac{(\bar{x} - LSL)}{3\sigma}\right] \qquad (12)$$

USL = Upper specification limit

LSL = Lower specification limit

$\overline{X}$ = Process mean

σ = Process standard deviation

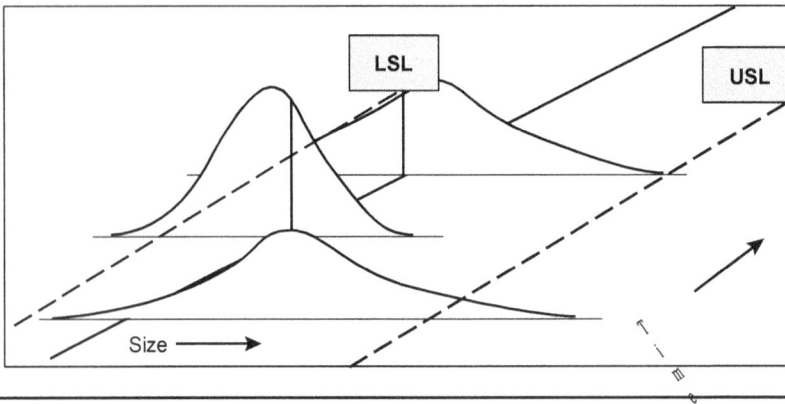

Figure 3.16 Process control.

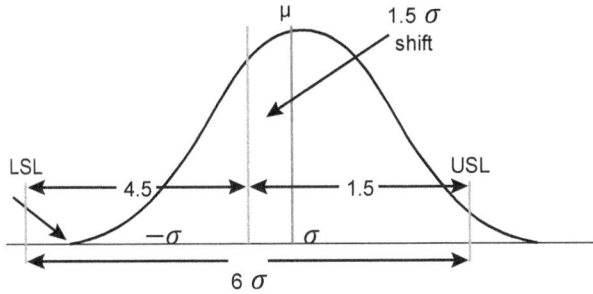

Figure 3.17   1.5 sigma shift assumption.

Processes that have crossed the customer specification limits are considered to be incapable of meeting their requirements (Figure 3.16). C_{pk} can be used to detect if the process mean has drifted. This is critical information for understanding the process performance and potential corrective actions. By the knowledge of the actual process location (mean), the process can be fine-tuned to be on target.

To create robustness in a process, meaning making the process insensitive to its natural 1.5 sigma drift, it is desirable to reduce process standard deviation, so that there are six sigma between the process mean and the nearest specification limit (Figure 3.17). In this case, when there is a drift in the process mean the process itself still stays capable of meeting the customer requirements (George 2002).

This is referred to as a Six Sigma process. Six Sigma as a metric is defined as 3.4 defects per million opportunities (DPMO). DPMO allows taking complexity of product/process into account. The rule of thumb is to consider at least three opportunities for a physical part/component—one for form, one for fit, and one for function, in absence of better considerations. The 3.4 DPMO is applicable when the process mean is assumed to have no more than +/- 1.5 sigma drift (Figure 3.18). In a 1.5 sigma shift, only 3.4 parts per million (PPM) fail to meet specifications. It is desirable to operate processes to be Six Sigma in the critical to quality (CTQ) characteristics and not the whole unit/characteristics. If the process is centered and has no drift, the DPMO reduces to 2 per billion opportunities, or 0.002 DMPO/PPM (Figure 3.19). The 1.5 sigma shift represents a more realistic picture of natural process variability.

The other related Six Sigma metrics are first pass yield (FPY), rolled throughput yield (RTY), PPM, Z-score or sigma level, and defects per unit (DPU).

$$FPY/RTY= P(x_1) . P(x_2). P(x_3) \ldots P(x_n) \qquad (13)$$

Where $P(x_n)$ is probability of success for a particular operation/process.

FPY is the probability of the activities going through the independent process steps without any rework or scrap. In other words, it is the proportion of the

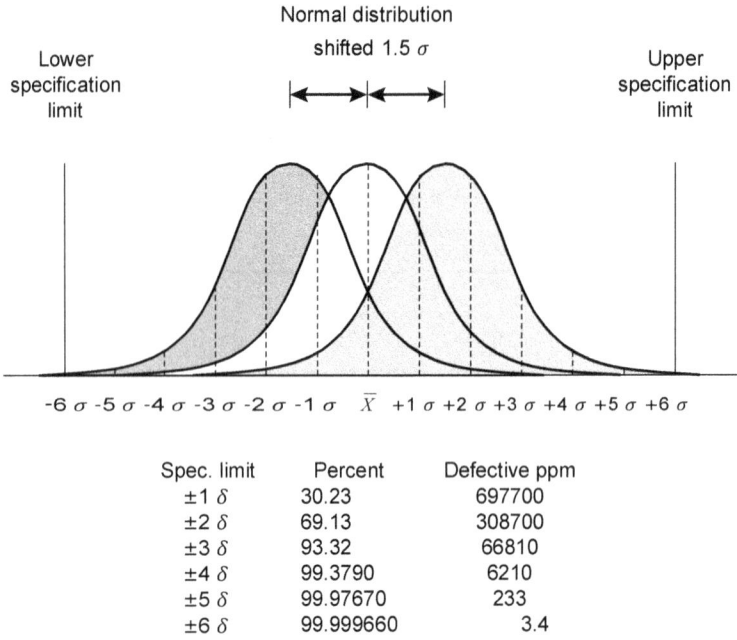

Spec. limit	Percent	Defective ppm
±1 δ	30.23	697700
±2 δ	69.13	308700
±3 δ	93.32	66810
±4 δ	99.3790	6210
±5 δ	99.97670	233
±6 δ	99.999660	3.4

Figure 3.18 Area under normal curve assuming 1.5 sigma shift.
Source: Breyfogle (2003).

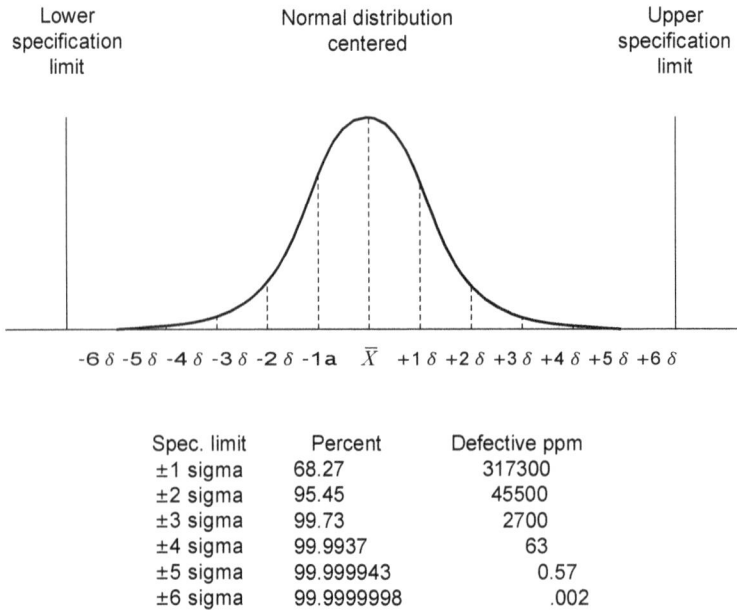

Spec. limit	Percent	Defective ppm
±1 sigma	68.27	317300
±2 sigma	95.45	45500
±3 sigma	99.73	2700
±4 sigma	99.9937	63
±5 sigma	99.999943	0.57
±6 sigma	99.9999998	.002

Figure 3.19 Relationship of sigma levels and PPM.
Source: Breyfogle (2003).

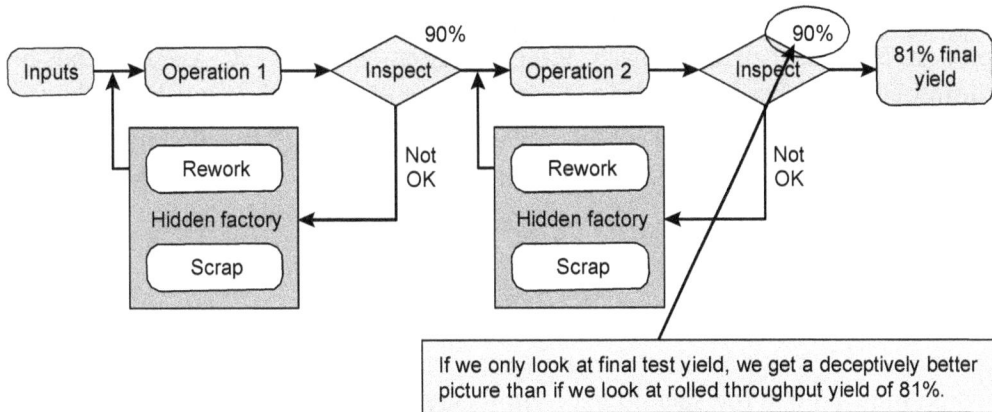

Figure 3.20 FPY in a two-step process.

process that can be produced without any defect the first time going through a system.

FPY is a metric that evaluates the system's performance as a whole. As more operation steps are involved, the FPY will get smaller. So it is very important to develop processes with simplified process steps. The more steps that there are in a process, the more opportunities that exist for failure. In Figure 3.20, parts are going through two independent process steps. The first process steps have passing rates of 90% each. This means that for every 100 parts going through them, 10 would be either reworked or scrapped. To estimate the probability of the whole system, we would use the Equation 13 and multiply the probability of successes at each process step. In this case, (0.90) X (0.90) would have a system yield of 0.81, or 81%. With only two steps in this process, the probability of a part successfully going through both steps the first time, without any rework or scrap, is only 81%. By determining the process FPY, additional information, such as PPM and DPU, can be obtained according to the relationship in Equations 14 and 15 (Breyfogle 2003).

$$PPM = (1 - Yield)\,10^6 \tag{14}$$

$$DPU = -lnFPY \tag{15}$$

Other Six Sigma measurements are as follows:

The Z-score is also referred to as sigma levels and is used to determine the number of standard deviations between the process mean and the critical region for that process.

$$Z\ Score = \frac{X - \mu}{\sigma} \tag{16}$$

This measurement is used to determine process goodness.

C_p, or process potential capability, is a measurement used to determine if the process is capable of meeting customer requirements at all. C_p assumes that the mean of the process is centered. This assumption frequently is invalid in the real world, but this is a good measurement to find out ideally how much of the customer specification could be met by the existing process (Gryna 2001).

$$C_p = \frac{|USL - LSL|}{6\sigma} \qquad (17)$$

An index of 1 would be the minimum acceptable level for C. A C_p of less than 1 would indicate that the specification limits are narrower than the process natural variation, and, as a result, a portion of the process would not meet the customer requirements. Thus, it is desirable to have an index greater than 1. For a process to be Six Sigma capable, the C_p index should be 2. This would mean that the process natural variability is half of the specifications, and if there are any minor drifts in the process mean the process would still be capable of meeting the requirements with a maximum amount of defect less than 3.4 DPMO. Some processes must have a much higher C_p index. For example, the pharmaceutical industry has process potential indexes of over 15. The higher the index, the more precise and repeatable the process would be. To illustrate correlation among C_p, PPM, and a, Table 3.6 samples some common values. Note that to use the process potential index the process must be normally distributed. This could be determined by inspecting the process histogram or plotting the sample points on probability paper.

By using these metrics, the process performance and health could be determined and cross-referenced. For example, the yield and its relationship with sigma level (Z-score) may be determined.

Process capability can be correlated with DPM/PPM for a given process. Based on the DPM, value goodness of a process can be assessed using Table 3.7.

Table 3.6   Relationship among C_p, PPM, and sigma level.

Cp	PPM	σ
1.00	66,813	3
1.33	6,210	4
1.50	1,350	4.5
1.67	233	5
1.83	32	5.5
2.00	3.4	6

Table 3.7 Sigma capability and DPM.

$\sigma'_{capability}$	DPM (2-sided)
6.0	3.4
5.5	32
5.0	233
4.5	1,350
4.0	6,210
3.5	22,750
3.0	66,810
2.5	158,687
2.0	308,770

Goodness of a process relates to the capability of that process in meeting the customer's DPM requirement.

Capability can also be computed if the DPM is known as follows:

$$\sigma_{capability} = 0.8406 + \sqrt{29.37 - 2.21 * Ln(DPM)} \qquad (18)$$

Six Sigma—A Methodology

In an attempt to drive processes to perform at 3.4 DPMO levels, it is necessary to develop a structured problem-solving roadmap and tools to achieve this. Motorola Corporation in 1987 developed the DMAIC (define, measure, analyze, implement, control) and DFSS (Design for Six Sigma) methodologies. The delivery of Six Sigma efforts was based upon creation of an implementation infrastructure "steering committee." This delegation includes a site champion and trained individuals, Green Belts, and Black Belts and the support of the process owners.

The steering committee is composed of representatives from all divisions or functions in the company plus the Six Sigma program manager. The committee meets weekly to review progress of projects, select people and projects, and attend to administrative issues.

The site champion sits on the steering committee and is responsible for several projects and assisting project team leaders by clearing roadblocks and mentoring them as needed. The site champion is trained in Six Sigma in order to be able to assist team leaders.

Process owners are typically managers who are responsible for the area where the improvement project is taking place. They set goals and objectives for the project leaders. Process owners sometimes take on the role of champion.

Green Belts are trained individuals who are also called Six Sigma specialists. They typically receive one or two weeks of training. Their responsibility is data collection and simple data analysis under direction of Black Belts. Green Belts may do individual projects where in-depth knowledge of statistical techniques is not required (Brussee 2004).

Black Belts are trained individuals who take on the role of project leaders, project team coaches, and change agents. Black Belts typically receive four weeks of training spread over four months. They are responsible for the financial outcome of their projects. Black Belts may also train and mentor Green Belts.

Master Black Belts are experienced Black Belts who typically go through an additional one to two weeks of training more focused on statistical approaches to problem solving and leadership and project management skills. Master Black Belts are primary trainers and coaches for Black Belts and Green Belts. They are resources to provide technical guidance in the proper application of the tools during project execution (Breyfogle et al., 2001).

The methodology applied for Six Sigma projects for process improvement efforts is DMAIC, as shown in Table 3.8. This approach is composed of a five-step approach that is customer focused with a project-based infrastructure. This methodology emphasizes providing extensive training in statistical quality tools. Therefore, the practitioners can apply actual quantitative data and apply statistical inference tools to logically solve process problems (Pyzdek 2003).

Step 1—Define

At this stage of improvement effort, the champion identifies and/or validates the improvement opportunity, develops the business processes, defines critical customer requirements, and selects team leaders for an effective project team.

Table 3.8 DMAIC process.

DMAIC	
Define	• Define the project goals and customer (internal and external) deliverables
Measure	• Measure the process to determine current performance
Analyze	• Analyze and determine the root cause(s) of the defects
Improve	• Improve the process by eliminating defects
Control	• Control future process performance

During this stage, the team is selected. The deliverables from this phase of the methodology are:

- Team charter, including mission statement and team objectives
- Action plans
- Process maps
- Quick-win opportunities
- Critical customer requirements
- Prepared team

Step 2—Measure

In this step, the objectives are to identify critical measures necessary for evaluating the success of KPIV and KPOV, meeting critical customer requirements, and beginning to develop a methodology to collect data to measure process performance, as well as understanding the elements of the Six Sigma calculation and establishing baseline sigma levels for the processes. The team maps out the existing processes to understand process flow and details. Some of the tools that may be used in this stage are: cause-and-effect diagram (C&E), quality function deployment diagram (QFD), preliminary failure mode effect analysis (FMEA), and measurement system analysis (MSA) to ensure that the measurement system is sufficiently accurate. The deliverables for this phase would be:

- Input, process, and output indicators
- Operational definitions
- Data collection formats and plans
- Baseline performance
- Productive team atmosphere

Step 3—Analyze

The objective of this phase of methodology is to stratify and analyze the opportunity to identify a specific problem and define an easily understood problem statement. It is important to identify and validate the root causes to make sure the *real* root cause has been identified. This is done by applying tools such as narrowing KPIVs to a vital few, collecting and analyzing data, and using histograms, box plots, and multivariant studies. To analyze output variables, use hypothesis testing to determine significant input variables. Correlation, regression, histograms, and so forth are all part of analysis of data. The result of this step is a list of a vital few input variables, Xs in the relationship $Y = f(x)$, (Pande et al., 2000).

Step 4—Improve

In this step of the methodology, the objectives are:

- To identify, evaluate, and select the right improvement solutions

- To develop a change-management approach to assist the organization in adapting to the changes recommended

In this stage the process model, $Y = f(x)$ needs to be established. Tools and activities supporting this stage could be design of experiments (DOE), in which a process mathematical prediction model is developed, as appropriate. Structured decision tools to select optimal solutions of qualitative input variables in order to optimize process performance need to be used. The deliverables of this stage would be:

- Process maps and documentation

- Solutions

- Change maps

- Implementation milestones

- Improvement impacts and benefits

- Storyboard

Step 5—Control

Objectives of this stage are:

- To hold the gains, understand the importance of planning and executing against the plan, and determine the approach to be taken to assure achievement of the targeted results

- To understand how to disseminate lessons learned and to understand standardization opportunities/processes

- To develop related plans

Typical tools used during this phase are development of a pilot plan and pilot solution, verification of reduction in root cause sigma improvement resulting from the solution, determining if additional solutions are necessary to achieve the goal, identifying and developing replication and standardization opportunities using SOP, and error-proofing techniques (poka-yoke). Then integrate and manage solutions in daily work processes in addition to integrating lessons learned. Further, identify the team's next steps and plans for remaining opportunities. Finally, compare improvements with the goals to ensure that objectives were met and turn the process over to the process owners (Pande et al., 2000). The deliverables at this stage are:

- Process control systems

- Standards and procedures

- Training

- Team evaluation

- Change implementation plans

- Potential problem analysis

- Pilot and solution results

- Success stories

- Trained associates

- Replication opportunities

- Standardization opportunities

In addition to DMAIC, another methodology—Design for Six Sigma (DFSS)—has been developed for achieving Six Sigma process capabilities for the design side. This attempts to involve the design process from the onset. The approach has proven to reduce rework and improve FPY because the design considers the process capabilities and functions with that framework.

DESIGN FOR SIX SIGMA

Design for Six Sigma (DFSS) is a process similar to DMAIC and is used for designing products and services. The goal is to incorporate robustness to achieve Six Sigma performances upfront in the design of the product or services. This is to match the production and operational processes capabilities with the design requirements (Juran & Godfrey, 1998). To accomplish these goals, design, optimize, and verify (DOV) is used; it is a popular methodology for designing products and services to meet Six Sigma standards. IDOV is a four-phase process: identify, design, optimize, and verify. These four phases parallel the four phases of the traditional Six Sigma improvement methodology: MAIC—measure, analyze, improve, and control.

Phase 1—Identify

The identify phase begins the process with a formal tie of design to specifications or the voice of the customer (VOC). This phase involves developing a team and team charter, gathering the VOC, performing competitive analysis, and developing CTQs.

Essential Steps

- Identify customer and product requirements.

- Establish the business case.

- Identify technical requirements (CTQ variables and specification limits).

- Determine roles and responsibilities.

- Set milestones.

Key Tools

- QFD (quality function deployment)

- FMEA (failure means and effects analysis)

- SIPOC (supplier, input, product, output, customer product map)

- IPDS (integrated product delivery system)

- Target costing

- Benchmarking

Phase 2—Design

The design phase emphasizes CTQs and consists of identifying functional requirements, developing alternative concepts, evaluating alternatives, selecting a best-fit concept, deploying CTQs, and predicting sigma capability (Juran & Godfrey, 1998).

Essential Steps

- Formulate concept design.

- Identify potential risks using FMEA.

- For each technical requirement, identify design parameters (CTQs) using engineering analysis such as simulation.

- Prepare raw materials and procurement plan.

- Prepare the manufacturing plan.

- Use DOE (design of experiments) and other analysis tools to determine CTQs and their influence on the technical requirements (transfer functions).

Key Tools

- Smart, simple design

- Risk assessment

- FMEA

- Engineering analysis

- Materials-selection software

- Simulation

- DOE

- Systems engineering

- Analysis tools

At this stage, attention should be given to the process steps or complexity. As shown in Table 3.9, any additional step in a process has a direct negative impact on process FPY and any complexity taken away from the process naturally improves its yield and sigma level capability by making it potentially simpler to produce.

Phase 3—Optimize

The optimize phase requires use of process capability information and a statistical approach to tolerance. Developing detailed design elements, predicting performance, and optimizing design take place within this phase. Table 3.9 depicts process overall yields vs. sigma levels. Desired sigma levels can be established and incorporated into the design.

Essential Steps

- Assess process capabilities to achieve critical design parameters and meet CTQ limits.

- Optimize design to minimize sensitivity of CTQs to process parameters.

- Design for robust performance and reliability.

- Use error-proofing, poka-yoke.

Table 3.9   Process overall yield vs. Sigma.

# of parts (steps)	Overall yield vs Sigma (distribution shifted 1.5(ð))			
	±3 σ	±4 σ	±5 σ	±6 σ
1	93.32%	99.379%	99.9767%	99.99966%
7	61.63	95.733	99.839	99.9976
10	50.08	93.96	99.768	99.9966
20	25.08	88.29	99.536	99.9932
40	6.29	77.94	99.074	99.9864
60	1.58	68.81	98.614	99.9796
80	0.40	60.75	98.156	99.9728
100	0.10	53.64	97.70	99.966
150	- - -	39.38	96.61	99.949
200	- - -	28.77	95.45	99.932
300	- - -	15.43	93.26	99.898
400	- - -	8.28	91.11	99.864
500	- - -	4.44	89.02	99.830
600	- - -	2.38	86.97	99.796
700	- - -	1.28	84.97	99.762
800	- - -	0.69	83.02	99.729
900	- - -	0.37	81.11	99.695
1000	- - -	0.20	79.24	99.661
1200	- - -	0.06	75.88	99.593
3000	- - -	- - -	50.15	98.985
17000	- - -	- - -	1.91	94.384
38000	Use for Benchmarking		0.01	87.880
70000			- - -	78.820
150000			- - -	60.000

Source: Motorola University (2004).

- Establish statistical tolerancing (Juran & Godfrey 1998).
- Optimize sigma and cost.
- Commission and start-up.

Key Tools

- Manufacturing database and flow-back tools
- Design for manufacturability
- Process capability models
- Robust design
- Monte Carlo methods
- Tolerancing
- Six Sigma tools

Phase 4—Validate

The validate phase consists of testing and validating the design. As increased testing using formal tools occurs, feedback of requirements should be shared with manufacturing and sourcing, and future manufacturing and design improvements should be noted.

Essential Steps

- Prototype test and validation
- Assess performance, failure modes, reliability, and risks
- Design iteration
- Final phase review

Key Tools

- Accelerated testing
- Reliability engineering
- FMEA
- Disciplined new product introduction (NPI)

Another approach similar to DMAIC is DMADV (define, measure, analyze, design, verify), as shown in Table 3.10. The two approaches are almost identical (Yang & EI-Haik, 2003).

Table 3.10 DMADV process.

DMADV	
Define	• Define the project goals and customer (internal and external) deliverables
Measure	• Measure and determine customer needs and specifications
Analyze	• Analyze the process options to meet the customer needs
Design	• Design (detailed) the process to meet the customer needs
Verify	• Verify the design performance and ability to meet customer needs

SUMMARY

The history of improvement techniques is certainly a checkered one. Not only have hoped-for results not materialized, but employees have often become cynical and half-hearted about trying new improvement efforts. Clearly identified improvements have not delivered the expected NP and ROI. There seems to be validity to the premise that we measure local improvements in one way and global improvements (NP and ROI) in another. T, I, and OE have been suggested as a way to bridge this gap, with T being treated as the most important measure to improve.

Having illustrated the limited results and lack of consensus about how to improve an organization's operations, our focus shifts to understanding the core problem. Maybe it would be helpful to understand how Ford and Ohno's management systems caused improvement. This chapter now will focus on the goals of different organizations; the need for global measurements like T, I, and OE; the fact that all organizations can be depicted as chains or networks; and that variability exists. The major implications are that real improvements can be measured only by their global impact, that T is the longest available lever, and that efforts should be focused heavily on bottlenecks or constraints and on reducing variability and dependencies.

WHEREWEWENTWRONG

Ford's system worked well because he was dealing with a highly integrated system producing only one product, which made it easier to manage with a holistic approach. But consumers' expectations and tastes began to morph as new options become apparent. The newer cars were fulfilling the customer's expectations in new dimensions such as prestige, amusement, hobby, and style, which was a significant departure from the original purpose of transportation.

The complexities grew for companies as they responded to the consumer markets and offered more products and varieties; the size, scope, and level of complexities grew significantly. Therefore, operations management became more difficult and required much more complex systems to manage the supply chain, manufacturing, throughput, materials, responsiveness, technology, human capital, energy resources, environmental effects, and infrastructures. These complexities made the measurement operations' effectiveness both more difficult and critical.

To solve this problem, companies dissected their organizations into parts and focused efforts on improving the parts.

Because most of the parts of these companies were not directly connected to the marketplace, new measures of performance were developed based largely on the cost concept (labor efficiency, product cost, investments), and they were initially very effective, because most costs varied directly with production volumes. Over time more of a company's costs became fixed and fewer varied directly with volumes, making the use of these local or cost measures not only obsolete, but counterproductive.

Most organizations focus their improvement efforts on reducing the direct labor costs. This may initially sound logical; we know that lower direct labor costs could mean lower operating costs, resulting in increased profits. What about achieving the lowest direct labor costs? Wouldn't zero labor costs sound good? Would it not imply that we have no direct labor? Can we run a manufacturing enterprise with no direct labor? So does this mean that we shut down all operations requiring direct labor? This obviously is not the right answer. If the direct labor cost reduction is not the answer, then what should be done to improve business profitability? The short answer is throughput optimization, as long as the market is not the primary constraint.

Shifting the focus to increasing throughput will allow the entity to reduce its operating costs as a natural outcome of increased volume. The higher the throughput, the more diluted the operating costs would become. This approach has additional benefits. The focus trained on increasing throughput directs the organization's talents toward creativity, innovation, and quantum leap approaches. Focusing on throughput improvement promotes thinking outside of the box of traditional profitability paradigms. By looking beyond common approaches, such as labor cost reductions, headcount reductions, etc., the organization's efforts are channeled to expanding the business, rather than shrinking it. This focus creates opportunities for increasing market share, which as a natural outcome may require additional development of the organization's infrastructure. This effect would create more jobs and more opportunities for social prosperity in addition to more profits. It is clear that increased throughput, with measured and synchronized efforts to contain operations expenses, yields higher profitability margins. The higher profitability allows organizations to pay more attention to their human capital, improve their internal and external training and development, invest in research and development, and further improve quality and reliability instead of taking shortcuts on quality and product performance. The outcome certainly would favor a more satisfied customer base and more involved and satisfied employees.

It is not a mystery that satisfied employees are more inclined to contribute to the company, and if they are given the opportunity to be involved and empowered they would be more likely to drive their own and their environment's creativity and productivity to higher levels. This behavior would further excite global progress and competitiveness, and the cumulative interaction effect will create prosperous environments for a higher employment rate. A society with a higher employment rate naturally possesses higher buying power, which is needed to stabilize the world economy.

In 2009, over 16 million Americans were out of jobs! Would the natural and expected behavior of these individuals be to purchase more cars, electronic gadgets, and luxury materials; receive more medical services; or invest in stocks, home improvements, vacations, entertainment, or food? Obviously not. How about the rest of the individuals who are employed—would they be inclined to overpurchase to make up for the lack of buying power of the 16 million? To the contrary, it is more likely that during the tough economic times the employed population follows the similar pattern as the unemployed, holding back due to the heightened insecurities and uncertainties revolving around fear of job losses. The aggregate effect of these behaviors is predictable and results in shrink- ing

market demands. This morphs into a vicious cycle that disrupts economic stability for most for-profit enterprises. Obviously, the pressure will be passed onto taxpayers in one way or another. Organizations have to be cognizant of this phenomenon and must deploy strategies to prevent its spiral effect. The key to organizations' cash flow revenue-generation stability is to operate below the market constraints and deploy measurements that address system constraints and protection of throughput. Therefore, the measurement systems should focus on guiding the organization to make throughput improvements. Measurements should also identify any hazards that could prevent throughput attainment.

Focus on the throughput aspect of operations requires total understanding of the processes, their attributes, their relationship from the local and global perspective, and their flows. It is critical to intimately understand the key factors that are capable of significantly throttling the throughput and to learn what type of process variabilities exist. We must understand processes' capabilities and how to statistically control them so that robust process capabilities can be reliably maintained.

Measurements focused only on direct labor costs can at times portray false pictures of the operations and leave opportunities on the table. The following example examines the fallacy of focusing on direct labor cost reduction as a primary means of reducing operating costs and improving profits.

Let's assume that we have an operation that has sales of $100k and its material cost is $35k. The direct labor cost is $10k, with $50k in overhead costs. So the operation's total costs before taxes and depreciation are $95k. This operation will have $5k profits, or earnings before interests, taxes, depreciation, and amortization (EBITDA).

$$\text{Profit Margin EBITDA} = (\text{Profits/Sales} \times 100)$$
$$\$5k/100k \times 100 = 5\%$$

Now let's assume that the organization is not satisfied with the 5% profit margin and wants to significantly increase it. Following are three feasible paths for meeting this objective.

Case I: Direct Labor Reductions

Management decides on the traditional approach to reduce the direct labor, say by 20%. The organization assembles kaizen teams to explore opportunities to reduce the direct labor costs. The teams are successful and identify enough improvements to shrink the labor costs by 20%. In this case, we will not reduce the material costs, because we assume that the same labor force is still capable of delivering the same amount of products, which we sell for $100k. So now the direct labor costs drops to be $8k ($10k $\times$ 0.20). As illustrated in Table 3.11, this change reduces the operating costs $93k, which improves the net profits to $7k, or 7% of the total sales vs. the initial net profit margin of 5%. So the 20% reduction of direct labor costs added 2% to the profit margin. This change may satisfy management, because the 40% increase in net profits sounds significant. $[(7k/5k) - 1] \times 100$.

Case II: Increase Throughput

In this case, management decides to improve net profits by focusing on throughput, meaning it wants to find ways to increase its marketable production by 20%.

Table 3.11   Benefits of reducing direct labor costs.

	Initial stage	Reduce direct labor
Sales	$ 100	$ 100
Raw materials	$ 35	$ 35
Direct labor	$ 10	$ 8
Overhead	$ 50	$ 50
Total cost	$ 95	$ 93
Net profit	$ 5.0	$ 7.0
% Increase		40%

Table 3.12   Benefits of increasing throughput.

	Initial stage	Reduce direct labor	Increase throughput
Sales	$ 100	$ 100	$ 120
Raw materials	$ 35	$ 35	$ 42
Direct labor	$ 10	$ 8	$ 12
Overhead	$ 50	$ 50	$ 50
Total cost	$ 95	$ 93	$ 104
Net profit	$ 5.0	$ 7.0	$ 16.0
% Increase		40%	220%

We won't assume improvement will save direct labor costs at this time, because we want to isolate the effect of throughput on profitability. This initiative is going to require more direct labor to support the additional 20% production. Direct labor costs will increase to $12k, which drives total costs to $106k (see Table 3.12). This may be counterintuitive to a company's direct labor cost reduction culture.

Net profit now climbs by more than 300%, to $16k! Additionally the profit margins soars to 13.3% of the sales. In this scenario, a 20% increase in sales improves the net profits by 13.3% which is more than twice the level achieved by reducing labor costs by 20%.

$$[(16k/5k) - 1] \times 100) = 220\%$$

Case III: Labor and Throughput Improvements

Of course the company can both improve its direct or indirect labor productivity by implementing continuous process improvement (kaizen) activities and better using the existing resources. Successful results means that when more throughput is needed, proportionately less labor will be required. Let us assume that company's kaizen teams improve labor use by only 10% (Table 3.13). This 10% would directly fall to the bottom line and change the net profits by that exact amount. In this case, the $1k improvement, improves the net profits by the same $1k. Net profit improves to $17.2k, or 17% of the sales. The improvement from the initial stage are now 224% greater.

$$[(17.2k/5k) - 1] \times 100) = 244\%$$

Although what we just discussed sounds simple and appears to display common sense, many managers have difficulty understanding and practicing it. It is the change agents' responsibility to have a sound grasp of these concepts and then lead their organizations' transformations.

Table 3.13 Benefits of increasing throughput and labor savings.

	Initial stage	Reduce direct labor	Increase Throughput	Increase Throughput + CPI
Sales	$ 100	$ 100	$ 120	$ 120
Raw materials	$ 35	$ 35	$ 42.0	$ 42.0
Direct labor	$ 10	$ 8	$ 12.0	$ 10.8
Overhead	$ 50	$ 50	$ 50.0	$ 50.0
Total cost	$ 95	$ 93	$ 104	$ 102.8
Net profit	$ 5.0	$ 7.0	$ 16.0	$ 17.2
% Increase		40%	220%	244%

A throughput focus has additional advantages, such as allowing companies to strategically adjust and position their pricing strategies. For example, if the price in this example was a determining factor for obtaining additional market share, this company would be in a more favorable position to reduce its prices and yet enjoy healthy profitability. This competitive advantage allows the company to strategically make offers to its marketplace that its customers may not be able to refuse. This strategy could lead to further strengthening company's competitive position. It may also contribute to competitors losing a foothold in that particular market segment, increasing the competitiveness of the company.

Measurements play a key role in determining organizational behavior. Measurements that promote the desired behaviors are vital to an organization, and of course measurements can degrade the organization's performance. Effective measurements focus on the elements that are critical to the organizations performance. Having too many measurements reduces their importance and confuses the organization. In addition, they may not contribute to elimination of process bottlenecks, promotion of the desired organizational behavior, or improvement in profits. So choose measurements that are meaningful and truly important to achieving the organization's global objectives.

I interviewed an executive, who had applied iTLS to improve his division's revenues. He told the following story:

> The head of my division I asked to put together a marketing strategy for our company. To give a little background on the company's situation, our company had 10 divisions. The revenue of each of the other nine divisions was over a billion dollars, and that our relatively new organization would also reach these levels. Our division's revenues were currently less than 10% of the revenues generated by the other divisions. The products

of our division were the aftermarket services. Our company had a centralized corporate sales and marketing team responsible for selling the services and products provided by all divisions. The problem was that our division sales were flat, and we were desperately seeking ways to increase revenues. We were mystified as to why our division revenues were low and not growing, even though we had the capability and capacity of delivering much higher throughput! So my boss asked me to put together a marketing strategy to increase our market share and revenues.

So our goal was to increase our revenues, and the marketing strategy was to layout strategies and plans to achieve this end. As I began my research process a series of facts and conditions surfaced. We had an opportunity to formulate a strategy for increasing market share by leveraging the company's current customer base by providing them aftermarket services. Also we decided to conduct a benchmarking study to see where our revenue level stood relative to our competition. We quickly discovered that our revenues were significantly lower than our competition which ignited a flurry of inquiries to discover the reason. We began an analysis of our current markets, size, segments, customers, and their potential and actual revenues, etc., and began talking to our sales and marketing teams.

While interviewing account managers and sales teams, I learned that our company sales force had very little knowledge about our division, its products, capabilities, strengths, and value-added services. I began digging deeper to understand the reasons for such a deep gap; knowing that we had conducted several educational and training sessions with the company sales teams. The sales teams were composed of experienced and intelligent individuals, so why did these folks know so little about our division's value-added services despite the fact that they had been trained? It is probably worthwhile to mention that none of the sales team members had voiced any confusion or lack of understanding of the training materials addressing our division products and services.

The typical assumption that physical constraints and capacities are the cause of lack of throughput soon was voided as we applied the iTLS process. There were some serious arguments that our plants did not have enough capacity to produce; therefore, sales were not pushing our products. As you can imagine, this had ignited hot debates and at times finger pointing within our division and between sales and operations. When we began to dig deeper during our interview with the sales team members, we discovered that the sales force was rewarded with incentives and bonuses based on the amount of their sales. As the mystery began to unravel, the core problem started to surface. The products and services that our division offered were significantly smaller in dollar value in comparison with the other divisions. Suddenly it became apparent why the sales force had no particular interest and excitement to learn and market our products and services. We also found that it took a salesperson the same amount of effort to introduce, market and sell our products as the products offered by sister divisions. Unfortunately, they generated much lower sales for the same effort when they sold our products.

So clearly, a salesperson that was being measured and rewarded based on the amount of sales, our division's products and services were not very attractive. This problem had persisted despite the fact that our division's services had an attractive double-digit profit margin compared to single digits for the manufactured goods being supplied by the other divisions. As I mentioned, our products and services were complex and required a significant amount of active effort to market them. This discovery exposed a basic conflict between our division's goal and the sales team's compensation system. The sales team certainly were responding and behaving according to their organizations internal measurements and optimizing their own returns. The internal measurement system for the sales and marketing department had not taken into consideration our division's needs for sales and were cherry-picking opportunities with larger accounts in order to increase their own compensation while not considering the impact on profit margins. The policy and its measurement system that drove this behavior had created sub-optimization use of the company resources, capabilities, and opportunities for growth.

Through application of iTLS, we mapped out the entire process and clearly identified the actual constraint to be the erroneous policy and its respective measurement system. We needed a compelling story to build our case to display the attractiveness of our market segment for the corporate sales and marketing organizations. We knew that we had to create what-is-in-it-for-them to entice them to listen! So we compiled all our internally focused market research studies and analysis and prepared a marketing strategy document which explicitly quantified and illustrated the total market potential, the company's probable potential, and target market segments. Within those target market segments, our plans identified target industries, and within those target industries we clearly focused on potential target customers to approach. We then arranged for a joint meeting with our division's executive team and the sales and marketing people. Our strategic plan was succinct and had enough useful information to convince corporate sales and marketing that there were feasible and viable opportunities. Then, it was jointly decided that it was in the best interest of the company to vigorously pursue the selected targets.

iTLS also guided our teams in developing a desired process flow that engaged the corporate sales resources with our division. IT systems were modified to expand our internal social network to improve cross-division communications. Our division services that were a natural extension of manufacturing, after-market services, were bundled up-front with the original manufactured products when sales were being pursued. We also arranged for regular training of sales teams and on-site involvement with our division. Further, in order to have a dedicated process owner for this drive, an experienced sales executive was dedicated to our division to bring focused leadership for market share expansion of our products and services.

We knew that we had to establish relevant and solid measurements to continuously guide and control the newly established process. To improve the existing measurement systems, we formulated a measurement model which included sales of our services as part of the simple computation algorithm that determined how much bonus should be paid to the sales force. The new measurement system credited the sales team through a weighted point system that provided opportunities for them to maintain their bonuses and incentives while selling our products and services. We also devised a program review mechanism to ensure effectiveness and sustainability of the approach with maintained sales and marketing accountability. I must also mention that our teams together modified the existing processes and procedures to ensure uniform implementation and sustainability of the program.

When I asked Ed what was next, he said: "Our team will rescan our processes to see if our process constraint has shifted elsewhere and of course we will go after removing that constraint. That is how we apply iTLS in our business."

This of course turned out to be an exceptional success story! What if Ed had not wanted to rock the boat and confront the centralized corporate sales team and their executives with his findings? What if he did not take actions for fear of not being able to get a buy-in from his senior management, or fear of losing his job or political popularity because his business unit was much smaller than the other divisions? What if the corporate sales team found his suggestions confrontational when Ed brought up the issue of modifying the payout measurement system? Would his suggestions have been interpreted as a political attack on sales and marketing executives (inferring that the sales team is not doing its job)? If Ed had not taken the action of building a solid business case for his division's position and presenting it quantitatively to the sales team, then Ed himself would have become the constraint in the process.

I am sure there are many other combinations and permutations of this situation that could have resulted in significantly different outcomes. It is not uncommon for organizations to act irrationally when policy or political constraints are discovered and confronted. The behavior of resisting change to the holistic improvement of an organization can certainly lead to its eventual atrophy and destruction, and this is the beginning of how things go wrong.

Ford, GM, and Chrysler are examples of how a combination of poor leadership, resistance to change, and political and policy constraints chokes an organization's progress and competitiveness. Great organizations with mammoth capital, resources, talents, and potential are brought to their knees and fall in favor of their competitors. Management's inability to apply sound measurement systems undermines improvement systems' full capabilities and leads to suboptimization of productivity, profitability, and prosperity of the organization. David von Drehle (2009) provides the following astonishing statistics about GM, illustrating how GM, which was considered "king of the road" in the 1960s, transformed itself into "a clunker" in 2009 (see Table 3.14). GM received over $20 billion in a U.S. government bailout in January 2009 but filed for bankruptcy in May 2009!

Measurement systems that focus on short-term, myopic, and local optimization strategies obviously drive behavior that fits those measurements. The effects of these measurements are typically observed in the form of staff confusion; conflicting goals, objectives, initiatives, and projects; taking shortcuts; and a lack of solid direction, longevity, and commitment to the served markets, its employees, customers, and the communities.

Another significant contributor to why things go wrong is the inability of an organization to implement and sustain its improvement projects and programs.

How many times have you been faced with project teams struggling to close their projects or project deadlines that have extended well over the intended time line? Whether you've used Lean, TOC, or Six Sigma continuous improvement methodologies, you probably have heard a variety of teams' responses regarding questions as to why projects have not closed on time or have failed to be completed at all. Often, the blame is placed on the project leadership.

The reasons for continuous improvement programs losing traction despite their potential for improvement are numerous. Dusharme (2004) surveyed team leaders in order to obtain information on the reasons for continuous improvement

Table 3.14 GM story.

	1962	**2009**
Sales	$105 bn	$30.9 bn (loss)
U.S. market share	51%	23%
U.S. employees	464,000	92,000
Net income	$1.46 bn	$4.4 bn (loss)
U.S. vehicle sales	4.2 m	2.9 m

projects not delivering the intended results. Respondents cited the following reasons in the following order:

1. Lack of management support

2. Lack of resources

3. Lack of management alignment understanding

4. Unreasonable expectations

5. Misunderstanding of what the continuous improvement approach is

As effective leaders in organizations, what can you do to ensure that your critical initiatives come to fruition rapidly? Clearly, the only organizations that survive today are those that show competitive leadership and agility. So you might ask how we could achieve the required leadership. Here are some suggestions that could significantly help you to improve a team's ability to complete a project.

One suggestion is to apply Mobilize, Organize, Speed up, Tie up loose ends (MOST), a principal of leadership that brings discipline, order, and agility to your continuous improvement project management (Pirasteh, 2005). MOST is a simple process that organizes project management and ensures that proper attention is given to your project efforts. MOST is discussed in more detail in later chapters.

As mentioned, the majority of reasons for the failure of CPI projects and initiatives fall on leadership's and management's abilities, responsibilities, and commitment. Almost all of the five reasons mentioned are typically controlled by management. Management leadership must totally commit to long-term involvement and growth of CPI culture.

Of course, it is leadership's responsibility to provide their teams with vision, leadership, and resources for sound project management. Management should insist that CPI and financial improvements are counted in a manner that shows that they are real improvements. It is also critical for the leadership to be commited. Commitment is long term and requires patience, passion, persistence, and understanding that sustainable continuous improvement efforts require the right cultures, and that building the right culture requires effort and time. It is not unusual for improvement teams to fumble and make mistakes when they are learning the system. It is no mystery that many great lessons have been learned as a result of those mistakes. Therefore, there should be some degree of tolerance for the implementation teams. This statement certainly does not imply tolerance for careless, uncalculated, frivolous risks. However, such an understanding would promote creativity and provide a foundation for quantum leaps, as team members understand that it is OK for them to take calculated risks.

When leadership and the business culture do not tolerate mistakes, negative inertia will quickly set in, team members will be apprehensive of taking any risks, and cultural motivation will switch from creativity to fear-based initiatives. Fear of repercussions, punishment, blame, and put-down in an organization's culture confines and dooms that organization to stagnation and the status quo. Taking away the barriers of fear encourages team members to take more action toward continuous improvement, and the cycle of learning improves. The cycle of learning refers to the experiences gained as a task or process goes through a full cycle, from start to finish. Some of these experiences could be positive and some could be undesirable, complex, or difficult. The undesirable or difficult experiences are typically improved because there are opportunities to repeat the cycle through improvement in the operators' understanding and skill sets. If there are more opportunities, the learning could be further refined by eliminating the undesirable experiences and repeating the positive ones. As the cycle of learning is repeated, one could expect to see the cycle time and process quality improve.

Effective leaders allow their teams to accumulate experience by empowering them to participate in training and application activities and encouraging them to implement project after project. These leaders understand that in order to do anything well, experience is essential. Experience is accumulated only by doing something over many times, *if perfection is the goal*. Malcolm Gladwell mentions the 10,000-hour rule as an indication and a requirement for developing outstanding and exceptional performance (Gladwell, 2008). The 10,000-hour rule is basically translated into doing something 8 hours, 2.5 days a week for approximately 10 years. Gladwell conducted an extensive research to understand what elements are the critical key factors in achieving exceptional, or what we may consider extraordinary, achievement. He studied the cause-and-effect relationships of all known conditions for some of the world's most successful individuals. Gladwell argues that allowing individuals to practice to become great at what they are doing is probably as effective, if not more, than being genetically gifted. This analogy, when examined against our typical expectations with CPI activities, requires some additional work!

CPI requires involvement of cross-functional owners doing the grunt work with deep understanding of the processes. During this process, coupled with the pressure to make changes rapidly and significantly, occasionally CPI teams make mistakes. These errors could be studied and applied as great educational topics for deeper and more accurate CPI implementation in the next cycle. The lessons learned from failures and mistakes can be as valuable as first-pass successes for organization's CPI initiatives and culture if used for knowledge improvement and not ignored or misapplied as punitive measures.

Unfortunately, this could be a conflict with management's short-term views and goals. Frequently, management leadership decides to implement CPI programs with the expectation of quick results. Often, organizations decide to apply CPI initiatives when their organization is at the verge of a financial heart attack or has already had the heart attack! The inherent conditions are typically stressful, pressuring management to take initiatives for a rapid turn in trends of current business results. At times, management is looking for a "silver bullet" to save the organization and take all the pains away, ignoring the fact that their organizations have arrived at the existing condition through a typically long process. The effort to overcome and deflect the profitability curve is also a process that could take time and resources and certainly is not a one-time event. Failure to consider this point pressures managements to become impatient and dissatisfied with their programs' progress and decide to either stop the progress or switch over to another CPI alternative.

Imagine an overweight individual who is told by his physician that if he does not lose 100 pounds he will face serious health repercussions. A typical approach is for the individual to gravitate toward a diet program. However, if he is impatient to see the effects of the diet program, he may be inclined to switch to another diet program, and this could go on. This individual must see his diet program and physical fitness as a way of life and not a short-term fix. If this individual does not commit himself to following proper nutritional guidelines and physical fitness requirements, it is unlikely that he will be able to attain a sustainable weight.

This type of management does not recognize the effects and importance of cycles of learning and experience model. A typical outcome is that management may come to view any initiative as "the program of the month." Managers may adversely view CPI initiatives as inconveniences instead of keys to their organization's productivity and longevity of their employment. Their strategy is to just hang on and eventually the program will fade away. This type of management would not be able to effectively benefit from the CPI initiatives.

What does it take to maintain a successful and sustainable CPI program? Leadership's total commitment to persevere, encourage, inspire, educate, and empower the CPI teams to solve problems over and over is a must. This promotes the development of the in-house expertise that is required to tackle various process improvement opportunities and develop problem-solving skills. The iTPS system addresses this long-term commitment as a critical success factor through the 4P philosophy:

- Philosophy
- Processes
- People
- Problem-solving

iTLS embraces this philosophy as an integral element of a sustainable operational ecosystem (Figure 3.21).

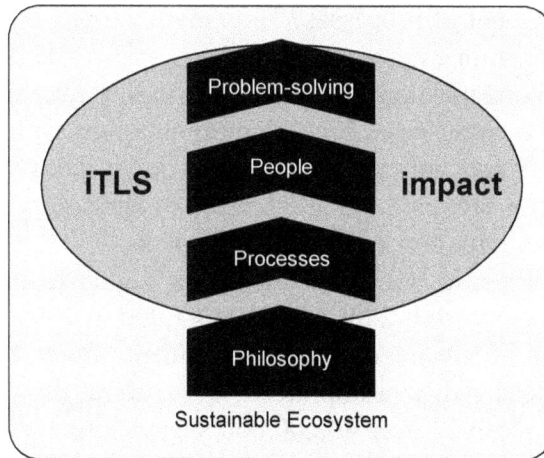

Figure 3.21   Sustainable operational ecosystem.

The premise of this model is that the organization needs to have an operating philosophy with a succinct and clear mission, vision, and set of values with total management commitment. These values and vision then are translated into specific sets of objectives that will move the entire organization toward a common set of goals with clear line of sight. These goals and objective are further translated into the processes that are capable of meeting the target objectives. Workers (people) are then trained, coached, mentored, and measured using those processes. Employees' growth and total involvement is the key here. The model suggests elevating the worker's skills so that they not only master competency in their required work processes but also can perform problem-solving at the root level, where the actual work is being done, and continuously improve their processes.

Management of CPI initiatives is a delicate responsibility and must be approached with long-term and global optimization benefits in mind. Short-term and myopic management practices focused on meeting the month-end, quarter-end numbers undermines this enormous capability, preventing CPI culture from fully developing. It is not unlikely to come across organizations that had invested in a CPI initiative, trained their workforce, obtained some favorable results through implementation of their CPI program, and then what do they do? They lay off the very same employees who were trained; learned the organization's processes, strengths and weaknesses; applied those experiences; and improved the company's processes!

What could be expected of the further growth or survival potential opportunities for this CPI culture? Would employees not perceive the CPI as an evil instead of a key to competitiveness and prosperity? What happens to the institutional memory? This is the invaluable experience that the employee has collected in helping to institutionalize processes in the company. What would happen to continuous improvement of processes? How many employees would be willing to participate in kaizen or improvement projects or provide their suggestions to further improve the organization's products, services, profitability, or efficiency? Would employees be enthused to become more involved with the organization's processes and issues and volunteer their services for improvement? Employee involvement has been proven a key element in organizational process improvements in conjunction with properly selected projects.

When General Electric (GE) introduced Six Sigma to its organization, the number of projects grew from 200 in 1995 to 47,000 in 1999 (Slater, 1999). GE published $2 billion in savings due to improvement efforts that were driven by employee involvement. Are you impressed? How about this: Toyota announced in 2001 that it had received over 40,000,000 suggestions for improvement from employees. This is about 2,000,000 suggestions per year or 50 suggestions per employee or one suggestion per week! Do you get that in your organization? Is it now a mystery why Toyota is capturing automobile markets worldwide while companies such as Chrysler and General Motors are going bankrupt? Toyota's commitment to continuous improvement through its TPS has been the key to its agility, productivity, and profitability. Toyota's long-term leadership commitment to its people, processes, and continuous improvement has been the key success factor. Toyota understands how to value, preserve, and improve the institutional memory of it employees and continuously improve it to perfection. To achieve perfection, Toyota also realizes the importance of experience cycles and their requirements.

The organizations that do not put this awareness to practice in benefiting their organization are in a constant loop of reworking what they wanted to do strategically in the first place. This is organizational muda, or waste!

Some organizations spend resources to hire talent, train, apply the training, and get some improvement results, and then they begin softening the intensity of their drive for pursuit of operations excellence through continuous improvement discipline. When these organizations are faced with financial difficulties, they attack direct labor costs, laying off the resources that they had trained to help them grow, rather than understanding the constraints and improving throughput. Then, if they make it through the rough time, they suddenly remember that they have been complacent with processes and quality improvements and need to work on continuous improvement processes. So they hire new resources and go through the cycle again and again. I call this "CPI tourism syndrome." In these situations, CPI practices and its practitioners are like tourists who visit an organization for a while, perform some show-and-tell, and when vacation time is over either leave or get kicked out. This is the constant organizational rework loop that leadership should avoid as a result of erroneous tactical thinking and lack of long-term strategic vision. During the 2008 American recession, which significantly impacted automobile manufacturing and its distribution channels, two of the Big Three automakers nearly collapsed and asked the U.S.

government for significant financial assistance as an alternative to bankruptcy, which for some of them did not help because the organizational heart attack had gone too long unnoticed!

These organizations were sunk in their local optimization illness. When senior management of GM, Ford, and Chrysler went to ask Congress for billions of dollars in financial assistance, to be provided by the U.S. taxpayers, they all flew to Washington in private jets while they were cutting jobs in manufacturing and the distribution channels where throughput was actually being converted to cash! What is wrong with this picture? This reminds me of an old story of a girl who was born into a very wealthy family and had a very comfortable lifestyle all her life. Naturally her perception of the entire world was a reflection of her own lifestyle. One day her composition teacher gave her class an assignment to write a short story about a poor family. Her story went something like this: "Once upon a time there was a very poor family living in London. They were all very poor, the husband, wife, and children were all poor. Their butlers and their maids were poor. Their driver and the gardener were also poor. . . ."

Interestingly, during the same time, Toyota sustained its health and operations and only fine-tuned its production by throttling it to match the market demands. What is interesting is that for a long time many organizational development and quality gurus such as Deming and Juran have harped on the criticality of systematic improvements, treating employees with respect, long-term planning, value of employee involvement, and so forth. Not all enterprises, however, have believed, understood, and followed these principals. Toyota and Honda are among the ones that listened carefully, understood and put every piece of advice into a well-disciplined and regimented practice. Management models that focus only on short-term goals will cripple their organization from creativity and progressiveness and actually promote employee apathy and disengagement of talents and commitment. It is not unlikely for such management models to constantly stay in expedite-and-chaos mode. Some of the indications of this phenomenon are high employee turnover and never-ending worry about meeting the next month's or quarter's financial goals. The operational variability that typically is an inherent byproduct of this model naturally delivers unpredictable performance behavior. Operational variability and instability adversely impact customer service, product quality and profitability, promoting waste and rework in discrete, transactional, and intellectual processes.

What about sustainability of CPI initiatives and efforts? This may be a familiar tune to many, where their organization adopted some form of CPI and did get some results but then was unable to sustain the gains or continue with the momentum! The organization may have gone through one or a few happy loops of positive outcomes, but the negative inertia prevailed, gradually slowing down the organization's enthusiasm and drive for operations excellence. A typical outcome of these situations is that people lose trust and become skeptical of the CPI efforts and uninterested in participating in those types of efforts any further. The organization and its leadership did not take the CPI initiative deep into its culture and possibly applied only some of its convenient tools and, like a child with a new toy, played with it for a while until becoming bored and then set it aside.

We have discussed Ford and how he lost his edge as market tastes and preferences changed. This change occurred because consumers' economic conditions changed. Consumers became pickier because they were wealthier and had greater buying power. The newness effect of the automobile had also worn off. These significant changes went unnoticed by Ford. His competitors, however, better understood the nature of these socio-economic changes and recognized that they needed to listen to the voice of their customers to understand their ever-changing needs and wants. The result was that customers substituted their products for Ford's.

A natural expectation may be that because these guidelines are common-sense and simple, this type of history should not be repeated. Many managers remain relatively unacquainted with their leadership shortcomings in how to sculpt their organization for continuous improvement. It is surprising how few managers can easily answer the following questions:

- Why is your organization not able to produce 20% more with existing resources?

- Why are you not able to complete 20% more projects, with the same resources and actually deliver most of them on time?

- Why does your organization lose sales despite holding excess inventory?

And how easily could they answer these questions:

- Do you know exactly what processes or operations are the most painful? Do you know where your organization is hurting?

- Do you know exactly what processes or operations are most effective and profitable?

- Do you have the proper alerts in your system to let you know exactly what is the next operational inconvenience or disaster?

- If you have an active and effective warning system, do you have specific containment and preventive measures for those alerts?

- Do you really know the problem?

- Do you really know the root cause(s)?

However, this phenomenon still keeps repeating itself. Many organizations that are offering products and services do not fully understand their own markets or customers or their customers' needs, wants, and challenges. They talk about part- nership, but do not become *one* with the customer, to not only understand their current business requirements and challenges, but to deeply understand their fu- ture strategic growth paths. These disconnect between the products or the service provider and its customers creates fertile ground for the competition to plant its own seeds of success.

Some organizations resemble a frog being cooked in a pot of water. If you put a frog in cool water and gradually turn up the heat, the frog will not jump out of the hot water and will eventually be cooked. Do not become the frog in your organization; become the change agent and lead your organization's CPI efforts to the next level.

As discussed earlier, it is appropriate to break down the complex processes and business components into manageable "chunks." It is imperative, however, to understand and maintain the relationship among all pieces of the puzzle and connect them at the global level with application of appropriate common vision, strategies, and measurements.

iTLS can act as the glue to connect fragmented pieces of the organizational performance puzzle for systematic and global optimization of profitability. iTLS glues together organizational performance improvement objectives with the core elements to achieve the right level of focus, elimination of waste and unneces- sary efforts, and containment of errors and variability in processes and decision making. If any of the core business requirements are suppressed, organizational profitability is significantly diminished. iTLS will bring focus to the core organi- zational objective of sustainable profitability and address how to achieve the most return on investments, with application of existing resources, to rapidly obtain at least 20% more projects completed, improve productivity by an additional 20%, and reduce operating costs while improving customer services by 20% or more.

Watch out for Fallacy of The Law of Familiarity

It is so exciting for people to become familiar with new CPI methods, tools, and techniques. Of course, this should be encouraged and promoted, particularly for the leadership management, so that they could better understand their CPI practitioners' activities and properly relate to them. However, familiarity with a concept should not be mistaken with expertise. For example, familiarity with the airplane concepts and parts, may not make an individual to be accounted and held responsible as a reliable pilot. Therefore, that individual may not be mistaken as an expert pilot and permitted to risk the lives of himself and others.

Unfortunately, frequently individuals become overly excited as they become familiar with a new concept and assume that sheer familiarity equals expertise and dive headfirst into the implementation while they have not fully explored and completely understood the concept in all dimensions entirely, its pit falls, do's and don'ts.

There is a clear distinction between being familiar with something and being an expert in it. Malcolm Gladwell in his book, Outliers discusses the 10,000 hour rule. This is a rule of thumb that identifies experts from novice. An expert is someone who has practiced something of her specialty for at least 10,000 hours (approximately 10 years).

Hopefully, leadership and managers recognize that distinction and not fall into traps of familiarity vs. expertise by positioning themselves or their personnel that are familiar with a CPI concept to act as expert implementors, before having a clear proof of their capabilities and effectiveness. The outcome of these decisions may not be favorable.

4
What Is an Improvement?

What is an improvement? It may initially seem like a trivial question; however, how do you know if you have made an improvement? Obviously, without a good measurement you would not be able to determine if any detectable and significant improvement has in reality taken place.

HISTORY OF "IMPROVEMENTS"

There is little doubt that Ford's and Ohno's management systems resulted in great improvement—individuals, companies, and countries benefited, so why raise the question of what is an improvement? The word *improvement* seems to define itself; it suggests making things better. However, it begs the question of what we are trying to improve. Over the last 50 years, adherents of many approaches have claimed that the systems improved organizations, yet on close examination many of these claims seem specious.

Many years ago "cost-reduction programs" were the fad. Each year we undertook a program to benefit our company by finding ways to reduce costs. We usually focused on specific operations to find ways to perform them faster or at less cost. One year we identified $12 million of cost reductions that passed the scrutiny of a screening committee whose role was to ensure that these ideas were valid. The next year we successfully implemented more than $8 million of these ideas.

When we ask audiences how many of these savings they think ended up in the company's bottom line, the reaction is always the same—little or none. The only way that so many people could give an identical reaction is if they had similar experiences. Those involved in such efforts inevitably raised the question, "Why didn't the company make more money as the result of our superb efforts to reduce costs?" The typical response was, "Well, we would be much worse off if we had not made these improvements." We heard the words, but always had that uneasy feeling that something was wrong.

Why is it that we, our colleagues, and so many audiences have the same skeptical response? We all knew something was wrong, but at the time we were not sure what it was. Clearly our improvements were not being translated into bottom-line results.

The problem isn't just that the efforts didn't yield the expected results. The larger impact often falls on those who worked so diligently to identify and implement these improvements. We have all seen our energies wasted despite having made heroic efforts to implement some improvement program and then get punished for our supposed success.

Let us explain this phenomenon. There was an industrial company that charged its engineers with implementing a particular improvement program. The record keeping of saving was rigorous, and by all accounts it had generated $30 million of savings over a three-year period, an incredible performance for a company with only $100 million of sales. Unfortunately, only a little over $1 million of these improvements ever reached the bottom line. The discrepancy was explained by, "Well, we would have been much worse off if we had not made these improvements." Unfortunately, in order to increase profits, over half of the people who worked so strenuously on this effort were let go.

Over the years our cost-reduction efforts were followed by other improvement schemes, among them was the computer system MRP, which morphed into MRP II and finally into ERP. Then it was the era of robotics fever. Others that have been pursued with great vigor were total quality management (TQM) and business process reengineering. Today the techniques of choice are Lean, Six Sigma, and TOC.

Viewed from a historical perspective, many of these efforts were abject failures and several were disastrous investments. Computerized MRP system and its successors promised to improve delivery performance, reduce inventories, and lower costs. A close examination of the results suggests that the opposite occurred. Even more discouraging is the fact that Japan's manual kanban system yielded dramatically better results in all areas. It's not that MRP didn't deliver some benefits; it's just that they were insufficient in most cases to provide a positive return on the investment.

TQM was initially received with great enthusiasm. It was our response to the Japanese and the lessons that Dr. Deming had taught them. A few years after the movement began, one of the major accounting firms conducted a study of the benefits achieved. Their conclusion was that fewer than 5% of the companies had achieved a satisfactory return on their investment and that the great majority of companies had a negative return on their investment.

I was once invited to a company that was celebrating the accomplishments of its TQM projects. The company had decided to use CPI and kicked off a series of projects driven by the employees. Employees had been told to pick a project and, upon its completion, they would receive recognition for their efforts. One particular project that received high recognition caught my attention. This project had to do with in-basket bins management improvement. The employee had cleaned up her in-basket area, clearly labeled and marked the area, and made claims of $25,000 in annual savings for reduced search efforts. What do you think? The effort of the employee to improve her work area was certainly commendable, but do you think that the company P&L will reflect the claimed savings of $25,000? Was the in-basket activity value-added activity? Do you think that the measurements for success were clear to the employees? What do you think the management's opinion and future directions for additional continuous improvement projects would be when the operation controller and executives were not able to realize the savings?

Next, business process reengineering (BPR) burst on the scene as the solution to the inertia of how companies were operating. It faded almost as quickly as companies realized that the expense of implementation exceeded the benefits.

If these historical efforts haven't worked very well, how have Lean, Six Sigma, and TOC performed? Based on some reported results, they have done pretty well, but many of these results need to be taken with a grain of salt. Motorola, the source of Six Sigma, reported annual earnings of over half a billion dollars. In the same press release, it reported that Six Sigma had saved the company over $2 billion in the previous year. If one does the arithmetic, it appears that in absence of Six Sigma the company would have lost $1.5 billion that year. It seems that we must be using one system to calculate cost savings and another to determine company profit.

Compounding this problem, and creating skepticism that results are being achieved, has been awarding the Deming and Malcolm Baldrige Awards for improvement to companies that have gone bankrupt, further indicating that something is amiss in how we measure improvements. If we are going to suggest that companies should adopt an improvement process and promise that if they adopted it that it would greatly benefit the company, then we are obligated to provide a measurement system that is sound and directly connected to provable bottom-line gains.

The purpose here is not to denigrate improvement techniques, but to question the validity of many claimed benefits. If improvement techniques do not translate into tangible bottom-line results, then it is difficult to validate their usefulness and their acceptance becomes more a matter of good public relations rather than actual results. Relying on the belief "that we would be much worse off if we hadn't made these improvements" is not comforting to shareholders.

HOW TO MEASURE AN IMPROVEMENT?

The starting point to answer this question is to ask ourselves, "What is the purpose of our organization?" It's clear that the goal or purpose of a publicly held company is different than of a public school, which is different from a federal entity. While we believe that iTLS can greatly benefit many types of organizations, this book will focus on organizations whose goal is to "make more money now and in the future, ethically." I believe that for-profit organizations and publicly held corporations are a large group that meets this criterion.

Some may question the appropriateness or accuracy of this last statement. Publicly held corporations often strive to meet other objectives, such as being good citizens; providing fulfilling, well-paying jobs; helping reduce global warming; and saving our precious Earth. We don't believe that such objectives are their primary goal. One way to answer this question is to look at it from the viewpoint of the owners, those who hold shares in the company, and ask, "Why did you use some of your money to buy this stock?" The nearly universal reply is, "To make more money." When a company becomes more profitable, shareholders usually benefit either through distribution of dividends or an increase in the share price.

When the goal of an organization is to "make more money," actions that enable it to do so are clear improvements. These, however, are mere words and lack tangibility. How do we measure making money? How can we tell if an effort to improve really resulted in more of the goal? These are valid questions that need answers, especially if we want to focus our improvement efforts on Archimedes' long levers.

Let's start with the some common financial measures of making money. Managers talk a lot about trying to increase their "bottom line." On a profit and loss statement the top line is the amount of revenue taken in, the sales. In between the top and bottom lines are many other lines, which generally represent how much of the revenue was spent on things like wages, insurance, materials, and taxes. The amount that remains after deducting all these expenses is the bottom line, or the net profit.

$$\text{Net profit (NP)} = \text{Sales/revenue} - \text{Operating expenses (OE)}$$
$$\text{Return on investment (ROI)} = \text{NP/Amount invested (risked)}$$

Net profit (NP) is an absolute measure and certainly one indication of how much money a company is making; however, it fails to take into account an even more important factor—the amount of money invested in the company. Every good investor weighs the expected return of their investment vs. the risk involved. An investment in a bank CD is very safe, but the return is on the low side. Likewise, a risky proposition needs to offer a larger return in order to attract investors. Return on investment (ROI) is a second and relative measure of making money.

Sophisticated investors go far beyond profit and loss statements and balance sheets in assessing companies; however, for our purposes we will use net profit and return on investment as two good indicators of making money. Unfortunately, there are problems with using these measurements to make day-to-day improvement decisions. First, they are historical measures; they tell us what happened in the past, not what will occur in the future. It's a little like driving a car by looking in the rearview mirror—the road ahead of us may be significantly different from the road behind us.

The second and more important problem is that they are often difficult to use. Ask a person who has a great idea on how to improve things about the impact on NP and ROI and you will probably get a blank stare. Ask a person who wants to improve things by purchasing a new piece of equipment about the ROI and he'll likely reply, "What does it need to be?" meaning, "I'll fudge the numbers if necessary to get it approved."

The point is that NP and ROI are often not very good tools to measure the expected impact of many decisions—decisions intended as improvements. Consequently, a new framework is needed in order to objectively judge improvement actions. TLS suggests an approach drawn from TOC, which relies on three measurements: throughput, investment/inventory, and operating expense, often referred to as T, I, and OE. Because these terms often mean different things to different people, let us define them.

$$\text{Throughput}(T) = \text{Sales/Revenue} - \text{Cost of raw materials}$$

Throughput is the money *generated* by the organization. It is the difference between what customers pay for a product and what the organization had to pay for the raw materials or inputs. In a sense, it is the *value added* that the organization has increased.

Investments/inventories (I) is the money that the organization invests in purchasing things it intends to resell. It is clear that inventory is an investment that organizations intend to resell, but how about fixed assets? Fixed assets like buildings and machinery are often needed to convert inventory into throughput. In a sense, we use up these assets in the process of creating throughput and resell them—the depreciation of fixed assets is usually a cost that is included in the price of a product.

Operating expenses (OE) is the money an organization spends in order to convert the inputs (raw materials inventory) into throughput (Figure 4.1). It includes wages, utilities, supplies, and the like.

Let's call these three measures of T, I, and OE operating measurements to distinguish them from the financial measurements of NP and ROI. Both sets of measurements encompass all the monies an organization generates, spends, and invests. In fact, these two sets of measurements can be easily related. NP is simply the revenue generated (sales) less money spent for materials and operating expenses.

$$NP = (\text{Sales/Revenue} - \text{Cost of raw material}) - (\text{OE})$$

Because throughput is sales less materials,

$$NP = T - OE$$

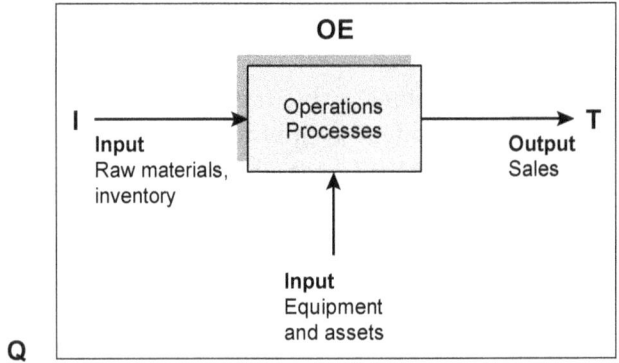

Figure 4.1 T, OE, I relationship.

ROI is simply NP divided by investment. Expressed in the operating measurements it is:

$$ROI = (T - OE)/I$$

Despite the fact that the definitions of T, I, and OE may differ somewhat from other usages of these terms, we have found that people intuitively understand them and the direction we would like them to move. When asked, "What direction would you like these measurements to go?" they immediately suggest that T should go up and I and OE should go down. When these measurements move in the suggested directions, both NP and ROI increase.

$$NP\uparrow = T\uparrow - OE\downarrow$$

What's the value of having two sets of measurements that simply provide two different perspectives on the same money? The financial measurements (NP and ROI) provide required information for reporting results to stockholders and tax authorities, but they have major deficiencies when used for making operating decisions. The operating measurements are not used for providing information to shareholders and tax authorities, but they are very helpful in making good operating decisions, even at lower levels in an organization.

Maybe an example will help. Suppose someone has an idea that they strongly believe will be a big improvement. They ask their manager for permission to implement it. A good manager, versed in the financial measurements, will want to know the real impact of the change and may well ask, "How much will it improve net profit?" The blank look or stammering that he gets in reply clearly indicates that few know how to answer the question. The manager then faces the dilemma of either relying on the promoter's intuition or rejecting a potentially good improvement.

If the same scenario is repeated using the operating measurements, the manager might ask how this change will impact the measurements of T, I, and OE. He may begin by inquiring, "How much will this change increase throughput; i.e., how will it affect our revenue?" He may well follow that with a second question: "Will it cause I (investment/inventory) to decrease?" Certainly he will ask if OE will decrease. The people promoting the change usually have knowledge and intuition about the impact of their suggestion. If all their answers are negative, this change is clearly not an improvement. If all are positive, we should immediately implement it. If they are mixed, some further evaluation may be needed. When organizations begin to think in terms of T, I, and OE, much better decisions are made much more quickly.

Having three measurements does create a dilemma. Are they all of equal importance, or is one somehow more important than the other two—should we give all of them equal weight or should our attention be more focused? One way to view this dilemma is to ask how much we could improve if we drove the measures to an extreme. Reducing OE is considered to be an improvement, but how far can we realistically drive it down? Reducing it to zero probably means we no longer have an organization. Obviously, there is some floor to the reduction of OE. How about I—if we drive it to zero, it means we have no assets or inventories. While it is possible to create such a company, for most existing organizations such a change would mean they are no longer in business.

How about T? We want to increase it. Is there a ceiling on T? Some might argue that there is limit in the marketplace, but few companies ever come close to owning the market for their products, let alone their capabilities. Logically, T seems to be the most important of the three measures. It might be useful to explore how the fathers of the first two waves, Ford and Ohno, viewed T. We will do that in the next chapter.

WHY DO IMPROVEMENT EFFORTS OFTEN FAIL?

Why is the history of improvement efforts so dismal? It certainly doesn't seem to be because of a lack of effort. Let's examine some of these efforts in de tail and try to understand how the identified improvements relate, or don't relate, to increases in the bottom line.

In many of our cost-reduction efforts, we identified specific opportunities to do things better. For example, we might have found some fixture that enabled a part to be produced in one minute rather than two. A savings of one minute per piece times the number of pieces needed per year times the worker's wage would give us a dollar savings. In our cost-reduction efforts, we identified hundreds of such opportunities and were able to implement many of them. So why didn't the savings show up in our bottom line? The bottom line would have been positively affected only if we reduced OE, eliminated some of the workers, or increased T; made and *sold* more products with the same labor; or reduced the level of inventory or the waste of obsolescence.

What typically happened was the opposite. We did spend a few dollars in making the new fixture (I/OE up), but we seldom reduced the size of the workforce. The worker often found a way to bury the saved time, often by making more parts (I went up). We may have gained some benefit if sales of the product using that part increased and we didn't add labor to make these parts. Cost-reduction efforts were largely focused on reducing costs (OE), and the people most affected, production workers, were highly motivated to keep their jobs. There was no way they were going to appear to be idle or underused.

In one of my seminars, one of the attendees told me a familiar story of how he led a team to improve his company's supply chain processes. They found they could eliminate three individuals, saving his department over $200k. It so happened that the affected individuals were close personal associates of the division vice president. The division vice president, upon learning of the project recommendations, praised the team and immediately transferred the three individuals and buried them in the operating expenses of another plant. Despite the team's efforts to improve their processes and reduce OE at an overall level, their division did not save that $250k, and also lost the time that the team spent on the project, thus increasing OE. The individual who told this story was disgusted and noted that the vice president's reaction did not go unnoticed. Even though the team members were praised for accomplishing an improvement, the overall team morale diminished and they showed no interest or enthusiasm for participating in another improvement project! Local optimization typically is wasteful!

How about improvements from investing in new equipment? Most industrial companies have rigorous financial hurdles for new investments, often two years or less. A two-year payback means a 50% return on that investment. If a company invests millions of dollars in such investments over several years, the company's overall return on investment should increase. Right? What are the actual results—little if any improvement! What causes this phenomenon? As noted earlier, when asked what the payback on a new piece of equipment was, the reply was, "What does it need to be?" We have become masters at manipulating the cost numbers to match the target. We seldom look at the real impact on T, I, and OE, let alone track the results of investments in these terms. The savings are almost always based on assumptions about local benefits, not their more global impact.

Similar stories can be told about other improvement techniques like TQM and BPR, so let's shift our focus to today's most popular improvement techniques—Lean, Six Sigma, and TOC. Often-touted Lean improvements are that the distance a part has to move has been reduced dramatically, sometimes by more than 90% and that the needed floor space has been cut by 40%. If we didn't reduce the labor to move parts or use the saved space to reduce outside storage costs, where was the bottom-line impact? Even books about Six Sigma often recommend counting saved floor space. They may be real savings if they allow a company to avoid the capital cost of building new facilities in the future, but they certainly won't affect today's net profit.

The importance of not generating the promised financial results is not the only factor that negatively affects a company. Even if layoffs are not used to improve profits, the people who worked so assiduously on improvement projects often become disillusioned. They have become accustomed to the "project of the month." It is no wonder that the most senior employees often adopt a wait-and-see attitude, expecting that this latest effort will fade away, like so many before it, or, even worse, the attitude of "We tried that once and it didn't work and then gave lip service to the improvement effort."

Improvement efforts have fallen short of delivering on enterprise-wide expectations. Many Lean, Six Sigma, and TOC implementations by themselves have had questionable financial benefits. Frequently, improvement efforts have claimed significant victories, without positively affecting bottom-line results. Those involved in improvement programs consistently blame top management for "lack of support" as a reason for lack of success in their efforts. Maybe this lack of support is tied directly to lack of bottom-line results. Leadership and top management support is the key to success of any improvement initiative. Such support is usually visible at the start of some new improvement effort, and maybe the reason it often subsides is because real benefits are not forthcoming.

5

The iTLS Model and How It Works

WHAT IS THIS iTLS?

iTLS, an acronym for integrated TOC, Lean, and Six Sigma, is a management philosophy that enables the creation of more permanent solutions to problems. It recognizes the existence of variability in nature and attempts to control processes statistically. iTLS is a methodology for understanding the real problem, establishing priorities, clearly defining the real need(s), and implementing practical solutions.

It is known that our abilities to learn and contribute increases exponentially as we acquire additional knowledge and experiences. Applying iTLS benefits from this very concept. Consider an expert in Lean techniques who has been contributing to your organization by removing wasteful activities from the processes. What if that same individual became an expert in Six Sigma techniques as well? Now she would be able to not only identify and remove waste but also implement solutions to reduce process variability to levels more acceptable to your customers. And what if she were also an expert in TOC? Most likely she would not fall into the trap of "the new hammer syndrome." (This is when someone has a new hammer, and it is the only tool she is familiar with. Everything then may look like a nail, and the person wants to use the hammer to fix problems.) Most likely, she would now be able to determine where to best focus improvement efforts and then apply the most appropriate tools and techniques.

iTLS is a new generation of continuous improvement (CPI) models and logically integrates the three powerful CPI philosophies, their tools, and techniques. iTLS harmonizes the interaction of the TOC, Lean, and Six Sigma in a synergic mix that yields significantly larger financial results than applying these techniques individually. Its implementation can improve a customer's experiences, lower costs, and build better leaders. iTLS focuses on delivering results through fundamental process knowledge and employs common sense, business knowledge, and scientific tools to improve the processes and products of a company. It is applicable across every discipline, including production, sales, marketing, design, administration, and service.

iTLS is an acronym for integrated TOC, Lean, Six Sigma, but there is more to it. iTLS is simply a management philosophy that enables you to reach a deeper understanding of a company's problems and then permanently solve them. Variability is a fact of life; iTLS provides tools and techniques to discover the sources of the variability and waste in processes and contain them within statistically acceptable levels. iTLS is a guide that enables you to understand the real problems in your processes, prioritize what needs to be done, clearly define the process control parameters, put in place practical and sustainable solutions, and then determine your next significant logical improvement opportunity for your system.

We use Toyota Production System methodology.
Why should we change?

You do not need to change, but you can add value to your CPI system capabilities. TPS has been a powerful process transformation methodology, but it is time to strengthen TPS with additional tools and techniques. Even the developer of TPS, Taiichi Ohno, recognized that the potential for improving TPS; thus we should not be reluctant to consider other possibilities. Lean is one of the three foundational pillars of iTLS.

We use Six Sigma methodologies, and we have invested
heavily in the program. Discarding it would be a political
disaster in our organization. So why should we change?

The same argument is valid for practitioners of Six Sigma or any other CPI methodology. You do not have to discard anything! All of the knowledge established in your organization is a positive foundation for your efforts to achieve higher levels of performance. What you have established is valuable and will be an integral part of iTLS. Six Sigma is one of the three foundational pillars of iTLS.

We use TOC methodologies, and we have claimed that TOC is
the only way to improve performances. Discarding it would be a
political disaster in our organization. So why should we change?

The same argument is valid for practitioners of TOC methodology. Your users are really interested in CPI results and outcome, not what acronym you use. Your users also would like for you also to continually improve your processes and upgrade your intellectual assets and capital. There should be no resentment in better serving your clients. TOC has had significant contributions to CPI and is an integral part of iTLS as one of the foundational pillars of iTLS.

What can be expected after initial implementation of iTLS?

Two conditions are necessary to sustain iTLS:

1. Leadership needs the stamina to go through iTLS steps and repeat them with vigor to significantly improve throughput and profits and gain or advance leadership in their industry. iTLS implementations expose hidden capacities as well as clearly identify critical problems. Leadership must leverage this to their company's competitive advantage and create a human culture of performance and profitability.

2. Leadership could toy with iTLS for one implementation loop and obviously get benefits; however, the idea of repeating the seven-step process after achieving significant gains can be met with a great deal of resistance, especially if it requires policy changes than many organizations are unwilling to accept. Oftentimes, organization leaders do not like to see the "real" issues and prefer to look the other way. This gives them the sense that "everything is OK." Exposure of long-standing issues may cause managers to fear that they will be exposed and perceived as ineffective managers.

I would like to share a story that may bring this problem closer to home. I met Ray in 2005. He was a junior executive in an international organization. Ray was passionate about iTLS and determined to make serious changes in his organization. Ray had been enthusiastically implementing iTLS in his division and had achieved outstanding results. His division reported such outstanding results in profits and quality and performance indicators that it became the envy of other divisions. Ray was promoted to head Operations Excellence for his division and encouraged to expand the process improvements process to other areas, such as business developments, engineering, quality, sup- ply chain management, and project management. Ray spoke in detail about the amazing discoveries he had made about what was hampering productivity and throughput. He had exposed these constraints through application of iTLS and was making changes that were focused on the throughput improvements. At this point, you might expect that the story ends with Ray becoming the division president and living happily ever after!

Reality turned out to be very different. Here is how the story goes: As Ray was repeating the seven-step process, he was discovering more and more fundamental problems within his division. Initially, the constraints were in production. But after cleaning up production issues and elevating it to a non-constraint state, deeper and more fundamental constraints became apparent. These constraints pointed to leadership shortcomings in plant management, lack of competence, human resources management and motivational apathy, lack of sales and marketing intelligence, information technology shortcomings and paralyses, and political and policy constraints. Ray's boss, who was the division head, became uncomfortable with the discovery of these constraints because he perceived them as a reflection of his inability to lead his division. After a while, he did not want to hear or know more!

Ray's boss, Arnold, was much happier when he did not know about these organizational issues. Arnold enjoyed the P&L calls with his plants and operations managers. As long as the numbers looked good for the month and the quarter, everything was just fine to him! Now, however, he was on a very uncomfortable grounds as he gained intimate intelligence about his own organization, and perhaps about himself, which made him very uncomfortable. Because of Ray's efforts, communication had improved, and bad news was now being elevated to higher levels rapidly, further annoying Arnold. Some of the bad news included the fact that some of his relatives and favored individuals who held critical positions in the division were not performing well! Arnold had been praised by the company president for running a smooth operation, but it was becoming increasingly clear that things were not as they seemed. Ray continued his efforts full force to expose more constraints, remove them, and then go to the next one, thinking that he had Arnold's approval. The situation became more and more awkward when some of these issues reached Arnold's boss.

Eventually, Arnold decided that he did not want to deal with solving real organizational issues and preferred the silence and peace of the past. Therefore, Ray's Operations Excellence organization was dissolved, and Ray was moved to an administrative function where he could do no more harm by enlightening the organization! Finally, Arnold got Ray fired to maintain his executive position.

To summarize, implementation of iTLS certainly provides multiple benefits; however, to sustain and grow your throughput, it is up to your leadership to continually repeat the iTLS seven steps.

How does iTLS work?

iTLS taps into the core capabilities of the three CPI methodologies and combines them with common sense (Figure 5.1). iTLS first uses TOC to bring focus to what needs to be improved, taking into consideration the global benefit, and then re-energizes the system to look for the next logical place for improvement.

Figure 5.2 depicts how the TLS model uses TOC, Lean, and Six Sigma to achieve higher levels of performance.

iTLS applies these three CPI approaches to produce something significantly better by capitalizing on the synergies created through their interaction with one

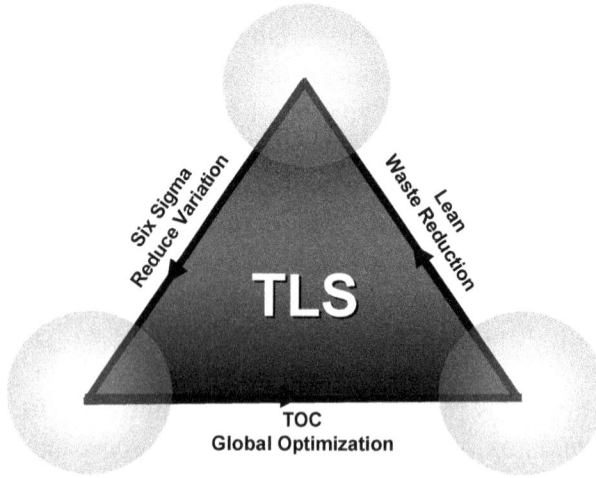

Figure 5.1 iTLS model.

another. Figure 5.3 conceptually illustrates the interaction of the three CPI components and how they relate to iTLS.

Figure 5.4 breaks down this interaction effect into comprehensible process steps to assist in understanding how to implement iTLS.

The iTLS model (Figure 5.1) uses Lean techniques to create a wasteless enterprise. Lean techniques are used to identify waste, remove it, and then implement process fail-safe strategies to prevent the same waste from recurring. The Six

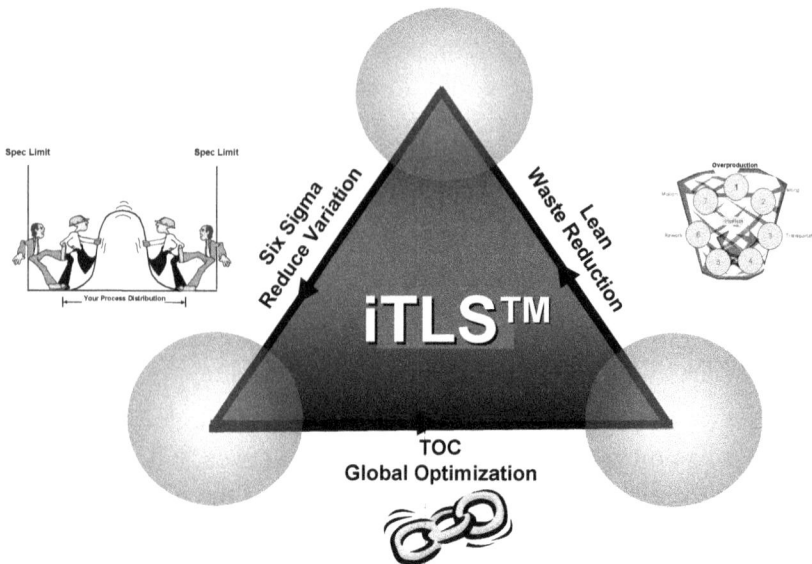

Figure 5.2 iTLS model.

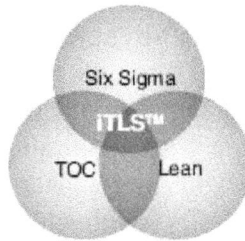

Figure 5.3 Integration of TOC, Lean, Six Sigma: iTLS.

Sigma tools and metrics are used to perfect the processes by understanding the nature of sources of variability (which is the error in the process), how variability affects the desired target, and the settings that should be established to limit the variability to a level acceptable to the customer. iTLS also plays a critical role in connecting strategic goals and objectives with process improvement efforts. The interaction effect among Lean, Six Sigma, and TOC creates much higher benefits than their cumulative effect. *It is critical to start with TOC.*

To illustrate this interaction effect, let's examine gold and copper when they are combined to form an alloy. Gold has a melting point of 1064.43°C, and copper melts at 1083.0°C. When the two metals are combined, their melting point drops to about 829–874°C. The alloy now has a melting point that is 200°C lower than the melting point of each individual substance. This

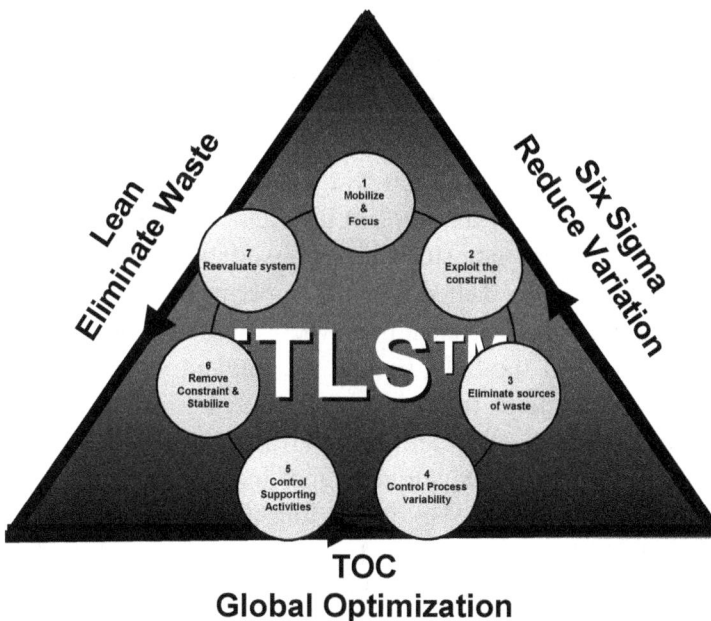

Figure 5.4 iTLS model.

interaction effect is not a simple cumulative function. Additionally, an alloy with about 10% copper will have a tensile strength of 60,000–100,000 psi. Pure gold, by itself, is weak, having a tensile strength of less than 20,000 psi when annealed; however, by alloying gold with copper (sometimes in conjunction with silver or nickel, and often a little zinc), gold alloys with higher strengths can be created. Also note that copper by itself has a tensile strength of about 32,000 psi, but the alloy interaction effect with gold will increase the tensile strength of the alloy up to five times that of pure gold and three times that of pure copper. The addition of copper hardens the gold, and gold–copper alloys are standard for coinage. Gold coins in the United States contained 10% copper, with the balance in gold.

When we discuss iTLS, imagine that we are discussing a CPI alloy made up of the right amounts of TOC, Lean, and Six Sigma. The interaction effect of these three methodologies in a iTLS model is what enables it to deliver results that are four to six times greater than if only Lean or Six Sigma are used. The important point is how the iTLS alloy is mixed and the formula that makes it so effective. The mixture discussed in this book is the tested algorithm that results in benefits four to six times greater than either Lean or Six Sigma. iTLS is the CPI alloy with mixtures that provide a higher performance.

Application of the right tool in the right place is the key to performance optimization. The iTLS process facilitates such an approach for process improvement.

I once had an opportunity to observe a procedure at a dental university where the senior dental students were working with patients as part of their practical training.

One of the stations that I chose to observe was for installation of implants. Two work stations simultaneously began their work with their patients at 8 A.M. One of the stations had a patient who was a 64-year-old man who needed two implants. The other station had a 61-year-old man who needed four implants. I decided to watch the first station. As part of the implant installation, it was necessary to use a drill to create a hole for the implant stud to be screwed into the lower-left mandibular. Another hole needed to be drilled into the upper-right maxillary. The student began by measuring the space, determining where the hole should be drilled and the angle and orientation of the hole, so that the implant would follow the same orientation, height, and angle as the rest of the teeth. The student previously had taken an impression of the patient's teeth, which was sent to the lab to create a stent template. He now needed to fit the surgical stent into the patient's mouth, which is where he encountered problems. He drilled four times because the hole and the template did not match. Each time he had to put away his tools, ask the patient to get out of the dentist chair, walk him down the hall 40 feet to the X-ray area, position the patient on the X-ray chair, put the protective cover on the patient, get the X-ray film, assemble the film on a fixture, position the fixture in the patient's mouth, take the X-ray, go to the film developing area, develop the X-ray, review it with an instructor for accuracy, determine if it needed to be retaken, come back, remove the protective jacket from the patient, reset the X-ray chair and camera by putting on plastic protective covers, escort the patient 40 feet back to his chair, change his gloves, and reposition his tools. Every time he drilled, this routine was repeated. The old man was upset and frustrated. He had lost some blood and would face excess pain after the anesthetic wore off.

Finally, on the fourth trial the dentist matched the surgical stent and completed the implant. I learned that the positioning angle was off by 1 mm! As I began asking the five whys and inquired for the root causes, it appeared that the surgical stent from the lab was not accurate. This student completed two implants in three hours, while the student next to him completed all four implants during the same time.

Could this process have gone smoother, with less rework and a happier patient? Certainly using the iTLS approach! Elements involved in measurements, materials used for the mold, lab process tolerances, and so forth all could have contributed to the template inaccuracy. All these elements could have been better controlled for superior results. The results could have been eliminating non-value-added activities, reducing the cost, putting tighter controls on tolerances for error reduction, and using fail-safe tools to prevent errors with the outcome of improved customer satisfaction and process throughput.

What is unique about iTLS?

iTLS is the only known CPI approach that is based on solid quantitative and empirical experiments. iTLS is a global approach that recognizes the combined power of Lean, Six Sigma, and TOC and capitalizes on their strengths. iTLS closes the gaps that exist among the CPI approaches by taking advantage of their strong interaction effect when they are combined in an effective sequence (see Chapter 5). Using the seven-step iTLS process in activity and project implementations will help you to maximize your profitability and throughput. iTLS can be applied in all process-based operations.

How is iTLS applied in a project or activity? What is the sequence of events?

iTLS has shown significantly better benefits in continuous improvement projects compared with Lean and Six Sigma methodologies applied alone. The combined TLS approach attempts to optimize the continuous improvement process using the following seven-step process (Figure 5.5):

1. Mobilize and focus.

2. Decide how to exploit the constraint.

3. Eliminate sources of waste from the constraint.

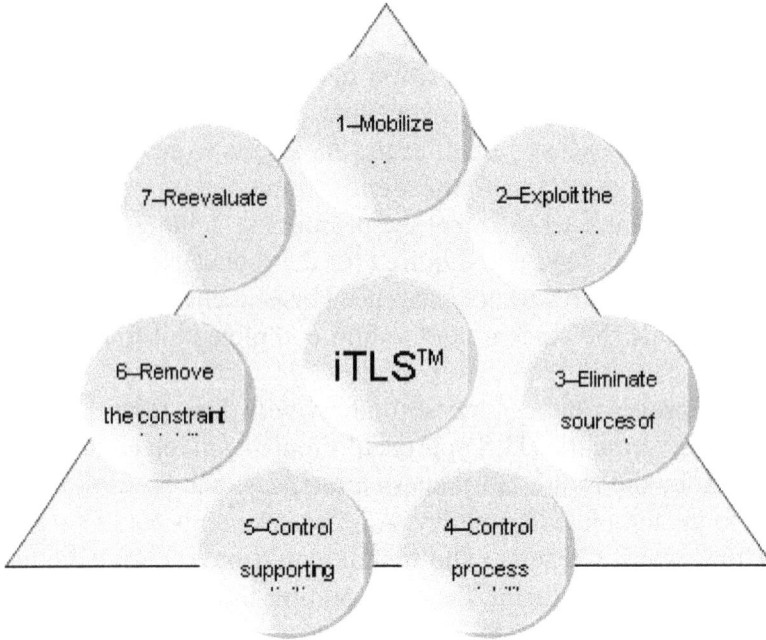

Figure 5.5 iTLS seven-step process.

4. Control process variability and error.

5. Control supporting activities.

6. Remove the constraint and stabilize.

7. Reevaluate system performance and go after the next constraint.

What does each iTLS step contain?

Each process step provides you with general guidelines for the typical input requirements, tools, and techniques you may choose to use and the outputs needed at each step of iTLS implementation. You should always consider the nature and environment of your business and the project's essential needs when choosing the tools and techniques. In some instances, depending on the scope of the project, you may not need to use each and every tool. As you follow the seven-step process, simply use common sense in selecting the tools needed to accomplish your scope of work. Therefore, it is imperative that you, as the individual managing a iTLS implementation, have adequate training in doing so. The training would prepare you to recognize which tools and techniques are necessary and sufficient to accomplish your objectives. Absent this training, you may waste valuable time and resources on steps and activities that are not necessary or miss essential tools that would have a significant impact on your final desired results.

iTLS™ 7-Steps

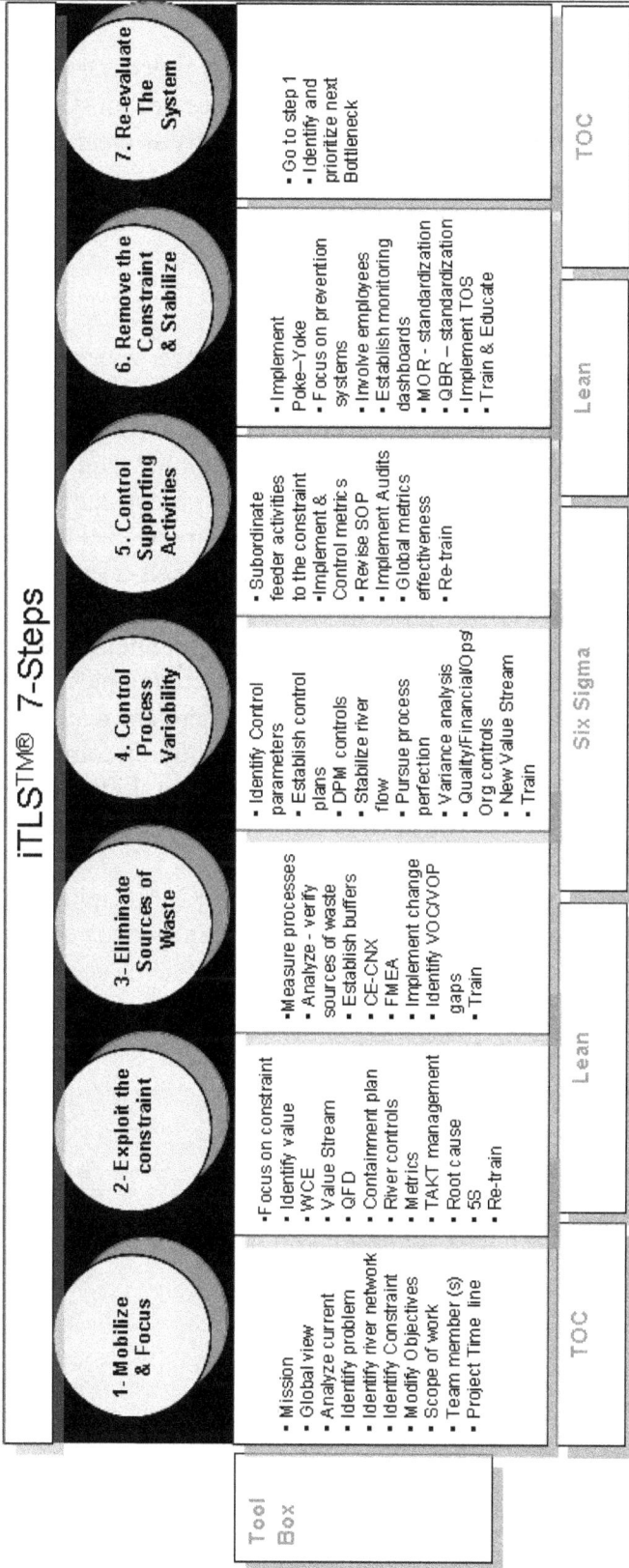

Tool Box

1- Mobilize & Focus
- Mission
- Global view
- Analyze current
- Identify problem
- Identify river network
- Identify Constraint
- Modify Objectives
- Scope of work
- Team member (s)
- Project Time line

TOC

2- Exploit the constraint
- Focus on constraint
- Identify value
- WCE
- Value Stream
- QFD
- Containment plan
- River controls
- Metrics
- TAKT management
- Root cause
- 5S
- Re-train

Lean

3- Eliminate Sources of Waste
- Measure processes
- Analyze - verify sources of waste
- Establish buffers
- CE-CNX
- FMEA
- Implement change
- Identify VOC/VOP gaps
- Train

4. Control Process Variability
- Identify Control parameters
- Establish control plans
- DPM controls
- Stabilize river flow
- Pursue process perfection
- Variance analysis
- Quality/Financial/Ops/Org controls
- New Value Stream
- Train

Six Sigma

5. Control Supporting Activities
- Subordinate feeder activities to the constraint
- Implement & Control metrics
- Revise SOP
- Implement Audits
- Global metrics effectiveness
- Re-train

6. Remove the Constraint & Stabilize
- Implement Poke–Yoke
- Focus on prevention systems
- Involve employees
- Establish monitoring dashboards
- MOR - standardization
- QBR – standardization
- Implement TOS
- Train & Educate

Lean

7. Re-evaluate The System
- Go to step 1
- Identify and prioritize next Bottleneck

TOC

Figure 5.6 iTLS seven-step flow and tools.

117

Figure 5.6 depicts the flow of the seven-step TLS process and notes which of the TOC, Lean, and Six Sigma tools and techniques are most appropriate at each step. We have attempted to make the process steps as clear as possible by identifying typical inputs, tools, techniques, and outputs so you have a road map for your CPI projects.

Step 1—Mobilize and Focus

To mobilize your CPI initiatives, you need to economize your resource utilization. You must focus on what it *is* that you plan to improve and *do* that. It should be your objective to get maximum benefit from your team's CPI efforts, which will offer ideas for future CPI initiatives. Therefore, the mobilization and focus step plays a key role in properly guiding CPI efforts. Your organizational and project management skills play a critical role at this stage and are needed to help you sell your project; obtain the needed resources; and, when finished, adequately close the project and recognize and reward the team members. It is also important to involve all stakeholders at the start of your CPI initiative and maintain open communication throughout the effort. Your organizational and communication skills will play a vital role in the success of the iTLS project. There are many brilliant and capable individuals who are unable to establish credibility or complete their key projects because they lack organization and communication skills. Pay attention to this requirement, and if you feel you need to brush up on those skills do not waste time in doing so.

The iTLS sequence begins with application of TOC principles (Figure 5.7). iTLS applies TOC techniques to ensure that global optimization is considered and

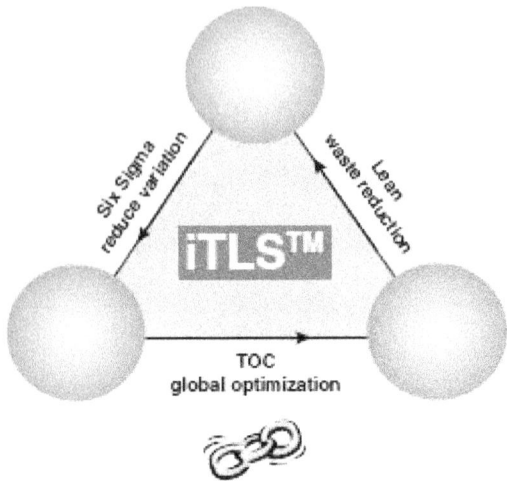

Figure 5.7 Application of TOC tools.

investigates the problem at hand from the 30,000-foot level. It is important to measure the organization's overall performance (the entire value stream) at a high level. The goal is to identify the existing or potential constraint(s) in the entire value stream that choke the free flow of throughput. Meanwhile, it is also essential to understand what river flow network you are dealing with so you can identify where the potential control points are and how you can better manage the flow of your operations river to relieve the constraints.

At this stage, problem definition needs to be reviewed and validated. Problems often are not articulated or well understood. This could cause project teams to work on the wrong issues or fuzzy targets. Developing the problem statement is both an art and science. An accurate definition of a problem statement can significantly improve root cause analysis and guide the project team to focus on what needs attention and avoid what does not. It is important to understand what is and what is not the problem, so that proper scope and boundaries can be established. This will significantly enhance effort optimization. In most organizations, resources are scarce and many improvement projects compete for the same resources. Therefore, do not to waste resources; focus them on the efforts that positively impact throughput. Figure 5.8 is an example of a problem statement checklist.

If the problem statement does not address the process constraint identified in step 1, it should be reconsidered. The potential risk could be that the problem-solving teams may be working on issue(s) that are not critical to the value stream and solving them may not change the overall performance of the system. Therefore, the problem-solving process should proceed only if the process constraint is considered to be part of the solution criteria. This will economize your resources and ensure that you are addressing the necessary issues.

The nature of the constraint(s) should be characterized using the guidelines in Table 2.2, so that focused cause-and-effect relationships can be established. For example, assume the process output rate is considered to be a problem. Instead of taking the approach of adding more production resources to increase capacity, the root cause(s) of the problem should be examined by using cause-and-effect analysis. What if the root cause were material shortages caused by ineffective purchasing policies? Obviously, solving a capacity problem would waste the firm's resources. Additionally, this alternative will not prevent the problem from reoccurring in the future. Refer to the case study "Inventory Management" in Chapter 9 for an actual example of a policy constraint costing a plant over $15 million dollars in excess inventory.

At this step you should clearly understand:

1. Why you are attempting to change something (processes, procedures, equipment, resources, etc.)

2. What specifically it is that you are attempting to transform and change

3. What you want the final outcome to look like

X	Describe problem symptoms specifically	
	Elements	**Findings**
	Who is the customer?	
	Who is/are the suppliers?	
	What is the customer requirement?	
	How is the current process performance relative to the customer requirements?	
	Where are the gaps in the existing process compared to the customer requirements?	
	Where is the problem visible in the process?	
	What happened?	
	Where did it happen?	
	What has recently changed in the process?	
	Has the process ever been there before?	
	Who is/are affected by the problem?	
	Is the problem chronic?	
	Is the problem sporadic?	
	What is the impact of the problem in costs (how much)?	
	What is the impact of the problem in quantities (how many)?	
	What is the impact of the problem in time (how long)?	
	How do we measure this process?	
	Is the measurement effective?	
	What would happen if we do nothing about it?	
	What is	**What is not**
	Problem statement	
	Write the problem statement	
	Tracking indicator metrics	**Findings**
	What are customer required metrics?	
	What are the existing metrics?	
	What metrics need to be put in place to track progress?	

Figure 5.8 Problem statement development checklist.

Note: Do not proceed to the next step if these three items are not clearly understood.

This information should be clarified in your project charter. Your project charter then will allow you to develop your scope of work and project plan in later steps. It is critical in this step to clearly identify the process constraint(s) and focus the project scope and efforts to resolve the constraint. Additional outputs should include baseline data (measurements) on current processes. This will help you to monitor progress both during and after implementation to determine if significant changes have taken place.

After clearly understanding what is it that you have to address, you need to establish your mission and analyze the existing process characteristics and performance. It is possible that after you have discovered the actual nature and attributes of the constraint(s), you may want to make adjustments to the objectives identified in the project charter. A number of formats are possible for the project charter, but make sure that your project charter contains the following information and avoid cluttering it with data that do not matter. The following essential information must appear in your project charter:

- Business need

- Project description

- Strategic plan

- Upper management approval

At this stage of the process, you need to set a time line for your project and develop your baseline project plan. With that information in hand, you identify possible team members and communicate your resource needs to the resource owners, functional managers, and so forth.

Outputs at this stage will allow you to advance to the next step of the iTLS process. You must clearly be able to quantify/qualify the following before advancing to the next stage:

- Do you have a sponsor?

- Do you know why you are doing this project?

- Do you know what the problem statement is and have you explicitly articulated it?

- Do you understand what the current process is with all relevant measurements/baseline metrics?

- Do you know where to focus? What is the constraint?

- Do you have the resources to accomplish your project?

Step 2—Decide How to Exploit the Constraint

Now that you have discovered the weakest link of your critical process, where throughput needs to be improved, the mobilized teams should develop a specific focus that addresses the organization's bottleneck (Figure 5.9).

Specify the value in the process. Value is identified by products, services, or activities that your customers are willing to pay for. All other activities and efforts that your customers are not willing to pay for, but are consuming your resources, are considered non-value-added and must be considered for elimination from the process.

There are a series of activities that you may consider overhead, burden, or cost of doing business, such as facilities, communication systems, information systems, financial systems, or management. The traditional value classification may refer to them as "business" value adds! Nevertheless, with global business environments changing rapidly, the logic for having all these items should be questioned, and their underlying business assumptions need to be challenged to ensure that all resources in the organization are driven to improve the throughput and the organization's strategic and tactical objectives.

In many organizations, the main focus is on direct labor management, efficiencies, and reduction. The value of overhead is not clearly understood in most cases. As long as departments' costs are within the budgeted percentages, they may remain under the radar; otherwise, department managers are forced to shave their resources to meet the budgeted and allowable percentages. Frequently,

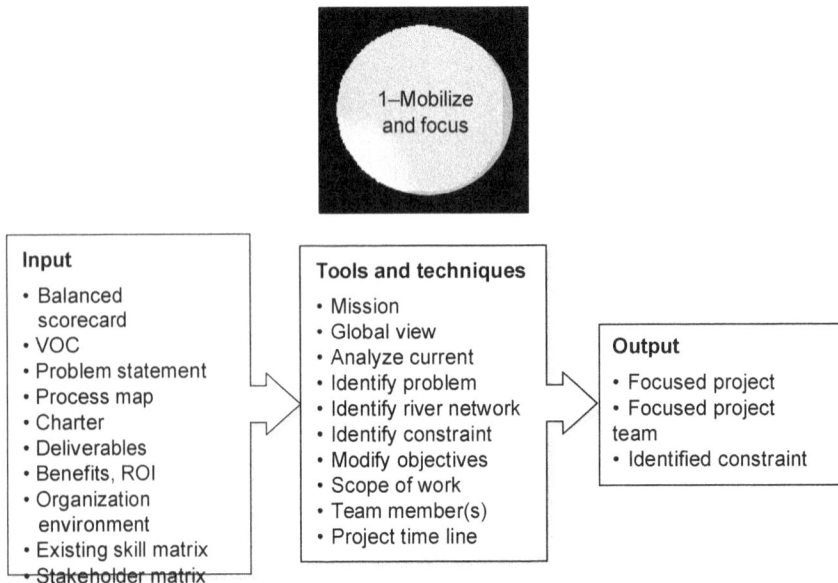

Figure 5.9 Step 1, mobilize and focus.

these resource-shaving drills are capricious and could seriously harm the organizational capabilities. Unfortunately, many of these decisions are based on meeting current quarterly or monthly budgetary targets, which usually focus on local optimization.

Value-stream mapping of the areas you are investigating will help you visually depict the flow of process steps and sequence of events. This would be the current reality of your processes. Also, you need to map the transportation logistics (see Chapter 2) of your processes to document the sequence of hand-offs, distances traveled, double- or multiple-handling opportunities, storage, buffer, inventories, and delays. You should also document how physical activities and information flow among resources. You should compare the value-stream throughput with the customer-required takt. You need to quantify how synchronized and balanced activities are as work flows from one step to the next by studying the value-stream map. What are the bottleneck(s) in the process to meet the takt, and what are the feeder activities into the bottleneck? Identify all non-value-added activities and develop plans to rapidly eliminate them.

Your goal should be to synchronize operations and the value-stream throughput with the takt, plus 10% (starting rule of thumb; you can fine-tune based on the desired statistical control), additional capacity reserves at the constraint resource. You should plan on kanbans or buffers to protect the bottleneck resource. It may be useful to redesign the existing processes after removing non-value-added activities in order to minimize transportation logistics and simplify the process steps. To sustain a smooth river flow, you should install control points after redesigning the process network (see Chapter 4). River flow networks provide excellent guidelines and strategies for material release and control for a demand-driven system that pulls work through the network.

The redesigned value stream should flow without interruptions or delays. You would use time buffers at control points or other strategic locations to ensure synchronous flow of work. Elimination of non-value-added activities typically opens at least 20% additional capacity at the constraint. The goal is to squeeze maximum throughput at the constraint.

A parallel approach of implementing 5S at this phase needs to be considered to bring order and discipline into the process activities (see Table 2.6). 5S would also assist in sustaining any process gain achieved and promote continuous improvement as a way of work life. The value added, which is the effort that the customer is willing to pay for, would be identified through a value-steam-mapping process. A waste-less value stream would be created by streamlining the activities, so that the queues and unnecessary inventories and work-in-process would be minimized. By implementing pull systems, the value chain would produce products or services only upon customer requirement. The focus would be to produce the required amount, at the requested time, to be delivered to the exact customer and location (Figure 5.10).

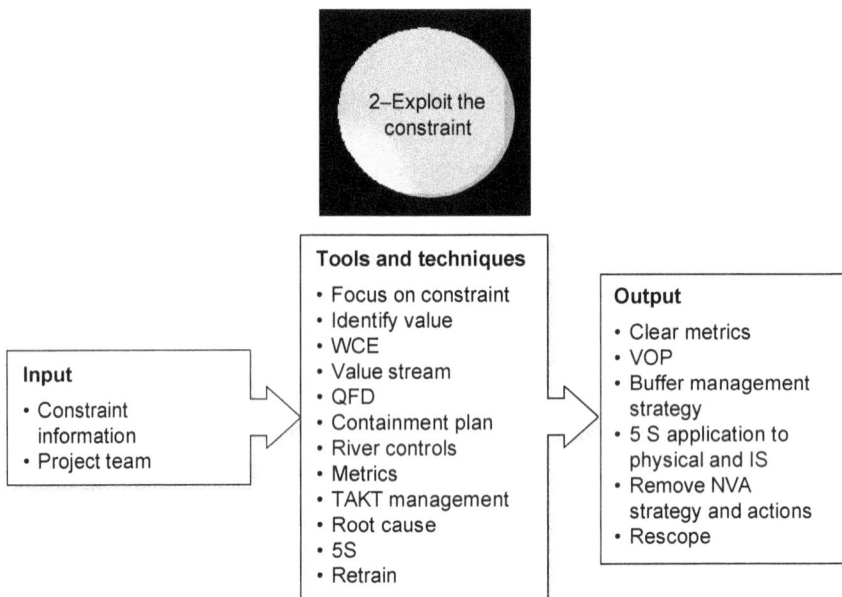

Figure 5.10 Exploit the constraint.

Outputs at this stage will allow you to advance to the next step of the iTLS process. You must clearly be able to quantify/qualify the following points before advancing to the next stage:

- What does your bottlenecked process river look like?

- Have you started 5S training and implementation?

- Do you have a detailed containment plan?

- Have you analyzed how to squeeze your bottleneck to maximize its output?

- Have you computed WCE at the constraint?

- What is your process capability, VOP?

- Do you know where the control points on the critical-process river are?

- Have you calculated your buffer requirements?

- Have you reviewed your scope to see if there are any changes required to

Step 3—Eliminate Sources of Waste

The goal of this step is to identify the root cause(s) of waste and remove them (Figure 5.11). It is necessary to formally follow the root-cause analysis process

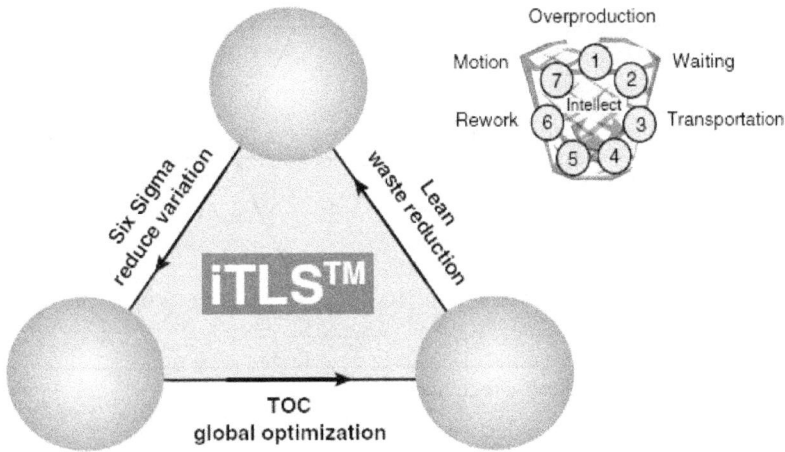

Figure 5.11 Application of Lean tools.

to clearly understand what is causing the NVA activities and how they could be prevented from reemerging.

Experienced practitioners may be tempted to solution-jump if the symptoms of a particular situation look and feel like something they have experienced before. Be aware of the "new hammer syndrome," in which you have a hammer and everything looks like a nail. Seldom is everything identical, so even though you may have a lot of experience dealing with similar conditions, we encourage you to go through the process of CE-CNX without bias and act as if it is the first time you have encountered such a situation. This ensures that you have an open mind and may enable you to look at the conditions from a new dimension.

In steps one and two, the sources of waste in the process will be clearly identified and targeted for improvement. Cause-and-effect analysis (CE) tools, such as the fishbone or Ishikawa diagrams (Figure 5.12), should be used to identify and quantify the sources of waste and process variability. A process is a combination of various activities (factors) that accomplish a particular objective. A process could also be explained in a simple mathematical model:

$$\text{Process: } Y = f(x); \; Y = f(x_1, x_2, x_3 \ldots x_n)$$

A process is made up of a series of input variables or factors that directly or indirectly interact with each other.

$f(x)$ is the process containing various variables

$Y = f(x)$: Response or result or an undesirable effect that needs to be investigated

X_n: Inputs assumed important (factors)

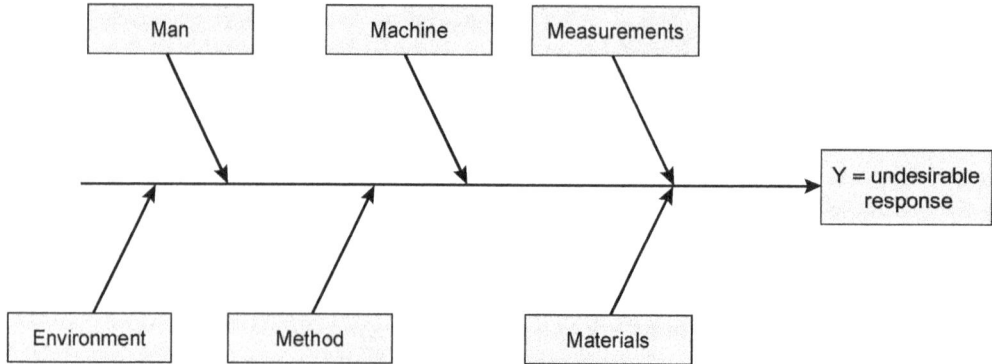

Figure 5.12   Ishikawa cause-and-effect diagram.

When a process is explained in a model format, it becomes much easier to analyze. The model could be used graphically and visually in brainstorming processes to identify the *vital few* factors that influence the process the most.

The Ishikawa diagram is a brainstorming tool that organizes assumed important input variables into general categories such as Man, Machine, Method, Materials, Measurements, and Mother Nature or Environment (6Ms). Obviously during the brainstorming process all variables are considered and tabulated under those categories on the Ishikawa diagram.

The brainstormed variables need to be investigated to determine how much each contributes to the undesirable effect. The number of variables that have been brainstormed could vary from a few to tens or hundreds. When these variables are many, their investigation could be time and resource consuming. Additionally, some of the variables could be aliases or redundant, so the input variables need to be screened to identify the key critical variables. Use of tools such as Pareto could help to screen out unimportant variables.

The CNX process could also be very helpful (Table 5.1). After brainstorming variables using an Ishikawa diagram, you could characterize each variable to constants (C), Noise (N), and X factors (X). Constants would be items that you know quantitatively will stay constant in your process and you are fully aware of their behavior and can easily control them. Noise variables are the factors that appear randomly and cannot be controlled, such as lightning. X factors

Table 5.1   CNX definition for factor screening.

C: Constant—controllable factor; we know everything about it.

N: Noise; common cause, random factors, such as ambient temperature.

X: X factor; experimental element; factors we think are contributing to the effect, but we don't know how much and how. But we want to find out and convert them to Cs.

are the variables that you suspect have a significant role in contributing to the undesirable effect, but you may not have a full understanding of their attributes, behavior, and measurements.

Characteristics of an effective CE diagram:

- Clearly define the effect to be investigated. Ensure that all team members understand the short phrase you use to describe it.

- Place the phrase describing the effect in a box (the head of the fishbone) and draw a line (the spine).

- There are two approaches at this point:

  - Brainstorm causes for the defined effect, and organize them after they have all been recorded into main categories and sub-causes.

  - Determine the main categories in advance, and write the causes right on the diagram as they are stated.

- In either method, continue to pursue causes and sub-causes until the root cause is identified.

- Root cause analysis could be done with the help of the Five Whys (Figure 5.13).

  - Ask "why?" multiple times to undercover the root causes.

  - Why does this occur?

  - Why does the condition exist?

  - Root cause would be the most basic reason a problem has occurred or could occur.

  - Ask "why?" five times.

  - Start with: "Why is this failure mode active?"

Check the logic in reverse direction:

- Probable root cause can cause symptom 4 to occur.

- Symptom 4 can cause symptom 3 to occur.

- Symptom 3 can cause symptom 2 to occur.

- Symptom 2 can cause symptom 1 to occur.

- Symptom 1 can cause failure.

- "Read" the chart backward from each root cause back to the effect to check the logic and check for completeness. For example, having

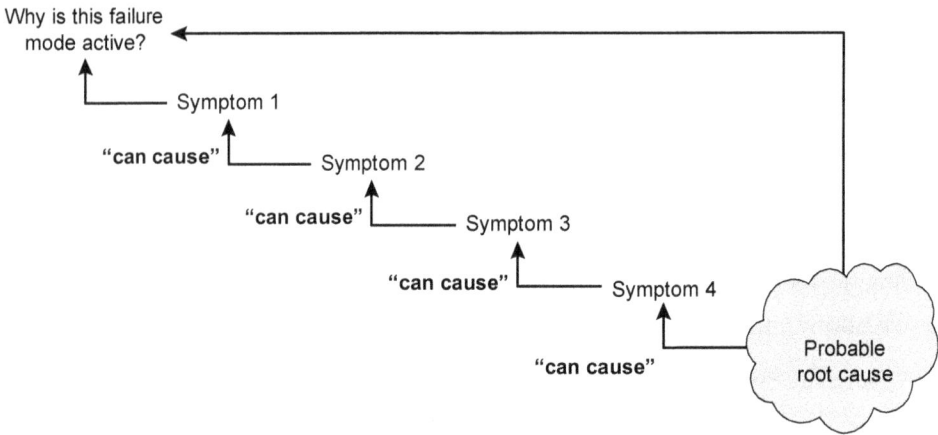

Figure 5.13 Five whys.

a lack of specifications causes unclear requirements. Unclear requirements cause loss of orders.

- When properly done, it should clearly show the cause–effect relationship.

- It should read logically from the end back to the beginning.

- The causes are only potential causes at this stage. This tool is usually a prelude to failure mode effect analysis.

After characterizing the input variables, C and N factors are screened out of initial investigation and only X factors will be focused on. X factors then are transferred to a failure mode effect analysis (FMEA) or process failure mode effect analysis (PFMEA) matrix for rapid prioritization (Table 5.2). FMEA/PFMEA uses a weighting system in which variables are quantified and can be easily put in order of priority, to prudently use resources on what is important. FMEA/PFMEA weighs each variable by frequency of occurrence (OCC), severity (SEV), and

Table 5.2 FMEA objectives.

Identify potential failures and prevent them from recurring.
Assess causes of failures quantitatively.
Evaluate the effects on the customer and value added.
Prioritize areas of focus.
Minimize risk of failure by choosing an appropriate solution.

probability of escaped detection (DET), and uses the product value as the risk priority number (RPN) to measure the combined effect of the three dimensions (Figure 5.14).

$$RPN = (OCC) * (SEV) * (DET)$$

Quick steps to construct a PFMEA:

1. Study the process/product to be analyzed.

2. Brainstorm the possible failures using CE.

3. Transfer X factors from CE as potential failure modes from step 2—iTLS.

4. List the potential consequences of each failure mode.

5. Assign severity (SEV) scores.

6. Identify current controls to detect the failure modes.

7. Assign occurrence (OCC) scores.

8. Identify current controls to detect the failure modes.

9. Assign probability of escaped detection (DET) score for each cause and control.

10. Calculate the risk priority number (RPN) for each line in the FMEA.

11. Prioritize the failure modes and causes based on RPN.

12. Determine the action to be taken.

13. Recalculate the RPNs based on the action plans.

To assign scores for SEV, OCC, and DET, use Tables 5.3, 5.4, and 5.5.

Various tools and techniques could be used at this stage to eliminate the sources of waste at the constraint. The tools mentioned here are the minimum requirements for the iTLS approach. You may choose additional tools as long as they make sense and are *necessary* and *sufficient*. One item that you should never overlook is team training. Investing in your people is one of the most important aspects during iTLS journeys.

Figure 5.15 is a summary of the essential requirements. You need to pay particular attention to your communication and organizational skills at this stage. Typically, during this stage significant process changes are identified and need to be implemented. Consequently, all stakeholders may need to be involved because several organizational aspects may be impacted. Sometime reorganizations are a necessity or policies have to be modified, replaced, etc. At this stage, you typically find many unpleasant surprises, poor practices, bad habits, limiting and

#	Process function (step)	Potential failure modes (process defects)	Potential failure effects	S E V	Potential causes of failure	O C C	Current process controls	D E T	R P N	Recommended actions	Responsible person and target date	Actions taken	S E V	O C C	D E T	R P N
1																
2																
3																
4																
5																
6																
7																
8																
9																
10																
11																
12																
13																
14																
15																
16																
17																

Figure 5.14 PFMEA.

Table 5.3 SEV scoring guide.

Rank	Description	Definition (severity of effect)
10	Extreme without warning	Failure could cause personal injury or create regulatory noncompliance. Failure will occur without warning.
9	Extreme with warning	Failure could cause personal injury or create regulatory noncompliance. Failure will occur with warning.
8	Very high	Failure renders the unit inoperable or unfit for use. Major production disruption (100% scrap).
7	High	Failure causes a high degree of customer dissatisfaction. Minor production disruption (sort and <100% scrap).
6	Moderate	Failure results in a subsystem or partial malfunction of the product. Minor production disruption (<100% scrap).
5	Low	Failure creates enough of a performance loss for customer to complain. Minor production disruption (100% rework).
4	Very low	Failure can be overcome with modifications to the customer's process or product, with minor performance loss. Minor production disruption (<100% rework).
3	Minor	Failure would be noticed by average customers, but can be overcome without performance loss. Some rework on line but out of station.
2	Very minor	Failure would be noticed by discriminating customers. Some rework on line in station.
1	None	Failure would not be noticed by the customer and would not affect the customer's process or product.

Table 5.4 OCC scoring guide.

Rank	Description	Potential failure rate
10	Very high	About 1 occurrence in 2 events ($C_{pk} < 0.33$)
9	High	About 1 occurrence in 3 events ($C_{pk} = 0.51$)
8		About 1 occurrence in 8 events ($C_{pk} = 0.67$)
7	Moderately high	About 1 occurrence in 20 events ($C_{pk} = 0.67$)
6		About 1 occurrence in 80 events ($C_{pk} = 0.83$)
5	Moderate	About 1 occurrence in 400 events ($C_{pk} = 1.00$)
4	Moderately low	About 1 occurrence in 2000 events ($C_{pk} = 1.17$)
3	Low	About 1 occurrence in 15,000 events ($C_{pk} = 1.33$)
2		About 1 occurrence in 150,000 events ($C_{pk} = 1.67$)
1	Remote	About 2 occurrences in one billion events ($C_{pk} = 2.00$)

unnecessary policies, irrelevant measurements, and so forth. You need to be considerate when managing change and respectful to the people involved and to the workforce that is impacted. If you work in a unionized environment, they should have been involved from the beginning of the process as one of your stakeholders and allies.

You must clearly be able to quantify/qualify the following before advancing to the next stage:

- Have you removed NVA processes from the process bottleneck?

- Have you squeezed everything possible out of your bottleneck?

- Have you addressed the root cause(s) of the bottleneck?

- Do you have detailed containment, corrective, and preventive implementation systems and plans?

- Have you computed WCE before and after improving the constraint?

- What is your process capability?

- Do you know where the control points on the critical-process river are?

- Have you implemented the required kanban/buffers at the control points to protect the constraint and throughput?

- Is the process throughput acceptable? Can VOP meet VOC robustly?

Table 5.5 DET scoring guide.

Rank	Description	Definition
10	Absolute uncertainty	The product is not inspected or the defect caused by failure is not detectable.
9	Very remote	Product is sampled, inspected, and released based on Acceptable Quality Level (AQL) sampling plans (C > 0).
8	Remote	Product is sampled, inspected, and released based on Acceptable Quality Level (AQL) sampling plans (C = 0).
7	Very Low	Product is 100% visually inspected in the process with moderate confidence of detection.
6	Low	Product is 100% visually inspected in the process with high confidence of detection. Product is 100% manually inspected using go/no-go or other gauges.
5	Moderate	Product is 100% visually inspected in the process with very high confidence of detection. Some Statistical Process Control (SPC) is used in process and product is final inspected off-line.
4	Moderately high	SPC is used and there is immediate reaction to out-of-control conditions. Subsequent assembly operations (prior to shipment) will be difficult to complete.
3	High	An effect SPC program is in place with process capabilities (C_{pk}) greater than 1.33.
2	Very high	All product is 100% automatically inspected. Subsequent assembly operations (prior to shipment) will be prevented from being completed.
1	Almost certain	The defect is obvious or there is 100% automatic inspection with regular calibration and preventive maintenance of the inspection equipment.

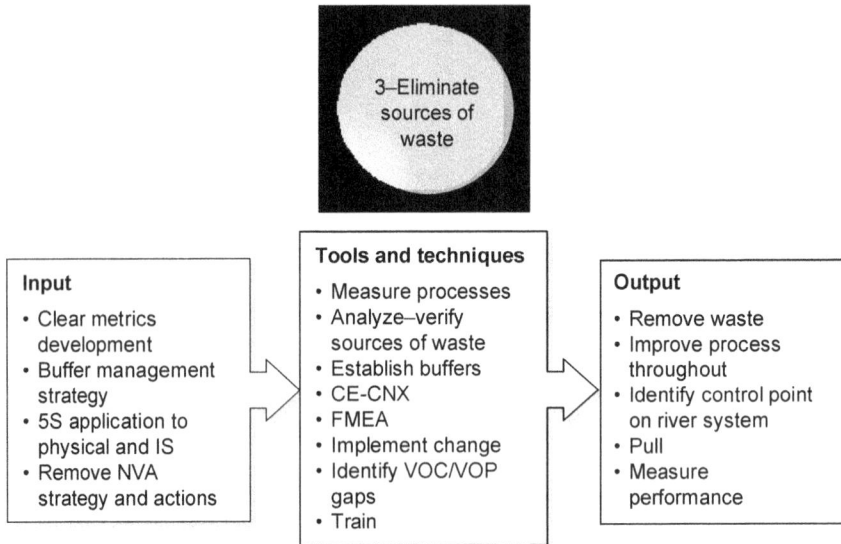

Figure 5.15   Eliminate sources of waste.

- Is your process completely demand driven? Are you *pulling* to the demand?

- Do you have plans for inventory management, levels, etc., after the improvements?

If your process constraint is not able to meet the required throughput and VOC, you must remap the process and make sure you understand what the root cause is. Seldom is the constraint the lack of physical capacity! Other factors need to be fully explored before redesigning the process to be able to meet throughput, quality, and profitability requirements. Make sure that you are looking out of the box and challenging all existing assumptions in order to find an appropriate solution. Existing assumptions could lock you in to developing just another version of what it used to be!

Step 4—Control Process Variability

After you eliminate or minimize the waste and have a smoother flow, your new process flow network should be established. At this stage, you would be using Six Sigma tools and techniques to control process variability (Figure 5.16). Ideally, the process input variables need to perform consistently and be repeatable with minimal variability relative to the customer's requirements. Obviously,

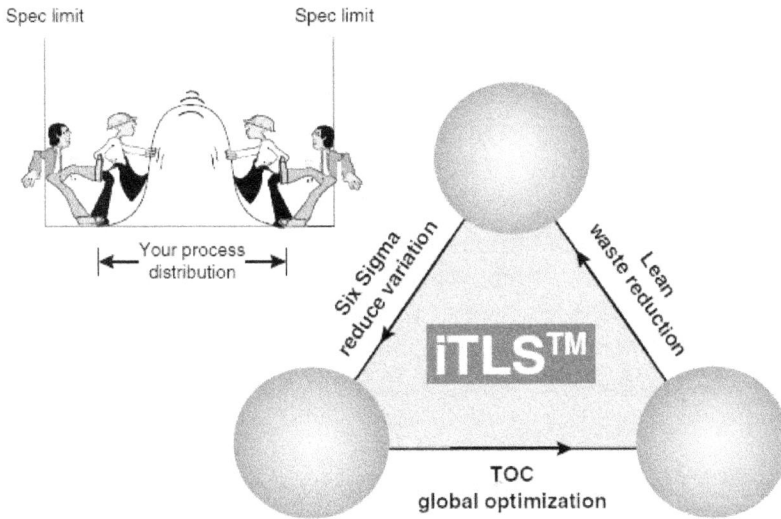

Figure 5.16   Application of Six Sigma tools.

the level of required variability is determined by VOC, or the customer's specification and the organization's strategies.

At this stage of the process, you want to make sure that your process is as error-free as your requirements. Your goal is to find ways to center your process distribution on the target defined by your customer specifications. This will make your process mean similar to your required nominal. Then you want to make sure that your process spread, or variability, is squeezed enough (determined by your customer specification limits) around your process mean. Your process spread, or variability, is the error in the process from the target. The narrower and more compact your distribution shape, the closer the process responses to the targeted performance. When you have centered your process and squeezed out as much variability, or error, as is required, you need to make sure that your process control limits are far enough away from your customer's specifications. This would leave some buffer space for random fluctuations of your process mean. The amount of buffer space you would design will depend on VOC and the economic feasibility of achieving it. This buffer space is measured in 'δ', (sigma). The more sigmas that you can pack between your process mean and the nearest specification limit, the more precise your process will be (Figure 5.17).

To pursue perfection considering the VOC, Six Sigma tools should be applied to identify and isolate the source(s) of process variation and systematically remove or minimize those variations. Certainly, it is necessary for the operations to have full understanding of the voice of process (VOP) by this stage. It is

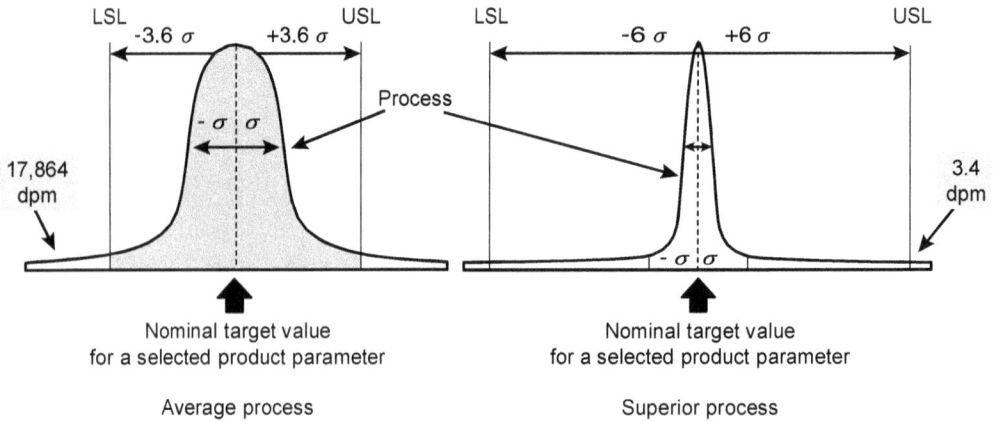

$\sigma_{capability}$	DPM (2-sided)
6.0	3.4
5.5	32
5.0	233
4.5	1,350
4.0	6,210
3.5	22,750
3.0	66,810
2.5	158,687
2.0	308,770

$\sigma_{capability}$ vs DPM

Figure 5.17 Comparisons of two processes.

necessary to quantify the process capabilities, C_p and C_{pk}, by comparing the VOC to the VOP, and determine the gaps, if they are detected:

$$C_p = \frac{USL-LSL}{6\sigma} = \frac{VOC}{VOP} \qquad (17)$$

USL: Upper specification limit

LSL: Lower specification limit

σ : Process standard deviation

The VOP is the natural variability inherent to that process. It is the random fluctuations of the process between the process's lower control limit and upper control limit. The minimum potential index for meeting the VOC requirement is 1.00; in reality this index could still cause over 67,000 unacceptable events per million. A better measure of process capability would be C_{pk}, with a minimum index of

1. In real-world applications, an index of 1.50 for most applications signifies existence of a somewhat robust process. Such a process could deal with normal and random fluctuations of a process and still deliver customer specifications with a long-term yield of 99.868% and about 1,450 errors per million. To create a typical robust process with a long-term yield of 99.99966%, the C_{pk} index should be 2.00, representing a Six Sigma process. This would allow for most random variability in processes, with no more than 3.4 unacceptable events per million. This may sound good for most industrial processes; however, for medical or pharmaceutical processes, a Six Sigma process may not be adequate. You have to make sure that the VOC is fully understood prior to designing any processes in order to make sure that your processes are able to deliver what exactly the customer is asking for consistently.

$$\text{Process Capability Index} = C_{pk} = min \left[\frac{(USL - \bar{x})}{3\sigma} \ or \ \frac{(\bar{x} - LSL)}{3\sigma} \right] \qquad (18)$$

$\overline{X}$: Process mean (arithmetic average)

Applying CE-CNX, DOE, and so forth would enable you to pinpoint which factors in your processes are responsible for the majority of the process variability. When the sources of process variation have been identified through the screening process, using Six Sigma's analytical tools, the critical few factors are identified for process control.

$$Y = f(x) \text{ or } Y = f(x_1, x_2, x_3 \ldots x_n)$$

During this stage, it may be necessary to perform Design of Experiments (DOE) to establish the optimal settings for the critical factors that have been identified. The DMAIC process, as well as DMADV (see Tables 3.8 and 3.10), would provide a guide for the team to follow logical steps to reduce or optimize process variability and establish processes that are capable of meeting customer requirements. Please refer to Chapter 3 for more information on the application of Six Sigma tools and techniques.

Taking the VOC for your processes, you can determine what PPM and DMPO levels they expect your processes to perform at. Then you can compute the desired standard deviation or normal variability that is required in your processes. That information allows you to establish the natural variability band for your desired process. This will give you a clear guideline as to what level of imperfection will be allowed for your process to operate without negatively impacting your customer requirements. Your aim would be to fine-tune your process to remain within the variability span. You need to establish control plans and use control charts to continuously monitor your processes' performance and ensure that you have adequate systematic approach to quickly respond to the trends, shifts, and outlier development in the processes. Use of control charts in conjunction with the C_{pk} index comparison are a reliable indicator or your processes' stability. They indicate process drifts to allow you to re-center your processes if specifically required.

Disciplined control of your processes through the method described will allow you to set up your processes and dial them for the PPM and DPOM levels required by the VOC.

It is also important to measure your value-stream performance at the global level to ensure that higher throughput levels have contributed to profitability and quality improvements. Hopefully, you have realized that these improvements are feasible, but they are not something you will do once and walk away from. It requires constant monitoring, measuring, and recalibration.

What can I do to ensure my measurements are reliable and credible?

It is very important for you to be able to trust your measurement system's performance, so you can make credible decisions relying on those measurements. A reliable measurement process should be free of bias, repeatable, and reproducible. It is also important to understand the precision and accuracy of the process performance of your measurement system as well as the process itself. Furthermore, you have to be able to understand, quantify, and isolate the process errors from the measurement error in order to make sound judgments and sustainably contain variability within the acceptable range.

What tools can I use to measure my measurement system validity?

You can certainly apply measurement system analysis (MSA). This book is not intended to go through all the quality tools, but we sometimes refer to those tools and techniques that we believe you must apply and certainly master. Therefore, let us briefly review the concept of MSA as a way of understanding how your measurement system is doing. Interestingly, the measurement processes and systems are also subject to the law of impermanence and natural variability. If these attributes are not understood, quantified, and taken into consideration when measurements are applied, then the final measurements may be contaminated with the measurement system's errors.

MSA is a quality technique that can quantify the measurement system's accuracy, precision, bias, linearity, reproducibility, and repeatability errors. MSA's purpose is to identify and quantify the sources of variation that affect a measurement system and minimize them to an acceptable level (Figure 5.18). Variation in measurements can be attributed to variation in the product itself or to variation

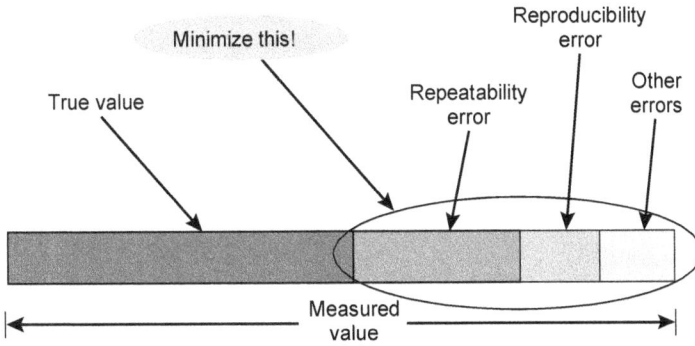

Figure 5.18 Measurement errors.

in the measurement system. The variation in the measurement system itself is measurement error.

Figure 5.19 summarizes the input, tools and techniques, and the output recommendations for this step.

At this stage of the process, it is important for you to be able to verify the following before moving on to the next step. Obviously these questions and points

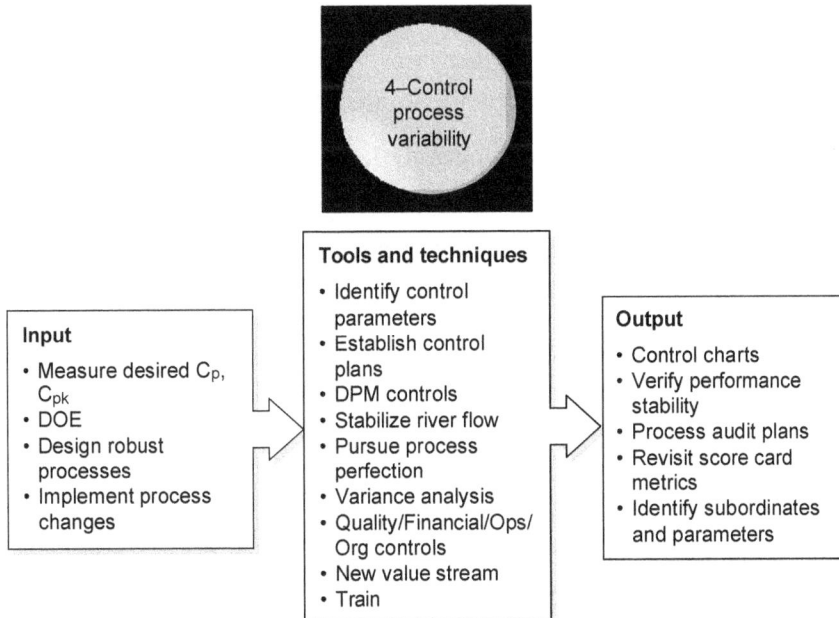

Figure 5.19 Control process variability.

only serve as a guide, and based on your processes and requirements you should include additional control factors, as necessary:

- Have you identified which process factors contribute most to the constraint process variability?

- Do you know if you have variability in "accuracy," "precision," or combinations?

- Have you identified measurements of "repeatability," "reproducibility," and existence of "bias"?

- Have you confirmed your data by conducting a Gage RR study?

- Do you know how to squeeze error out of your processes at the constraint?

- Have you put in place proper control charts at bottleneck and buffer areas?

- Have you identified which processes (subordinates) are providing critical input to the bottleneck?

- Have you identified subordinate parameters and their control plans?

- Have you completed FMEA and control plans for the bottleneck and buffers?

- Have you implemented the new value stream redesigned for the desired control levels?

- Do you need to train and implement new metrics?

- Do you need to make any changes to the policies and procedures?

- Have you identified an audit system with clear guidelines for inspecting critical factors and their associated parameters, frequency of audit, auditor training, and so forth?

Step 5—Control Supporting Activities

Upon establishing the optimal process variable settings, it is necessary to establish standard operating procedures and control mechanisms to ensure that the process's critical factors will remain in statistical control and will not vary significantly over time. Application of fail-safe (poka-yoke) devices and statistical process control is essential to sustain the process gains and provide an early warning system to prevent process variability (see Chapter 2). At this juncture, any abnormal variability must be investigated using an iTLS problem-solving tool (Figure 5.20). This tool needs to be used at the place where the variability is observed and should include the actual employees involved in the process. The team needs to take ownership in the problem-solving and the development of containment and preventive plans. Additional engineering and technical assistance certainly needs to be provided to the team to develop effective poka-yoke to minimize variability.

The rapid problem-solving worksheet should be used daily at all buffers and bottlenecks. The purpose is clear: to constantly involve the work teams in monitoring, controlling, and continuously improving the process's performance. This tool is used in conjunction with the control charts on your takt board. When the workers identify an abnormal deviation, they must immediately collect data and begin the problem-identification and problem-solving process. The quality of problem-solving is critical to the sustainability of the solutions identified and put in place. A work team that is trained in problem-solving and disciplined to follow the process each and every time will play a critical role in error reduction at your critical processes. We recommend that you institute a reward and recognition program for work teams that sustain their processes.

As part of good operations management practice, the management teams should walk the work and operational areas every day, at least at the beginning and

Problem				
Root cause	**Plan to resolve**	**Responsible**	Member	Date
1. Why:	Containment			
2. Why:				
3. Why:				
4. Why:				
5. Why:				
	Prevention/Poka-yoke	Schematic		
Operator:				
Supervisor:				
Quality:				

Figure 5.20   iTLS rapid problem-solving worksheet.

end of every shift, with the department managers and review every takt board. Any problem identified on takt boards that may need management intervention should be responded to immediately. A periodic review of rapid problem-solving work-sheets could help in promoting deeper understanding of work processes, issues, challenges, and solutions. This understanding should facilitate better control of the processes that are feeding the bottleneck. Frequently, best practices that emerge from these efforts can easily be copied in other applicable areas.

If the non-bottleneck processes feeding the constraint incur significant disruptions, they can starve and adversely impact the bottleneck. Starvation of the bottleneck impacts the entire system's throughput capability. It is imperative to maintain smooth and consistent flows of activities at the processes that feed the constraint (Figure 5.21).

Up to this point, you have gone through much effort to improve your river flow with harmonized feeders to make sure that your river will not flood or suffer droughts, while feeding its end customer. To ensure sustainability of your leveled river flow, periodic control monitoring must be in place. The following would be a good checklist before proceeding to the next step:

- Are all critical feeder processes and their significant factors to the constraint identified?

- Have the constraint protective buffers been established and tested to make sure that feeders will not starve the constraint?

- Have the organizational, operational processes been modified and properly documented?

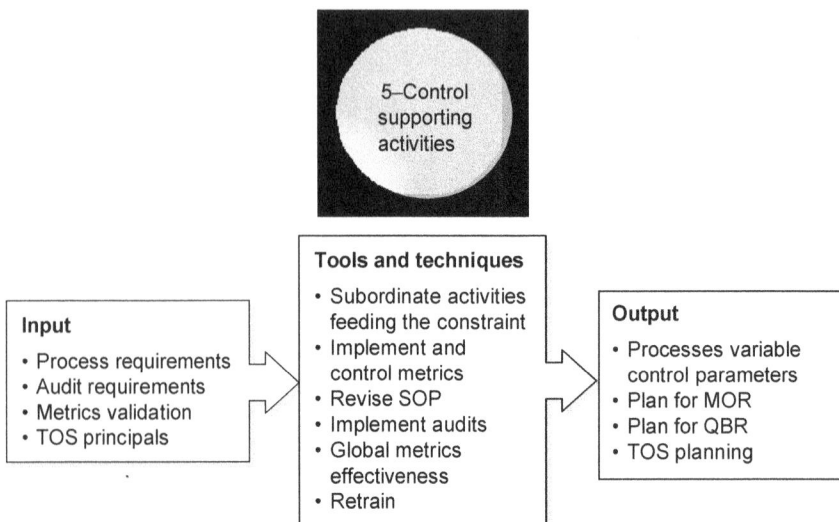

Figure 5.21   Control supporting activities.

- Have relevant standard operating procedures (SOP) been established to support any process changes?

- Have audits been established with clear elements to validate each constraint's health and subordination of feeders?

- Have the work teams and their management been trained on any new changes?

Step 6—Remove the Constraint and Stabilize

Application of step five activities will protect the bottleneck operations and will elevate them to a level of capability that is not considered a process constraint. Of course, it is necessary to monitor the operations and resources to ensure their health and performance consistency over time. Process audits can be extremely effective, so it is also necessary to design audits to monitor process performance to ensure that the process gains are maintained. If any deviations are observed during the audit processes, they should trigger corrective and preventive action plans.

What are iTLS suggested monitoring systems?

Dashboards can be used to monitor the performance of critical operations, daily. Dashboards should include global measures that not only measure the local bottleneck performance, but also the throughput measures. These dashboards should be reviewed with cross-functional process owners and departments, including the subordinated activities for any fine-tuning. With today's information systems, it is feasible to have real-time visibility into such measurements. Dashboards should include flags for any out-of-control conditions. At the operations levels, it is important for the workers and people who actually are performing the tasks to be fully engaged in the measurement process and dashboard management. Frequently, it is assumed that when we talk about dashboards or takt board we are referring to the manufacturing processes, but the fact is that as long as you have activities, processes, and tasks it really does not matter if the workers are performing manufacturing, discrete processes, or transactional processes. You can use the same dashboard and takt board concepts to monitor and control the work. Workers should fully understand how their work is being measured; what the key performance indicators (KPI) are that satisfy quality, performance, and costs; and how they are performing against those KPIs. Workers should be involved and clearly understand the root causes of any performance gaps in their KPIs and know what they should do to improve the metrics. Obviously, the KPIs and metrics used to measure these critical processes must be effectively tied with incentive plans for the workers and address the question of "what is in it for me?" Hence, it is important that you involve human resources (HR) as an active team members in your CPI projects and activities. HR could assist with ensuring that your processes are harmonized with company policy and procedures and, if changes are required, that they are integrated properly into the enterprise environmental assets. Additionally, HR could assist in communications and developing policies and practices for reward and recognition programs to connect performance metrics with worker evaluations, compensations, incentives, promotions, and so forth. Early involvement of HR in your CPI activities could prevent worker grievances and operational disruptions that might undermine your efforts. HR also needs to have some level of ownership in the development of your teams' new processes to assist in further safeguarding the success and sustainability of the new process improvements (see Figure 5.22).

Employees at each work area, discrete or transactional, should have a kickoff meeting at the beginning of every shift to review performance metrics from the previous day or shift at local and global levels, understand gaps and pipeline expectations, and plan their activities for their shifts according to the needs and priorities of the operation. It is helpful to have visual takt boards at each work area; they should clearly depict the status of work, trends, issues, and solutions to the issues that may arise during work.

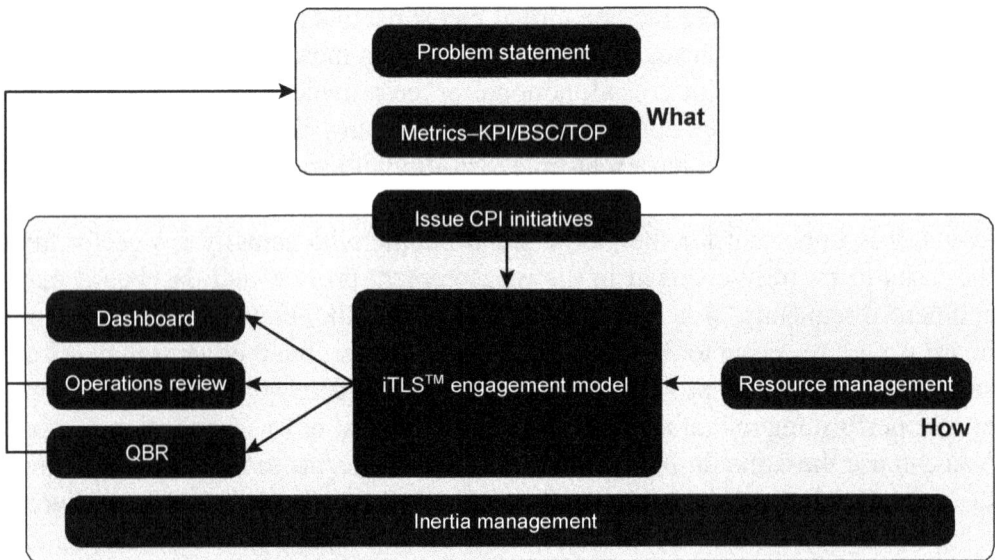

Figure 5.22 What and how for iTLS monitoring model.

What does a takt board setup look like?

A takt board is made up of three boards (two cork boards and one center white board). A takt board is basically set up as four major areas (Figure 5.23 and Picture 5.1). These four focus areas communicate and broadcast specific functions and objectives:

1. **What do you want me to do?** The central section, as shown in Figure 5.23 and Picture 5.1, is where instructions to process and operate particular activities needed for operations or production (it could also be kanban cards) are clearly broadcast. In this area it is specified:

   a. What to process; what parts or activities

   b. Where to process; which work area, cell, line, and so forth

   c. How much to process; the required amount to be produced or processes

   d. When to process; takt rates and time requirements for the processing parts

2. **How am I doing?** The right wing of the takt board is dedicated to the TOS metrics and other critical measurements. We encourage employees to manually update these measurements on a real-time basis (Figure 5.24). We realize that a number of automated solutions are available, but we feel that the workers somehow need to be engaged in the process, so they pay attention to the trends, shifts, and outliers developing in their measurements. The tally sheets need to document performance to takt for the current day and also be able to show the monthly trends. This will improve employees' understanding of their status, where they stand relative to the goals and objectives, and how the process has been doing in the short term and longer term. The objective is to engage the employees in problem identification and problem-solving in real time and as frequently as possible. The goal is for the workers to reduce the frequency and severity of their issues. Use of control charts enables workers to develop a deeper understanding of their processes, which would prevent any significant issue from arising that would impede them from achieving their objectives. Use a color-coded scheme to provide visual indication of the health of each metric.

3. **Need help:** The left wing of the takt board is dedicated to "Need Help" and "Can Do." On this board, employees post areas or items that they need help with and that require their supervisor's intervention.

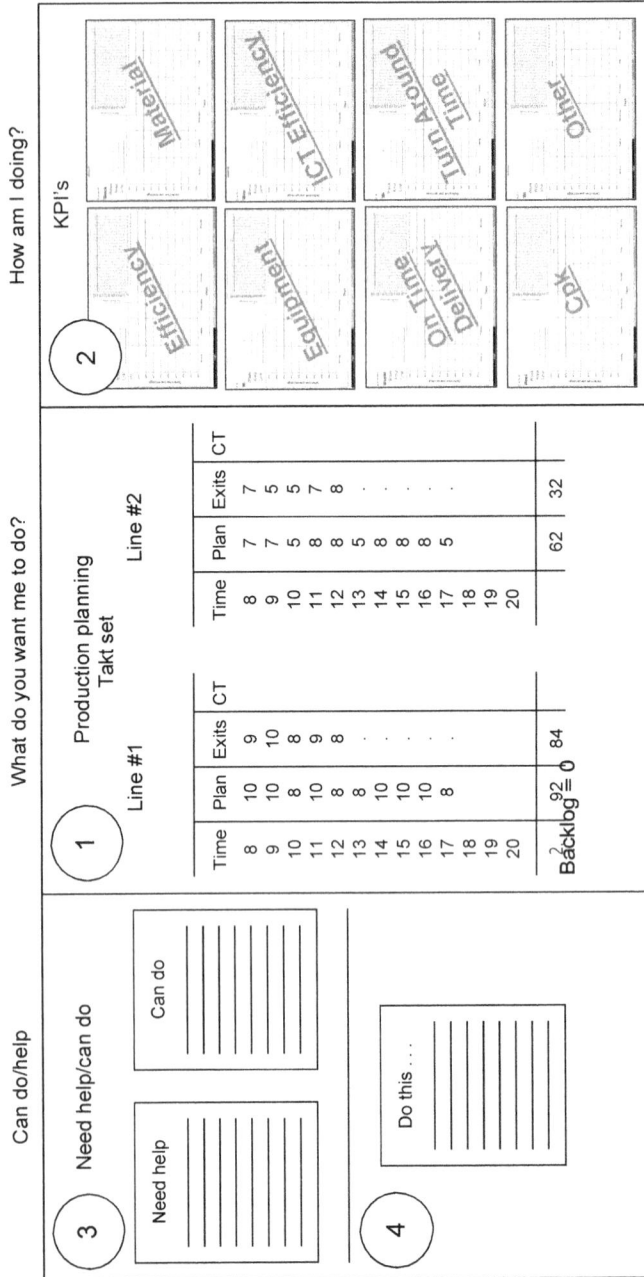

Figure 5.23 Generic iTLS takt board layout.

4. **Do this:** Solutions to the problems that were identified in section 1 are posted in this area. The objective is involvement of employees in problem-solving and process awareness and expanding the cycle of learning. During the shift meetings, this area will be reviewed by all employees, so the cycle of learning transfers to all. Frequently, this process results in realization of best practices that could be applied by other workers or other departments and functions. This particular area also would be a focus point for the management daily walk to identify problems, quality of problem-solving, and needs for training or development. Also, when best practices are identified, communicate them and, if applicable, standardize those best practices to benefit the enterprise.

Tatk boards should be reviewed by each area supervisor or manager on an hourly basis. Supervisors need to note any *need help* requests for their immediate action.

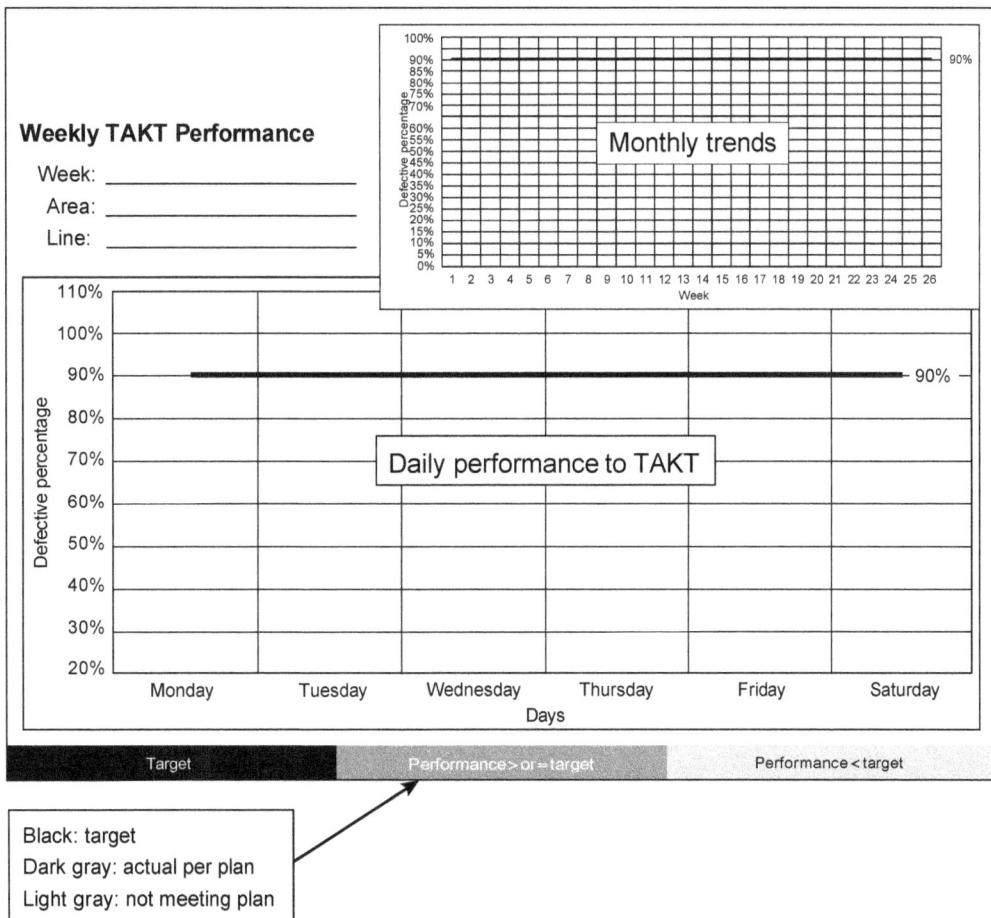

Figure 5.24 Generic iTLS performance tally sheet.

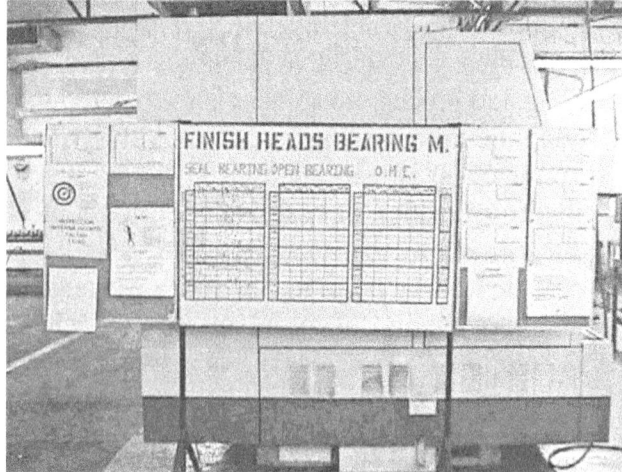

Picture 5.1 Takt board set up in a shop-floor environment.

Please note that need-help requests are not urgent and do not result in immediate line shutdown. These are issues that workers could not immediately solve or were out of scope of their influence; improving them will facilitate performance enhancements. Urgent items must be dealt with immediately.

Figure 5.25 depicts inputs, tools, and techniques and output of step six of the iTLS process. With this step you ensure that the resources that were identified as process constraints are no longer posing a threat to the flow of your process river and throughput integrity.

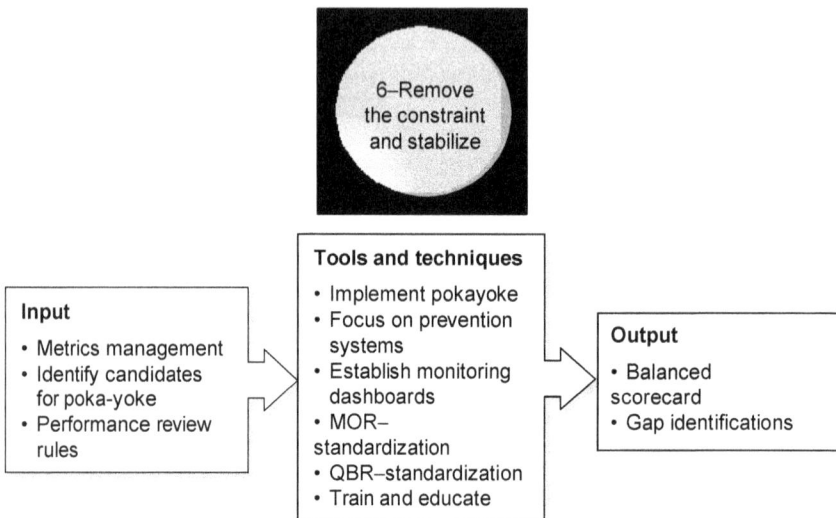

6–Remove the constraint and stabilize

Input
- Metrics management
- Identify candidates for poka-yoke
- Performance review rules

Tools and techniques
- Implement pokayoke
- Focus on prevention systems
- Establish monitoring dashboards
- MOR–standardization
- QBR–standardization
- Train and educate

Output
- Balanced scorecard
- Gap identifications

Figure 5.25 Remove the constraint and stabilize.

To ensure that your process river flows do not have any significant obstructions, or bottlenecks, you may need to consider the following items. As mentioned previously, you may need to add additional relevant items to the checklist, depending on the scope and requirements of your CPI project to validate, before moving on to the next step:

- Have you implemented fail-safe mechanisms for your processes, to ensure controlling their variability?

- Have you trained your workers on problem-solving?

- Do you have solid corrective and preventive-action systems that are well understood and practiced by your workers?

- Have you established your takt boards?

- Have you established your measurement dashboards?

- Have you updated your balanced scorecards?

- Have you established monthly operational reviews and quarterly reviews to ensure that your processes are sustaining the gains designed for?

- Has the system throughput improved? How much? Does it meet your design parameters?

Step 7—Reevaluate the System

This critical step has a tendency to be set aside, particularly when things are progressing smoothly. To minimize chances of neglecting this step, it is necessary to implement scheduled audits of the system. The iTLS implementation team must reevaluate system performance at the global level to investigate where the bottleneck has shifted. Also, it is important to ensure that application of statistical process control (SPC) tools, such as control charts with process capability information and PPM performances, are effective at this stage. Any process mean shift, trends, outliers, or process spread changes must immediately be investigated for root cause analysis. Consequently, corrective and preventive measures are taken to ensure process stability and control (Figure 5.26). When a new bottleneck emerges, the team needs to go to step 1 of the iTLS process and begin the process over.

At this point of process, you should not walk away from the project and assume that the CPI job is done! You must ensure that you know where you need to focus next. Make sure the following points are considered:

- Have you gone through project close phase and obtained stakeholders buy-in?

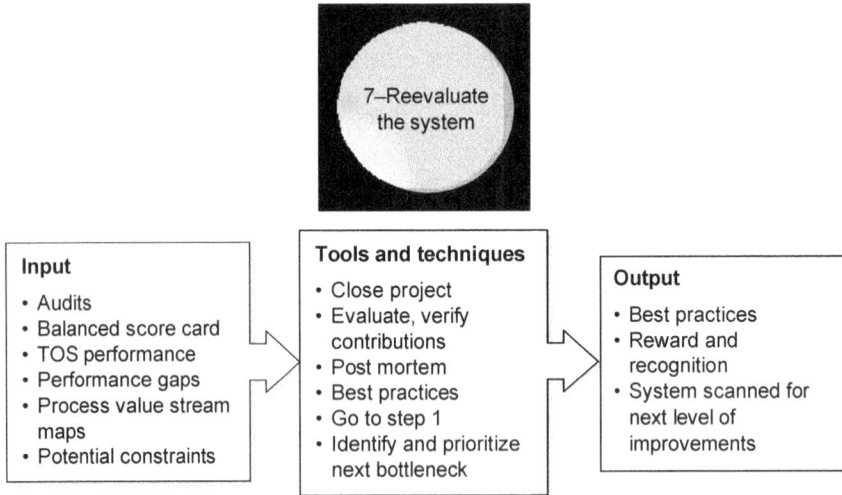

Figure 5.26   Reevaluate the system.

- Have you reviewed the throughput improvement results with your financial controllers and obtained verification and approvals?

- Have you assessed the entire project and documented lessons learned?

- Have you established follow-up communication plans with stakeholders regarding the lessons learned?

- Have you remapped your process value stream?

- Have you identified the potential bottleneck of your system for the next level of improvements?

- Have you established your champions' reviews to communicate the improvements for potential best-practices knowledge transfer?

- Have you modified documentation that needed to be updated due to the need for process changes due to emergence of the new best practices?

- Have you established standardization of the best practices globally in your organization?

- Have you processed your reward and recognition for the team players?

- Have you planned for your project charter for the next level of improvement?

How do you know that implementation of iTLS has been successful?

Your initial project charter has established the expected deliverable and the requirements in order to improve the river flow of your processes. Also, at the beginning of the project you established the project baselines. The measurements of your process throughput improvements and their contribution to your overall system compared with your process baseline are the indication of your process success and the degree of improvement. Your financial controllers and your customers should be able to tangibly verify the impact of your effort on the throughput improvement in terms of profitability, speed, and quality improvements.

You could consider the measurements shown in Figure 5.27 when comparing your improved processes with the baseline.

Measurement	Baseline	Improved process	% Change
DPM/DPMO			
C_{pk}			
Rework $			
Process cycle time			
Transportations/movement			
Customer satisfaction			
Inventory $			
Throughput $			
Operating costs $			

Figure 5.27 Baseline assessment.

What is the roadmap for implementation of iTLS as an organization-wide program?

iTLS implementation is straightforward and logical. The iTLS road map is composed of the following 21 steps. It is imperative to consistently apply these steps in a well-disciplined manner. You need to ensure that your iTLS champions and project leaders fully understand the road map and follow it. Figure 5.27 illustrates the overall road map and flow of initiatives for successful implementation of iTLS. Element number 1 in the road map should not be overlooked. Obtaining upper-management buy-in is critical to the success of your efforts.

1. Obtain upper-management support and sponsorship to launch a continuous improvement program. Upper management needs to visibly and actively show support and invest in education, training, and institute reward and recognition systems.

2. Apply iTLS as a global approach for continuous improvement methodology.

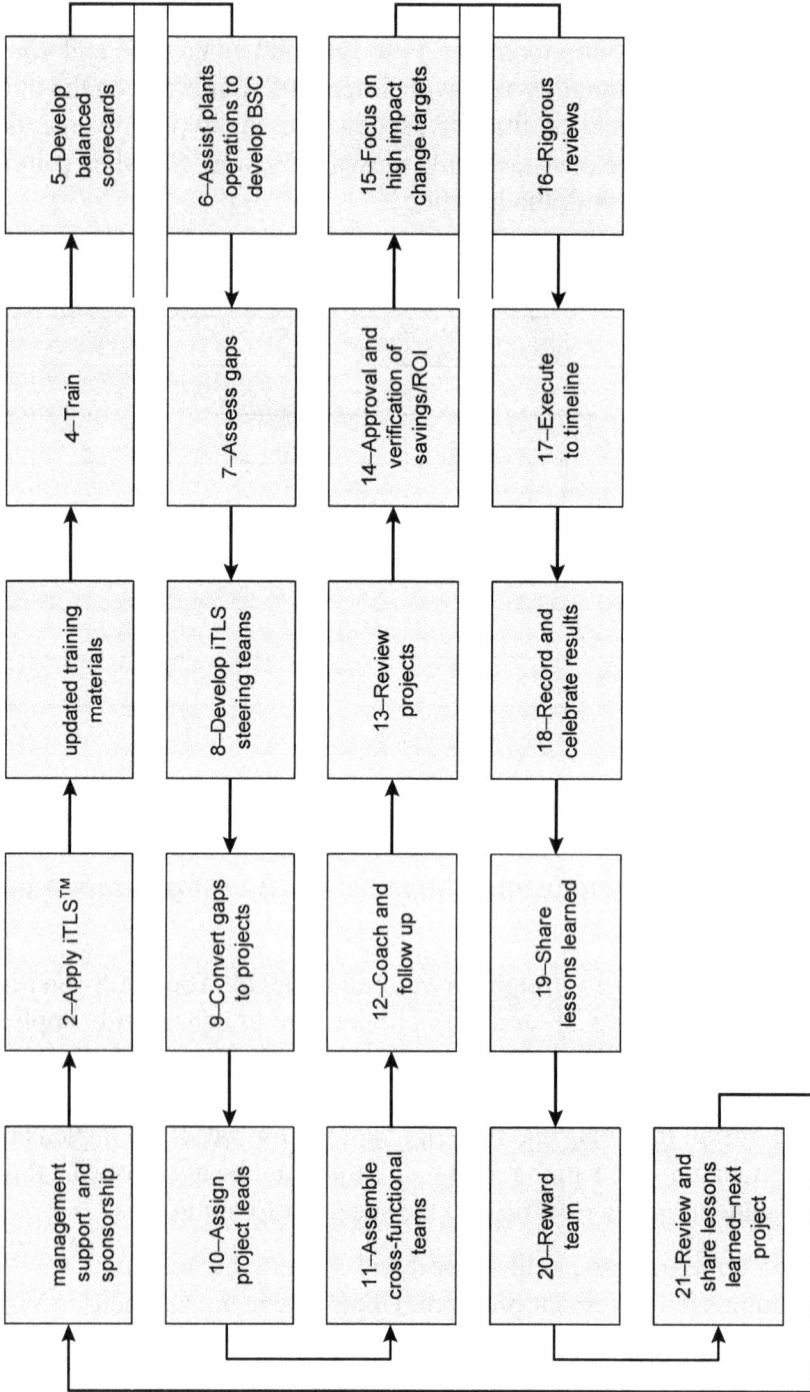

Figure 5.28 iTLS implementation road map.

3. Use updated training materials and trainers.

4. Do not take shortcuts in training. Train employees in iTLS methodology applications. Start by training upper management, sponsors, champions, and team leaders. Training is an important element of the employee-empowerment process. Training without practice is not effective. It is important to engage the trained individuals in real-life problem-solving and continuous improvement process immediately during their training process.

5. Management must establish organizational goals and objectives by developing organizational key process indicators. This process is called developing an organizational balanced scorecard.

What is a balanced scorecard (BSC)?

A balanced scorecard is a document developed internally by the organization's management. The goal of the scorecard is to develop a tool to provide the line of sight from an organization's vision to individual goals. The balanced scorecard contains traditional financial measures that consider long-term capabilities and customer relationships.

Why are there so many organizations that are disappointed with implementation of their strategies and tactical plans? There are many reasons for the root causes of these disappointments. I will focus on the most frequent causes. It is important to also note that, in most cases, the causes of these disappointments are interaction effects of several factors that make the situations more complex and undesirable.

As we learned in simple process stability analysis, we know that there is nothing in the universe that is unchanging and permanent. There are degrees of variability in everything we know. We know that (J, sigma, or standard deviation, when applied as measurement of process variability, is real. Every time multiple measurements are involved, we know that it is highly unlikely that all measurements will be exactly identical. That is why we assign tolerance limits to processes to account for these variations. What appeared as stable and unchanging, such as mountains, rocks, and continents, have now been shown to be ever-changing. Why has this reality not fully permeated into our organizations, particularly when we are putting together strategic plans? Why is it that organizations continue to use the same approaches, strategies, and tactical plans as decades before, pretending that the environment is static?

The ever-changing environment requires constant research to map the changes, trends, and shifts and their effects on the business in order for the organization to respond, however subtle (Mintzberg, 1993). Organizations clearly need to integrate change planning and management as a natural and continuous effort throughout the life cycle of an organization. The culture must be tuned to strive for global optimization and teamwork. This may create a contradiction with some common management approaches, such as traditional cost savings, particularly for larger organizations.

For example, an organization that has multiple locations or plants puts pressures on its managers to cut costs. As a typical response to immediate cost-cutting, managers reduce personnel and operate with minimal resources to become invisible on the corporation's radar screen. When it comes to strategic planning, the operations that have cut resources too deeply do not have the proper skilled resources to dedicate to thoroughly perform this critical activity. Further, the measurements focus on the local efficiencies, which forces front-line managers to allocate the minimum amount of resources and typically delay the process to the last moments of requirements. The plans that are put together in the last moment suffer from the "student syndrome" and often lack thoroughness and the necessary depth and breadth.

In these types of settings, cross-departmental coordination becomes a serious challenge. Often local measurements incent each department to maximize their local efficiencies even when they cause inefficiencies in other departments. Disagreements and interdepartmental frictions add in effectiveness.

The combination of a lack of resources and the unwillingness of managers to ease off on territorial controls and work with planning teams and cross-departmental resources, combined with assumptions that the business environment is static, result in questionable strategies. In the end, these strategies may not have the necessary relevance for successful implementation, because they have not adequately been researched and developed and they may not be well connected with the organization's overall objectives. If the outcome of this planning is another version of past plans, disappointments will be a natural outcome (Figure 5.29).

An alternative to this type of strategy development is conceptually simple and effective, but it requires conscious effort to execute, because cultural development, especially at the executive level, is essential. An organization needs to develop its critical success indicators and measurement at the global level and then translate them with crisp granularity to the operations level. When clearly communicated, these measurements will set the tempo for the desired organizational behavior. It is critical to consider real-world changes to the business environment, customer needs and wants, markets, competitive activities, and so forth as an input to the strategic planning process. Certainly reduction of operating costs is a real-world consideration to most organizations, but continuous process improvement to streamline process and eliminate waste from processes to increase throughput is a preferred approach to layoffs and headcount reductions.

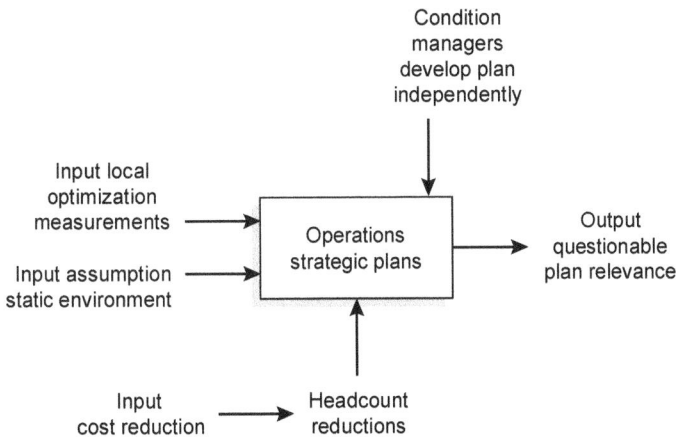

Figure 5.29 High-level model for undesirable outcome of strategic planning.

Organizations' operating cultures should embrace collaborative work environments and transparent cross-departmental efforts to maximize overall organization profitability. This type of operating ambient is empowered, encouraged, and rewarded by the executive leadership. An organization considers what resources it needs to develop strategies consistent with and directly connected to the organization's overall objectives. The planning team must be intimately familiar with the organization's overall plans and quantitatively aware of the changes taking place in the marketplace, customers, economy, rivals, and so forth. Their research and plans must be transparently shared with the front-line and field managers and ensure that all operations' input have been fully considered and that there is buy-in from the operations managers and the stakeholders to the strategies, tactical plans and their measurements, and reward systems. The plans must accommodate new market intelligence and environmental-change data to maintain relevance. Strategic planning is a continuous effort and should be treated as live documents that needs to operate with valid and fresh data. The outcome of this type of planning effort certainly offers higher probabilities of the successful implementation of the strategic and tactical plans (Figure 5.30).

Organizational metrics are derived from the organization's vision, mission, and core values. Therefore, clarity and thoroughness are critical, because everything else in the organization are tied to them.

It is common for organizations to spend significant efforts on developing their mission, vision and strategies, road map, and so forth. The executives and upper management get together, perhaps at an off-site location, spend a few days going over elaborate presentations, action plans, and objectives, and possibly close the summit with a a game of golf or other event. After their closed-door sessions, however, communication to the rest of the organization is often stifled. What was discussed and decided does not get passed out and down to all levels

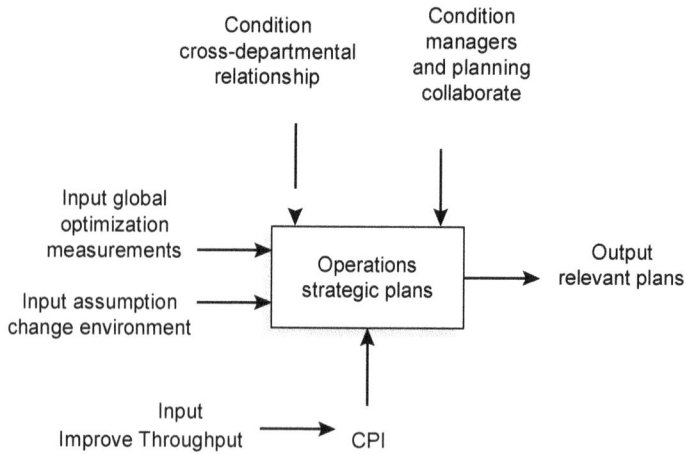

Figure 5.30 High-level generic model for collaborative strategic planning.

of the organization with clear and measurable objectives and metrics. The organization's reaction and input to those objectives and measurements frequently is not solicited, and valuable input can be totally ignored.

The organizations should create future value through investment in customers, suppliers, employees, processes, technology, and innovation. As part of active planning, individual performance plans should be part of group performance plans that are driven by business unit initiatives. Business unit initiatives must be driven by the organization's vision; mission and strategic goals should be well communicated to all levels of operations (Figure 5.31).

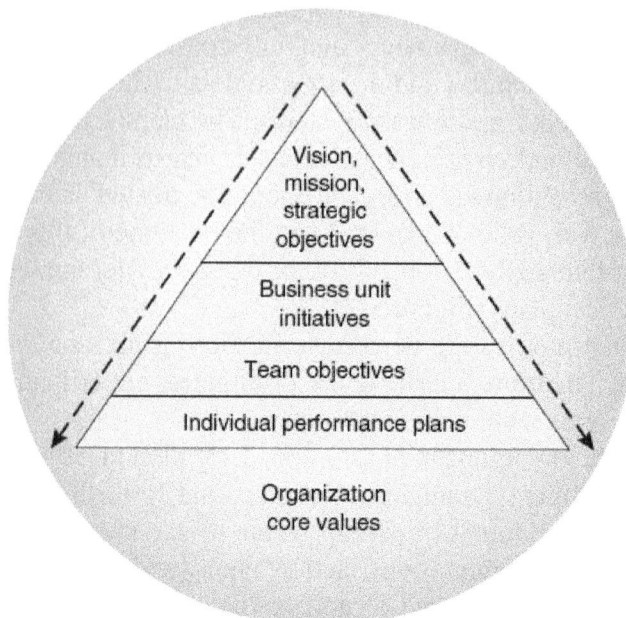

Figure 5.31 Conversion of firm's core values to balanced scorecard.

Organizations must develop a clear vision, mission, and business strategy so that they can succinctly define the KPIs that measure their operational success. One of the effective ways of translating the organization's strategy to tangible KPIs is using balanced scorecards (BSC). These balanced scorecards need to be cascaded throughout the organization. The balanced scorecards contain key process indicators applicable to all functional levels of the organization. For example, an organizational strategic-level BSC needs to be broken down to the functional organizations, such as finance, engineering, product development, research and development, manufacturing, logistics, marketing, sales, supply chain, and so forth.

Each functional organization (divisions, departments) will apply its KPIs from the BSC as a line of sight to focus their efforts. The focused efforts will attempt to align the organization's efforts for achieving the optimal collective results. Each functional organization should measure its capabilities against the KPIs from their BSC and their targets and then identify any gaps in the KPIs and use the identified gaps as targets for its CPI initiatives. Gaps in KPIs would clarify the need for change and improvements, and the iTLS process will begin. The contributions of any CPI initiative identified in this way should positively impact the KPI and the functional level BSC. The rollup of all improvements from functional operations should significantly improve the overall organization's KPIs.

Identification of process gaps further highlights the need for training programs to enable resources to operate and perform at the optimal levels.

All of this enables the organization's leadership to have total awareness of what is critical, what needs to be measured, what those measurements are, how they should be measured, how frequently they should be reviewed, what should be done when gaps are found, and so forth.

The balanced scorecard is not only a measurement system; it is also a management system that enables organizations to clarify their vision and strategies and translate them into achievable objectives. The balanced scorecard provides feedback around both the internal business processes and external outcomes in order to continuously improve strategic performance and results. By fully deploying the balanced scorecard, strategic planning transforms into the nerve center of an enterprise to control its variability from targets. Recommended dimensions to be covered in a balanced scorecard should include the following:

> *Customers and markets*—When assembling their strategic plans, organizations often spend a tremendous number of resources and effort on competition analysis and intelligence gathering. Obviously, understanding how the competition is doing business is helpful, but the focus is wrong here. The organization should be focused on the markets and the customers. Instead of wasting significant effort to understand what the competition has done, it is more valuable to understand what the customers' needs are now and in

the future. Using this information, the organization can determine its performance gaps, core strengths, weaknesses, opportunities, and threats if it doesn't do anything differently. Becoming too focused on a particular competitor may not allow the organization to effectively lead the market and rather guide it down the industry-lagger path.

The focus should be on the markets and their customers, with clear understanding of what their needs are, where the market is heading, and how future changes in environments might impact customer behavior and needs. These needs should be fully compared to the organization's current core capabilities. The organization then needs to quantify what it would take to fill the gaps, and then decide if it makes strategic sense to go through the exercise.

Using the gathered intelligence, the organization can objectively map out its action plans and define measurements that produce the desired organizational behavior. The functional management then deploys the objectives and measurements with solid links to the organizational objectives, which, in turn, are also strongly linked to the markets and customers.

Price—Price is the organization's pricing strategy by market and by customer, considering the internal capabilities and opportunities. The operations river network needs to be fully considered in order to more strategically price products and services in the marketplace.

Services Feedback—Organizations provide products and services to the marketplace, and it is critical to fully understand the customers' experience. Customers' experience and perception must be tracked and used to continuously get closer to the heart of customers and the marketplace. The most popular method of obtaining such feedback is using surveys. It is important that these surveys be designed objectively and specifically and avoid generalization or vagueness. Also, surveys must be unbiased and truly provide information, which could be either good or bad.

Delivery performance—Delivery of products and services is critical to the customers. As enterprises develop smoother operation flow, their dependence on fast and reliable deliveries become more pronounced. Some of the critical delivery performance indicators are on-time delivery, quality, and consistency.

Quality—As businesses become more direct from the origin to the point of use, dependence on high-quality products and services increases significantly. Error-free products and services will win the customers and marketplace. Today, when you purchase a laptop you may place your order online and receive your product directly from the manufacturer. What may shape your perception of the quality of what you received would be how the product was delivered. How was it packaged? Did it work as you expected? What if you had an issue with the laptop and had to send it for repair? How was it handled? How easy was the process? When the repair was done, did it work as you expected or did it require rework? It would be no mystery that customers are attracted to higher-quality products. Low- and unpredictable-quality products will work themselves out of the marketplace eventually. What is the sales pitch for Lexus and Toyota?

Products or features—Product or service features are another selling point of what you offer to the marketplace. Obviously, your products and services will constantly be benchmarked against your rivals, and the closer you meet the marketplace expectation the more successful your sales will be. Understanding the marketplace and the customers' needs and wants will be the key to how successfully you will design and offer your products and services. This knowledge will allow you to effectively balance your products' and services' features vs. cost. Organizations must understand this element and closely monitor it as features change with the environment. Think about Hummer vs. the Toyota Prius hybrid. Toyota was working on developing hybrid technology while big cars and gas guzzlers were popular. What has happened to Hummer production and its once- popular features?

Learning and growth—It is the social and professional responsibility of organizations to continually grow their internal capabilities. An organization's human capital is its biggest asset. This is an asset that can grow and continuously contribute to organizational growth and profitability when managed properly. Human capital needs to constantly be challenged and trained.

This serves several simultaneous purposes that are vital to the health of the organization and its people. Continuous training keeps employees updated, more relevant, and flexible to assume responsibilities that require more skill and decision making.

Organizations would be the beneficiary of effectiveness gained from a trained and skilled workforce while employee job enrichment and satisfaction improve. You should identify what particular useful skill sets would help throughput of your organization and devise plans accordingly to grow your organization to those levels of competency and excellence. Developing your human capital allows your workforce to make better decisions, especially during emergencies and critical situations. Typically, during these situations critical and emergency decisions are made by the lower-level people in the organization and not the top management. You need to have plans, measureable objectives, and metrics to measure employees' training and learning objectives.

Going through the development of a balanced scorecard could be an eye-opening venture for managers. Through its development, managers could discover how much information is perhaps missing that would be valuable in effective decision making (Figure 5.32). The gap identification of BSC should not be taken lightly.

With the balanced scorecard, the organization's performance gaps are identified. Gaps would be the difference between current performance and the organization's goals. These gaps should be identified as projects for the organization. The trained and empowered iTLS teams should manage these projects. Any improvement would improve the critical indicators on the scorecard.

6. Help all plants and operations develop their key process indicators and scorecard.

7. Assess gaps in current performance against the scorecard goals. Identify the constraint gap.

8. Each plant must develop its iTLS steering teams and select an iTLS champion to chair the steering teams to provide cross-functional

Strategies and objectives	Current year initiatives	Future business imperatives	Business dimensions
Vision: Our overriding purpose—how we will deliver value to customers **Mission:** Who we serve, what services we provide, and how we achieve competitive advantage **Strategic objectives:** Goals we must accomplish to achieve our vision		What we need to do to build the capability to achieve our strategic objectives	**Customer and market** **Price** **Service** **Delivery performance** **Quality** **Product features** **Learning and growth**

Figure 5.32   iTLS generic layout for balanced scorecard.

support to team leaders and review their progress systematically. (See MOST, Figure 7.1.)

9. Convert the constraint gaps to projects that can be delivered by trained individuals.

10. Assign projects derived from constraint gap determinations to trained leaders. It is critical for the team leaders, who act as project managers, to be well versed in project management practices. Team leaders can apply their company-approved project management methodology. We do prefer application of critical chain project management methodology to significantly reduce resource waste and bring focus to the project and its implementation effectiveness and speed.

11. Leaders need to assemble cross-functional teams to solve assigned projects/problems. Strong project management skills are necessary to effectively deploy this step.

12. Champions are responsible for coaching and following up with trained individuals to deliver projects.

13. The steering team and champions must review projects periodically to monitor project progress, facilitate changes, and provide continuous support to the teams.

14. Obtain approval from upper management and the financial controller on tangible savings and estimated improvements for prioritizing which areas to expend resources.

15. Focus on high-impact change targets. Projects should be allowed only on gaps that are the system constraints.

16. Conduct ongoing, rigorous reviews. If it is discovered that the teams have deviated from their targets, realignment should be considered. Also, if it is revealed that the project contains no return on investment or tangible benefit to system performance, the project should be stopped and/or reevaluated in order to not waste the organization's resources. It is permitted to modify the scope of work when it makes sense to do so. It is also important to document these changes and their root causes for the lessons learned.

17. Execute time lines and time-buffer management. When the project schedule is established and time lines are agreed upon, it is important to manage the projects closely and optimize project completion due dates. We recommend implementation of critical chain project

management techniques to better benefit and manage project random variability and guard against student syndrome or Parkinson's law.

What is critical chain project management?

Critical chain project management (CCPM) is a project management technique that is driven from the application of TOC. CCPM adds duration buffers that are non-work-schedule activities to manage uncertainty. CCPM assumes that most tasks contain a 50% uncertainty buffer and that the stack-up impact of these buffers superficially lengthens the project implementation cycle. Imagine that if every task contains a 50% buffer to protect it from the probability of tardiness. It is highly unlikely that *all* tasks will be randomly late, as the events are not random any more. By removing these non-work buffers and placing them at strategic locations to protect the process constraint (critical path) via feeder buffers (subordination activity), the process is more efficiently managed. The protective buffers will only be utilized where a delay really occurs. Because it is not likely that all tasks will be late and consume all of the buffer allowances, the project total cycle time will most likely be shorter. The worst case, which would be if all tasks were late and consumed all the buffers, would be no different from the traditional scheduling method. The CCPM hypothesis includes the following:

> *Existence of Student Syndrome*—Most students, despite having ample time during their study period, prepare for their exams at the last minute. Therefore, their entire time of attending school is not all used for the exam preparation and is used on other things. The same analogy is applied to completion of tasks on a project.

> *Bad Multitasking*—Resources are more effective working on one task at a time instead of working on multiple tasks simultaneously, jumping from one to another and back and forth. This is similar to the concept of single-piece flow of JIT vs. batch processing. As we have discovered, batch processing superficially stretches the process cycle time and hides inventories and errors. One-piece flow, in contrast, significantly reduces the process cycle time and increases quality, because there are no inventories to hide errors and process deficiencies. CCPM applies this concept in managing resources working on the critical path or constraint in project management scheduling.

> *Parkinson's Law*—This concept says that the work expands to fill the time available for its completion. The suggestion is that the available times assigned to the tasks may not be most effectively

used and the work is superficially stretched. CCPM strives to better manage these time allowances.

18. Record and celebrate results.

19. Share lessons learned within the professional teams and organizations. It would be beneficial to create a repository of your iTLS projects and efforts undertaken in the organization and make them available to the organization's members. These projects could be used as best practices and replicated throughout the organization, as applicable. Other members could learn from experiences of the teams, and when dealing with similar problems or issues they could apply the lessons learned to reduce problem-solving cycle time
and efforts. Using internal management information systems in the organization could serve as an effective means for making the team projects transparent and easily accessible to the users globally throughout the enterprise. This database could also be used for internal benchmarking purposes.

20. Reward and recognize the team members for results.

21. Take advantage of the lessons learned and proceed to the next project based on the scorecard requirements.

How is implementation of iTLS different in benefits gained?

Empirical data have shown that TLS typically delivers 4–6 times higher financial results than either Lean or Six Sigma applied alone.

What is in it for the customers and shareholders to implement iTLS?

iTLS implementation could significantly improve throughput and reduce operating expenses, while improving quality. These improvements could enable organizations to provide their products and services at lower prices and higher quality levels to their customers. Shareholders would have higher potentials for profitability and business excellence.

What type of organization can be successful in sustainable implementation of iTLS?

The goal of a healthy for-profit organization could be making profits now and in the future. Profit organizations obviously have a binding obligation to their shareholders at the local level to provide the maximum return on their investments. At the global level, however, organizations are also obligated to a

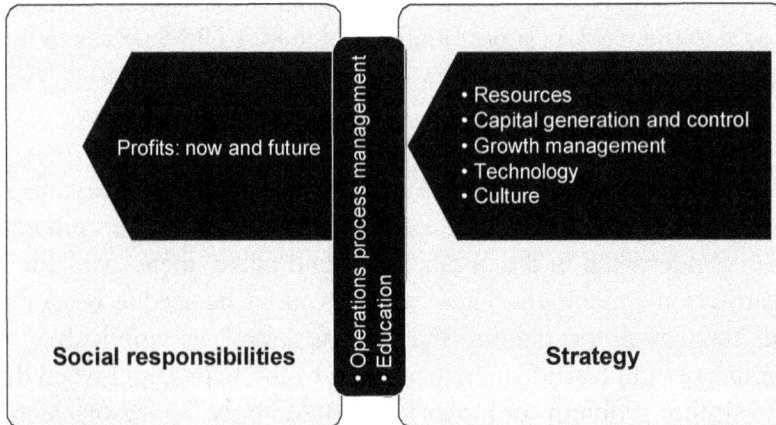

Figure 5.33 Organization's responsibilities.

series of social responsibilities to positively impact their community, society, environment, and, on the larger scale, the universe. At the strategic level, companies must integrate their technologies with their resources, cultures, and capital/ wealth generation while managing the organization's growth (Figure 5.33). Organizations must develop a clear vision, mission, and business strategy so that they can succinctly define the KPIs to measure their operational success.

Are there differences between growth and sustain strategies with iTLS?

This is an interesting topic that frequently does not get the proper attention when considering CPI implementation in organizations. Many organizations, while wishing to grow, would also like to sustain gains in productivities and processes. The environment and management style requirements for growth we believe are somewhat different from the strategy for sustain. The two strategies are as fundamentally different as the characteristics that are inherent to growth and sustain (Figure 5.34).

The growth strategy needs to create an environment that enjoys challenges and rocking the boat. The culture would welcome flexibility, creativity, innovation, teamwork, and changes. Its standard operating procedures tend to be fluid and are documents that could rapidly change as the processes change. These organizations need to move faster in thinking, decision making, and taking actions and accepting higher levels of risk. Leadership needs to be involved in fostering changes, learning, accountability, and continuously inspiring the organization toward innovation and rapid improvement. Leadership should also be prepared to learn about the organizational shortcomings and issues and to face those challenges to resolution. This type of organization moves fast, transforms rapidly, and morphs into

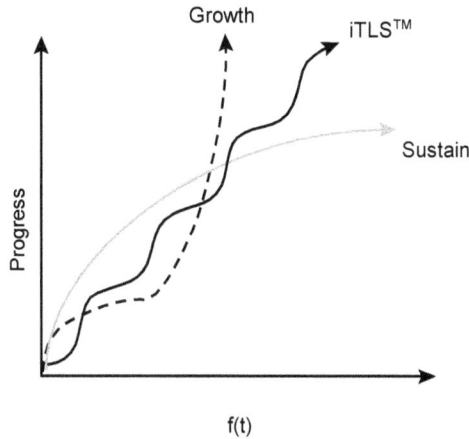

Figure 5.34 Different operating strategies.

new strategies with agility. This strategy calls for flexible equipment in cellular arrangement, with modern but light investment in capital equipment and assets. This strategy rewards innovation and change. The majority of throughput growth would come from new markets, customers, and applications.

The hold or sustain strategy is an organization that does not respond to changes rapidly; its standard operating procedures are inflexible, with lots of red tape. The organization's culture enjoys a smooth operation from day to day and does not prefer to rock the boat. Leadership is more hands-off and may not wish to hear bad news or learn of issues or systematic flaws. This type of organization is slow to change and innovate and perhaps is invested heavily in capital equipment and assets. This strategy rewards not making much noise and keeping things calm. These organizations tend to focus on the same customers from the same markets.

iTLS promotes a TOS that is growth oriented, pushing for what needs to be changed. However, iTLS also works heavily on strategies to control the system performance to maintain its gains until the next level of improvement. iTLS can facilitate rapid responses to strategic directions, while optimizing resource utilization to affect what matters the most.

Why is iTLS a competitive advantage?

iTLS focuses an organization's resources to address what is important and effective. It further guides the organization to remove waste and minimize variability, creating processes that are fast and error-free. An organization that is flexible, fast to respond, and able to provide reliable products and services at more competitive prices would certainly be able to better position its offerings in the marketplace.

How does an organization get started?

Follow the iTLS road map shown.

Does iTLS have different classifications for training levels?

iTLS recognizes the following classification referring to the training levels for the practitioners:

- Project sponsor
- Champion
- Specialist
- Expert

What are the definitions for these classifications?

Project sponsor: Project sponsors are project owners or the functional project managers. They most likely will have a direct organizational link to the iTLS champions. They own the project and ensure, using their organizational authority and leadership, that process changes are implemented and sustained in their areas of responsibility. By having the functional managers leading and facilitating projects, the probability of resistance to change from middle and front-line leadership is reduced. Specialists and project champions should report to the project expert and, in turn, to project sponsors.

Champions: The iTLS project champions are individuals who have taken part in project selection, own the project's implementation, and report to the project sponsor and senior management.
Champions are accountable for project deliverables and results; change management process rollout; training; facilitation; and promotion of iTLS. Champions prioritize projects, budgets, and resource allocations and develop a CPI road map. They should have authority and influence in the organization to obtain resources. Champions work closely and cross-functionally with iTLS specialists, iTLS experts, HR, finance, technical, and so forth to ensure the project's progress, health, and organizational development. Champions' major roles includes cross- communication with the iTLS steering team and project team leaders (specialists/experts) to remove and break down barriers preventing the change process. Specialists and experts report directly to the champion.

Specialists: The specialists are the individuals who are being developed as iTLS practitioners to become experts. Specialists have gone through iTLS training and are familiar with the iTLS process and application of its tools. They participate in various project teams, gather data, develop solutions, and implement the improvements. To minimize resistance to change and maintain improvement benefits, specialists should be involved in developing
solutions and improving their own processes. Active involvement of specialists in improving their own processes enhances their sense of ownership and pride.

Experts: Experts have had complete iTLS training (as in Black Belts and Master Black Belts) with 4500 hours of hands-on team leadership experience in application and implementation of iTLS.
They have the responsibility of developing specialists, leading specialists and teams in achieving their project objectives and targets by implementing iTLS methodology. Experts should be excellent project managers, with the ability to mentor and coach team members to achieve process improvements with optimal resource levels. Experts should be able to teach iTLS to others and be open- minded in learning, accepting, and applying new solutions and best practices. They play a role in process standardization and stability within their organizations.

How do they function together?

- Project sponsors identify what areas need improvement.

- iTLS champions assemble project teams, break down barriers, and provide resources to the project teams and are accountable for project deliverables. Champions are responsible for promotion of continuous improvement processes and their effectiveness. Champions work with an organization's team members cross-functionally in substantiating and verifying a project's true value.

- Experts provide local leadership and project management and are accountable for project implementation and results.

- Specialists work together with experts and project local owners and workers developing solutions to improve their processes.

What is a proposed iTLS project or activity timeline?

We believe that projects or activities must be implemented with agility, otherwise the implementation will drag on. A typical project should take less than seven weeks, or 560 hours, to complete. If a project cannot be completed within such a time frame, the scope perhaps is set too wide and needs to be broken down into smaller chunks. In many instances, when a large scope is broken down into chunks, these project scopes can be better synchronized or parallel processed as long as there are available resources. Projects that take longer than seven weeks to complete need to be reviewed to understand what the root-cause is that pro- longs the project's completion. The iTLS approach itself should certainly be used to discover the root cause(s).

Implementation of iTLS would bring about the following benefits:

- Fast, significant improvements, as measured by the global metrics and net profits and ROI.

- Rapid improvement in overall company performance.

- The organization gains simple tools and techniques that can be applied to continuous improvement in all business dimensions, from strategic planning to operation execution.

- Employees gain tools and techniques to continuously improve their sphere of process influence.

- The organization develops a self-driven culture of continuous improvement and problem-solving.

What are the minimum tools required by an iTLS project?

- Remember the following flow sequence:

    PF --> CE-CNX --> PFMEA -->CP

- Based on the nature of the projects, the need for application of various tools can vary. However, in most cases, the following would be the essential tools recommended by iTLS:

- PF: Process Flow (Understand the location of the constraint and VA/NVA)

- CE-CNX: Cause and Effect relationship with CNX characterization

- PFMEA: Process Failure Mode and Effect Analysis for prioritizing

- CP: Control Plan and SOPs

NOTES:

6
iTLS Study and Results Summary

HAS A MORE GLOBAL FOCUS WORKED?

We can now respond with confidence to our old friend who remarked about iTLS, "That's an intriguing idea, I wonder if it will work." The application of iTLS, which provides a more global focus and more tools for implementing a CPI initiative, not only worked, but also proved to be extraordinarily effective. iTLS delivered results that were four times greater than when Lean or Six Sigma were applied.

Most organizations producing products and/or providing services are urgently striving to increase productivity, attain quality leadership, and achieve higher efficiencies. Customers are asking for cost reductions while at the same time demanding higher quality. Companies that are not prepared to respond to their customer requirements and cost parameters are at risk of being replaced by domestic or international rivals possessing these capabilities. The company in this study is a global organization with 21 plants and 211 team leaders employing various process improvement methodologies. The company had over nine customer escalations from their major customers in 2005, putting their continuing business and credibility in danger.

The company was eager to find a solution. It had been using several different process methods, including just-in-time (JIT), Lean, Six Sigma, and TOC. Managers tended to use the method they were most comfortable with or that had shown the best results for a given type of project. At the upper management level, however, there was concern that the best management program was not being deployed at each plant location.

Determining which approach would result in the most long-term benefits was an ongoing challenge for the company. Upper management struggled with the problem of which process improvement approach to choose. A decision was made to select from among Six Sigma, Lean, and a new method that I developed that integrated TOC, Lean, and Six Sigma (iTLS). Management's goal was to achieve maximum cost savings and quality benefits by using the adopted improvement process company-wide.

Initial Conditions

An experiment was designed to collect data over a 2.5-year period to determine the effectiveness of the three methodologies. The results were analyzed to determine any statistically significant difference among the three methodologies. The success of each methodology would be determined by its aggregate contribution to the verifiable financial savings resulting from its process improvement projects. These savings were validated with plant controllers and senior management.

The new iTLS approach and the existing Lean and Six Sigma programs were included in this pilot effort. The results of these improvement projects were reported and examined. The data were gathered over 2.5 years from 21 plants where 211 team leaders had been trained in and were using one of the three methodologies. These plants completed 105 projects cumulatively over the period of the study. The plant management and controllers reviewed these projects for accuracy in claimed improvements, savings, and approach. Although the results from all projects were documented, the plant personnel and the trainers were not aware of the comparative research because the experiment was designed in a double-blind fashion to remove as many potential biases as possible.

The goal was to provide the company with data needed for a quantitative decision to select the process improvement approach that best fit its quality and financial savings requirements. The company was already measuring and tracking a series of key process indicators, and they became the drivers for project selections. Some of these measurements were on-time delivery, warranty costs and customer returns, inventory reduction, cycle time reduction, and cost of scrap.

The team leaders used one of the three methodologies mentioned above for improving these measurements. A plant in this study was defined as a production facility that was fully capable of prototyping, designing, producing, and distributing customer products. They were located in various regions of the United States. Only U.S. operations were studied in order to limit the impact of cultural, socio-economical, political, and other influences on the results. The approach for assigning the plants a methodology was a natural process due to their local preference, expertise, and experience with a particular methodology.

- 11 plants applied Six Sigma methodologies

- 4 plants applied Lean

- 6 plants applied iTLS

Which Method Is More Effective?

In several phone interviews with trainers and implementers in each region, the authors discussed the three methodologies and asked the trainers the following question: "Among Lean, Six Sigma, or iTLS, which of these methods do you believe is most effective?" Trainers inevitably responded that based on their personal experience that his or her approach was most effective. Some senior managers claimed that there were no significant differences between the three methodologies.

In the experiment, the determining criterion for effectiveness was the verifiable financial impact or benefit to the organization. You may ask why just dollars were used and not other measurements for determining the effectiveness of the three methodologies. The fact is that most organization leaders are well acquainted with the cost world. That is the way they are measured, and as Eli Goldratt put it clearly: "You tell me how you measure me, and I will tell you how I will behave." Because the cost world is what many organization leaders understand, why not provide the results in a language that they can easily relate to? If we employed conceptually new measurements, like T, I, and OE, we might have created resistance and a conceptual bottleneck to accepting the results.

To simplify the measurements and not get entangled in philosophical differences, I chose the cost measurement, which is well known to the majority of our business leaders.

To formulate the experiment, the following conditions were assumed for analysis:

- Initial claim (null hypothesis: H_o: $m1 = m2 = m3$) assuming that there is no difference between contributions received from the three CPI methodologies, or that all methodologies produce similar results.

- Challenging claim (alternative hypothesis: H_a: $m1 = m2 = m3$) claiming that the results of savings between the methodologies were not the same, or at least one of the methodologies was significantly different than the others. The analysis used significance value of 5% (P-value, $a = 0.05$). Where:

  $m1$ is the average $ savings for use of Lean methodology.

  $m2$ is the average $ savings for use of Six Sigma methodology.

  $m3$ is the average $ savings for use of combined iTLS methodologies.

One-way analysis of variance (ANOVA) was used to test the hypothesis assumptions (Table 6.1).

Table 6.1 One-way ANOVA.

Source	SS	df	MS(=SS/df)	F{=MS(Factor)/MS(error)}
Between	SS (factor)	$a - 1$	SS (factor)/df factor	MS (factor)/MS (error)
Within	SS (error)	$\sum_{j}(n_i - 1)$	SS(error)/df error	
Total	SS (total)	$\left[\sum_{j=1}^{a} n_j\right] - 1$	i = a data point within the jth group (factor level) j = the jth group (factor level) a = total # of groups (factor levels)	

First, let's compare Lean and Six Sigma to examine if there are any significant detectable differences in the average amount of savings achieved. The following sets of assumptions were constructed to examine this hypothesis:

H_o: $m1 = m2$; Lean and Six Sigma contributions are similar.

H_a: $m1 \neq m2$; Lean and Six Sigma contributions are significantly different and not similar.

$a = 0.05$

Comparing the average amount of financial savings from Lean and Six Sigma projects ($m1$ and $m2$), the results indicated that the averages were very much alike, with methodologies producing about the same amount of benefits. This basically meant that average contributions from Lean projects in our study were very similar to the average contributions from Six Sigma projects. The initial claim assumed earlier could not be rejected, that $m1 = m2$. The P-value, or significance indicator, was 0.622, which indicated no statistical significance between the two averages.

The conclusion from this result was that if we launched more Lean and Six Sigma projects, we will have a 95% chance of seeing the same level of results and that there would be no difference in benefits from the two types of projects. If the P-value had been less than 0.05, then one could have asserted that observations in this study did not have much chance of being the same and should the observations be repeated under same circumstances as the original study they would yield dissimilar results.

Figure 6.1 depicts ANOVA results and suggests that even though there are some differences between the Lean and Six Sigma measurements, it is highly likely that the measurements were coming from the same process. In other words, the Lean and Six Sigma observations were like different samples of the

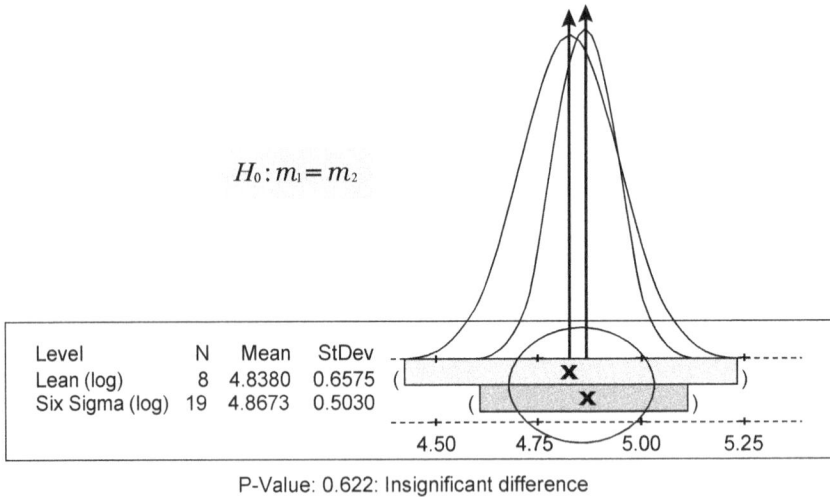

$H_0: m_1 = m_2$

Level	N	Mean	StDev
Lean (log)	8	4.8380	0.6575
Six Sigma (log)	19	4.8673	0.5030

4.50   4.75   5.00   5.25

P-Value: 0.622: Insignificant difference

Figure 6.1 Lean and Six Sigma benefits.

same overall process. Note in Figure 6.1 that the natural variability of the Lean and Six Sigma processes are very close together.

Now that it has been established that Lean and Six Sigma have similar contributions, let's treat them as one process and now compare it with iTLS—the combination of the three CPI methodologies. Our assumptions will be similar to the previous example, and we'll follow the same analytical logic. Our first assumption is that Lean, Six Sigma, and iTLS are the same in terms of their contribution results. Our alternative, or challenge assumption, would be to argue that at least one of the three CPI methodologies is contributing more significantly than others. Let's set up the framework as:

- Initial claim (null hypothesis: H_0: $m1 = m2 = m3$) assumes that there is no difference between the contributions from the three CPI methodologies and that they produce essentially the same results.

- Challenging claim (alternative hypothesis: H_a: $m1 \neq m2 \neq m3$) assumes that the results of savings between the methodologies were not the same or at least one of the methodologies was significantly different from the others. The analysis used a significance value of 5% (P-value, $a = 0.05$).

In performing the same analysis, a significant difference was detected between the two groups (Figure 6.2). The group composed of Lean and Six Sigma appears to be almost one process; however, the average iTLS project's contributions were shifted dramatically to the right and indicated a measureable difference. The significance indicator, P, was at 0.000, meaning that there is an almost 0% chance that this shift in the averages was due to normal process variability. We have to

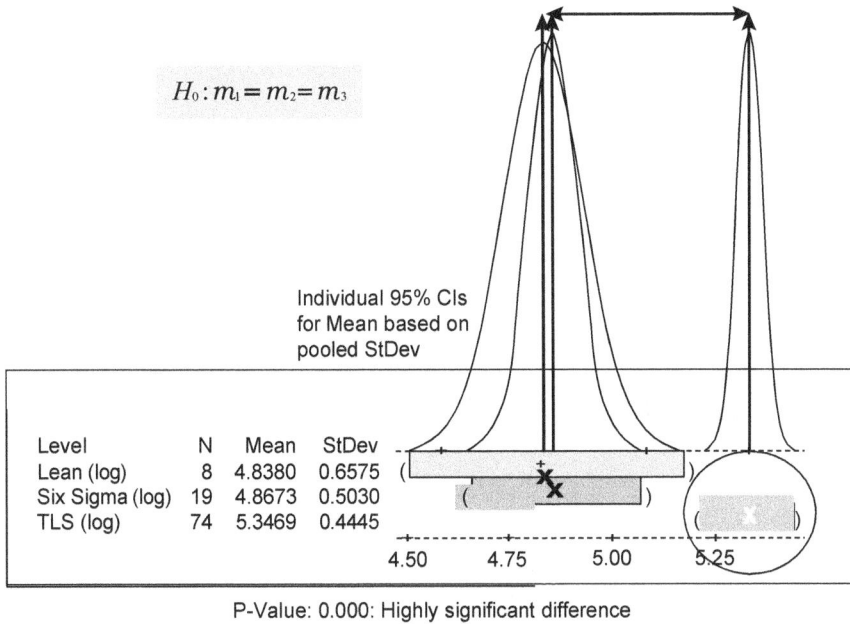

$$H_0: m_1 = m_2 = m_3$$

Individual 95% CIs
for Mean based on
pooled StDev

Level	N	Mean	StDev
Lean (log)	8	4.8380	0.6575
Six Sigma (log)	19	4.8673	0.5030
TLS (log)	74	5.3469	0.4445

4.50   4.75   5.00   5.25

P-Value: 0.000: Highly significant difference

Figure 6.2   Lean, Six Sigma, and iTLS benefits.

conclude that the iTLS averages are coming from a process that is significantly different from the Lean and Six Sigma grouped data. The data clearly indicates that the null hypothesis assuming that all three CPI methodologies contributed the same needs to be rejected. The interaction effect of the three methodologies creates a new process that is very dissimilar from either the Lean or Six Sigma processes.

Further statistical tests, such as Fisher's F-test and chi square tests (Triola 2004), verified and validated these results.

Findings

The iTLS process improvement methodology appeared significantly more effective when compared with the Lean and Six Sigma methodologies in delivering higher cost savings to the company. More important, the iTLS methodology provided 89% of the total savings, while Lean contributed 7% and Six Sigma 4% (see Figure 6.3). During this study, 101 projects were completed using the three methodologies. Data indicated that iTLS projects delivered, on average, 2.591 times higher savings than Lean and 3.866 times higher than Six Sigma.

The study also showed that the plants that used iTLS were able to complete more projects in the same time period than plants using the other two CPI approaches. In a postmortem interview with the team leaders, it also appeared that the iTLS projects experienced less rework than plants using the other two methodologies. The iTLS teams claimed that they had a sharper focus on the location

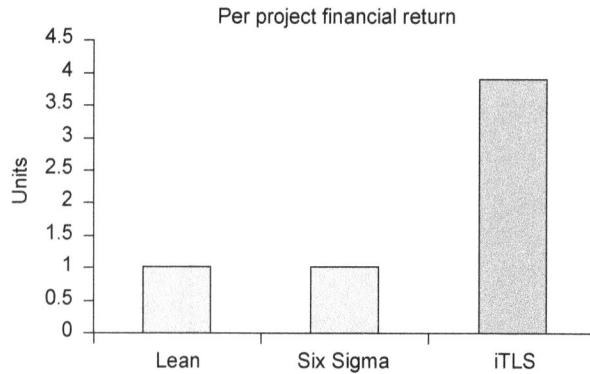

Figure 6.3 Lean, Six Sigma, and iTLS financial returns.

of the bottleneck in their process chain and improving the bottleneck made an immediate contribution to the targeted results.

The plant managers immediately saw the benefits from iTLS projects, which encouraged them to create more teams and make more resources available for improvement activities. Obviously, the more directly that projects addressed the plant's needs and constraints, the greater the improvement in throughput, quality, and process cycle times, on-time deliveries, and customer responsiveness. These positive effects encouraged plant leadership to continue with the process improvement activities and remove non-value-added activities and variability from their processes. These changes increased the stability of their processes and the ease of managing them.

While the Lean and Six Sigma teams claimed that they had also worked on important projects, after completing their projects the teams had difficulty connecting improvements to the bottom line of their plants. This lack of visible contribution to the bottom line and differences of opinions between the project teams and operations management had in the past damaged the credibility of CPI activities. As a result, plant managers were reluctant to assign resources to work on more CPI projects.

This situation was also frustrating for the teams that had worked hard to complete their projects. Some teams claimed significant contributions by reducing setup on some projects. Yet the P&L of the plant managers showed no significant improvement. Further investigation indicated that many teams did high-quality work, but because their activities were not focused on a constraint in the value chain their contributions did not result in either reduced operating costs or improved throughput. Additionally, many of these teams ended up reworking their projects or changing their scope after having expended considerable effort when they became aware that the project they had chosen was not in alignment with the organization's needs, objects, and targets.

Table 6.2 illustrates the contribution of each of the three methodologies per project, the number of projects the teams started, and the number of employees who were trained. More people used iTLS, because users were able to achieve quicker and more tangible bottom-line benefits. Therefore, the plant managers were motivated to invest resources because they received tangible results.

The amount of total contributions from the iTLS project teams dwarfed that from the two other teams (Figure 6.4).

The results of this study may assist similar firms in their decision making when choosing between the Lean, Six Sigma, or TOC improvement methodologies. Combining the three concepts delivered much greater results because TOC focused improvement efforts so that Lean's waste-reduction tools and Six Sigma's statistical tools were used where they would have the most impact.

Currently, some firms have combined Lean and Six Sigma approaches to generate favorable results. "In merely six years Pella has more than doubled its sales in a relatively slow growth industry while, at the same time, increasing its profitability by 250%, without an infusion of additional capital or resorting to layoffs. Mercedes Truck Operations in Brazil, in the heart of the traditional automotive industry, demonstrated that manufacturing process excellence is cross cultural. Maytag is building an innovative machine to compete with third world labor rates and manufacturing production methods. Vermeer is not only improving its existing manufacturing, it is using Lean Six Sigma concepts to design and develop new machines and products" (Sharma & Moody, 2001, 6).

The iTLS approach is simple and comprehensive. Before we discuss its operating process, it is critical to go over the requirements for its sustained success. A continuous improvement approach using iTLS starts with preparing your organization for change. Education, training, new measurements, and constant coaching are required to systemically implement the iTLS model and sustain its power to lead your industry and market sector.

Top management must truly commit to its deployment and the building of a culture of continuous improvement in order to ensure ongoing gains. It is not uncommon for management, as soon as they face the slightest budgetary inconvenience, to cut their CPI and Operations Excellence activities. This is particularly

Table 6.2   Lean, Six Sigma, and iTLS Comparison.

	Lean	Six Sigma	iTLS
Savings $/ project (multiple)	1	1	4
Number of projects started	34	55	179
Number of people trained	251	435	512

Contribution % to realized savings by method applied

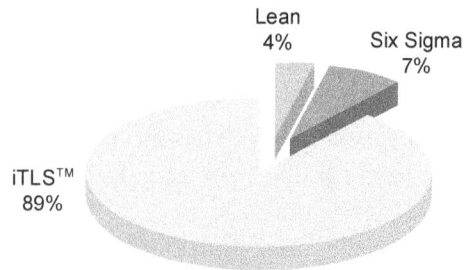

Figure 6.4   Contribution percentage by method applied.

true when CPI has been effective for them! This may sound counterintuitive, but it is true. I interviewed a number of managers in various organizations concerning this particular topic. Following are some of their responses:

- "Now things are going well and *hopefully* they will sustain themselves, so I do not immediately need this . . ."

- "Everything is going so smoothly, what do I need this team for? We do not have any other problems for them to *solve* . . ."

- "I am not in charge of operations anymore, so we can afford losing the CPI team and benefit from the *cost savings* . . ."

- "I am under tremendous pressure from my boss to cut costs, and cannot afford the *luxury* of CPI . . ."

- "As soon as businesses pick up we may put the team back together, but for now we cannot *afford* CPI teams . . ."

- "They were always in *our way* . . . not *allowing us* to do what we have always done. In our plant we know exactly what needs to be done and we have done it that [way] for a long time. We do *not need* someone else to tell us what to do . . ."

- "We let 80% of our *black belts* go . . . they *made* too much money!"

- "We cannot hire any CPI experts . . . we are in a financial pinch . . ."

So what do you think about these responses? Are any of them familiar to you? Do you think that the culture of CPI was really dominant in these environments? Did these managers believe and understand the power of CPI and its value? Did they understand their role in a global sense in the organization? Were they thinking locally or globally? Were they thinking short term or long term with the objective of *making profits now and in the future*?

I have not met a real change agent who did not have to deal with some of these cultural challenges and constraints. Changing a culture does not happen by itself, and as a change agent you should not expect to step into an organization that is already prepared for you with open arms. That condition is a rare event! You should, however, be prepared to face resistance to change. Actually, if you are not facing any resistance, you may not be changing anything! You may need to reevaluate what you are doing; it may be the same *old thing* that they have been doing!

It is up to you to determine how to get the buy-in from these managers and their associates. We must also *influence* their interests. They must clearly see and feel that there is something in it for them to join your efforts. It is up to you as how to change human networks through implementation of metrics and measurements that impact and shape behaviors that are in line with our new model. We must connect the way the organization is measured with compensations and reward systems for the people in it. It's useful to have an audit program to ensure a connection between these systems and to promote this connection. We will discuss that more in the next chapter.

Now let's discuss on a high level the sequence of events in implementing the iTLS. To begin the process, we use TOC to take a system's view and focus our attention and resources on the system constraints or core problems first. This is a critical step. Taking a TOC approach safeguards the organization against local optimization or sub-optimization of the system. When constraints have been identified, then Lean techniques eliminate much of the muda from the processes and Six Sigma offers a sequential problem-solving procedure, the DMAIC cycle (design, measure, analyze, improve, and control), and its statistical tools so that potential causes are not overlooked and viable solutions to chronic problems can be discovered. "If you do just Six Sigma, you're not going to maximize the potential of your organization. You have to do both," says Mike Carnell, president of Six Sigma Applications. "Lean's really an enabler for Six Sigma" (Carnell et al., 2001).

iTLS, by utilization of three methodologies, interdependently, in the right sequence, has proven to deliver results that are significantly larger than the sum of each alone. This multiplicative benefit gained is due to the positive interaction effect among the right mixture and application of the three methodologies.

The iTLS model has been implemented internationally across numerous organizations and business systems with excellent outcomes.

7
River System
Optimization with TOS

The application of iTLS™ in your operations should provide you with techniques and tools to increase system throughput, lower costs, and improve responsiveness and quality. The result should be a smooth flow of work through the processes and networks your organization uses to create its products and services. One of the main objectives is to create value-added products and services and to continuously and ethically grow profits. To accomplish this goal, an organization must continually expand its capability to serve new and growing markets with the products and services they desire.

In order to accomplish this objective, organizations need to adopt a system-oriented paradigm, one whose primary focus is generating more revenue. The old cost-world paradigm has outlived its usefulness and has become a millstone in today's competitive world. This chapter illustrates some of the negative effects of this cost-world orientation and how a throughput operating strategy (TOS) and iTLS™ can be combined to form a new paradigm for holistically managing our organizations and generating dramatically better results.

Operations are expected to continuously improve in order to effectively serve their customers. There are tremendous opportunities for combining TOS and TLS to increase throughput, shorten lead times and improve delivery performance with very low incremental production costs. Improvement efforts should directly impact throughput and customer experience. Understanding the appropriate Throughput Operating Strategy (TOS) for your environment and how to implement it will be a key in achieving better synchronized operations.

A TOS is an effective vehicle for moving from a cost-oriented to a throughput-oriented world. It involves:

- Understanding your network shape(s)

- Selecting the control points

- Gearing internal behavior to the control points

- Driving marketplace actions based on internal improvements

As we noted above, we believe that almost all functions have a considerable amount of excess or unnoticed capacity. The use of iTLS, coupled with an understanding of the shape(s) of your networks for procuring, producing, and delivering products and services, is a powerful tool for exposing and capitalizing on this capacity.

iTLS implementation requires you to understand your processes—their value stream and flow. Understanding how products and services are logically procured, produced, and delivered is a necessary first step. These flows define the characteristics of your river systems. Four shapes form the basis of all river systems. While all organizations generate throughput by converting inputs into outputs, the flow of materials doesn't always resemble the flows inherent in the automotive industry. We call the four shapes A, V, T, and I because when the flows are depicted in a vertical fashion, they resemble these shapes. These four shapes, or combinations of them, represent a company's river system. With this information and the selection of strategic control points to manage the flows, it is possible to derive how each river system should be managed. It is also possible to illustrate how the use of inappropriate local measurements results in undesired behavior and poorer financial results. Both insights are very long improvement levers. In order to understand how to capitalize on them, we should first explore the characteristics of each of these four shapes.

A NETWORKS

An A network typically involves the assembly of a large number of parts or components in order to produce one or a few products. The convergence point is where components and subassemblies from various sources come together to produce an end item. The resulting network roughly takes the shape of an A. Much of the equipment used in A network is general purpose; that is, it can be used to make a wide variety of parts.

The number of steps or resources needed to provide components for an assembly can vary from many to a few. A characteristic of A networks is that a variety of elements converge to form a single end item. Airplane manufacturing is an example of a large A network. The challenge in A network is to synchronize the flow of materials so that everything is available at assembly when it is needed. Two other characteristics are common in A network. Individual resources may be used in more than one feeding leg and more than once in a particular leg, and some of these legs many involve many different operations in order to complete a component for assembly.

It is clear how we would like work to flow in an A network—everything arriving at final assembly just before it is needed. Unfortunately, reality is very different. Typically, there are a large number of shortages that require expediting coupled with large component inventories that are not yet needed. Often these component shortages cannot be resolved in a timely fashion, and the nearly

Processes	Product manufacturing laptop computers	Number of separate products produced at each stage

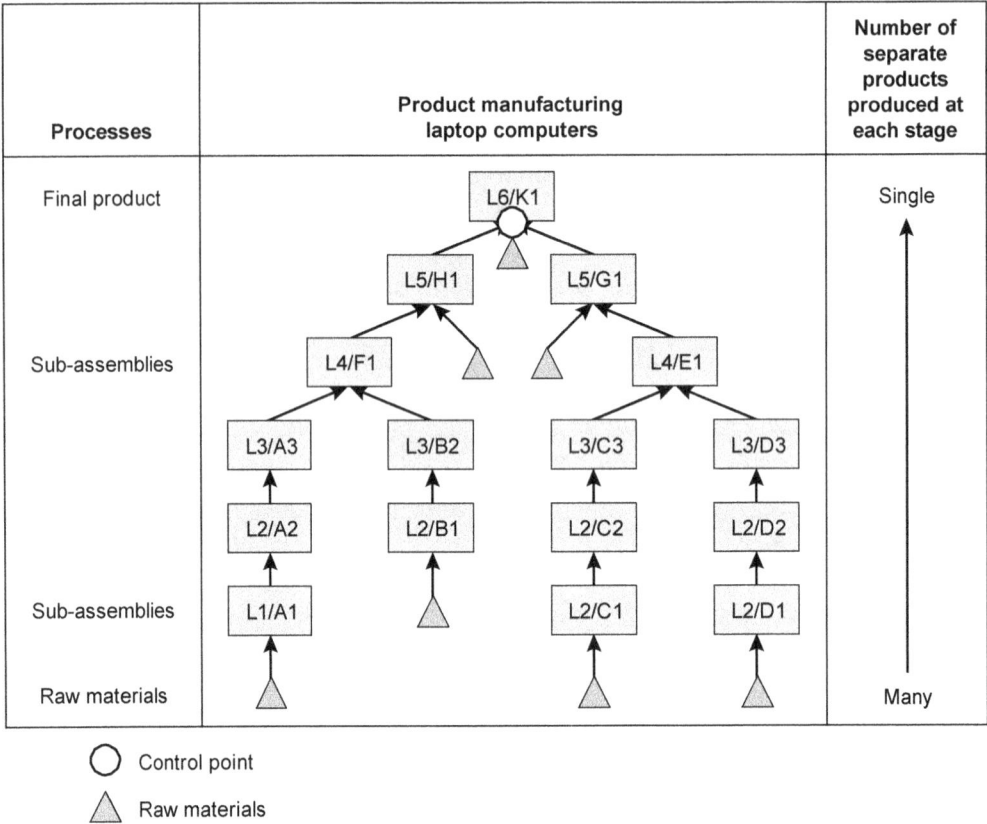

Figure 7.1   A river flow operation network—laptop computer manufacturing.

finished product, missing key items, is set aside and work shifted to the next assembly. In the case of aircraft assembly, this often means moving the partially finished aircraft from the assembly line to the tarmac. When the needed components finally arrive, they will be installed in less-than-ideal conditions.

In large A networks the effects are almost always the same:

- There are both shortages and excesses of items at assembly.

- Expediting is constant and intensive, resulting in large amounts of overtime and the frequent breaking of setups.

- Component lead times are much longer than necessary—parts are worked on a small fraction of time they are in process.

- Items are purchased and produced in larger-than-necessary batches (economic order quantities).

- Bottlenecks appear to be constantly floating even though there are rarely any real bottlenecks.

It's hardly a picture of a smooth, fast-flowing river system. The real question is why—what prevents the creation of something similar to Ford's and Ohno's river systems? We believe the cause is the continued use of local, cost-accounting thinking, which drives the wrong behaviors. If the person running a particular operation has a choice of working on several jobs, which will he work on first? Most likely it will be either the easiest one or the one that has the loosest standard. Is this the item that is needed for the next assembly? Probably not. What if this particular operator has a choice of working on a second item that requires little or no setup, even though it may not be needed at assembly for several weeks, versus working on a critically needed part that will require a major setup and loss of productive time? Which will he choose? Undoubtedly the one that makes his efficiencies look the best. If an expeditor appears, his priorities will change and may cause him to break a setup, something workers are very reluctant to do.

This wrong-headed thinking is compounded by "cost-plus" contracts, which greatly magnify the problem. Cost-plus contracts compensate companies on how much work they have done, regardless of whether those items are needed now, and not how many finished products they have delivered.

Traditionally, the flow of work in an A manufacturing network is typically managed by some sort of MRP system. Production may be based on either firm orders, which can be subject to change, or a forecast. Materials are often ordered based on an economic order quantity (EOQ), which tends to result not only in larger batches to get better pricing, but also in higher levels of inventory and a greater risk of obsolescence. Having excess raw materials or purchased components available tempts production planners to release work into the system earlier and in larger batches than necessary in order to maintain high efficiencies, increase absorption, and enable earlier billing on cost-plus contracts.

Local efficiencies are calculated based on the number of hours earned (based on some standard) vs. the number of paid hours. Therefore, the goal of this efficiency model is to produce as much as possible in a department and push it on to the next department, regardless of whether they need it now. These local efficiencies are largely independent of their actual contribution to the total system. Each department supervisor will independently strive to maximize his/her efficiencies even though they may be causing dams and rapids in the overall river system. Instead of a synchronized flow, excess inventories and shortages are created, coupled with the premature consumption of resource capacity, which may result in future temporary bottlenecks. Large batches move like waves through the system similar to rabbits moving through a python.

Process improvement activities in each department naturally focuses on its individual needs. Let's assume that a surface mount technology (SMT) board department is under management pressure to improve its efficiencies. The department manager decides to reduce the amount of time spent on setups in order to show better efficiencies. The project sounds reasonable, but we should be aware of a caveat. If the setup reduction increases production levels so that items are produced even earlier than are needed, it probably didn't immediately improve the overall system; it may have made it worse by delaying the production of other more-needed items. The problem with improving a specific operation without considering its impact on the entire system is that it may translate into lower rather than higher system profitability.

Traditional management of A-type river systems masks large amounts of capacity and hurts synchronization, because the objective is to keep people and equipment busy rather keeping material moving. If the amount produced was not needed at that time, it will eventually sit idle, creating a dam at a downstream operation. This premature use of capacity masks the amount of capacity available and delays the flow of items needed more urgently at final assembly.

Large batch processing is a favorite operating principal for managers judged by local measurements. Producing smaller batches requires more setups, which often show up as a loss in their efficiency measures. Managers prefer to set up an operation and run it for a long time because it both maximizes their efficiencies and reduces the effort they must expend. Frequent changeovers are such a threat to managers that they push back on the production planners or find ways to combine the smaller batches to reduce setups. Unfortunately, large batch sizes limit customer order flexibility and adversely effect on-time deliveries. A large-batch processing model that is forecast driven magnifies the problem because inherent forecast inaccuracies often result in the production of items that eventually end up as write-offs. It should be understood that striving for efficiencies and producing in large batches is not a shortcoming of front-line managers and workers, but the direct result of management's model for managing A networks.

On-time delivery in traditionally managed A networks can be a nightmare and require extraordinary efforts. Producing large batches and prioritizing work based on efficiencies create imbalances in the flow. The result is that components needed to complete customer orders must be expedited. MRP systems are not typically oriented to system synchronization and in fact can compound the problem through multiple levels in their bill of materials.

I recall viewing a printer production line where mountains of semi-finished printers were piled on pallets prior to the final process. They were all missing an 80-cent plastic component (fuser pad) that was coming from Asia. A $300 product could not be converted to cash due to the missing 80-cent component! This component part was less than 0.3% of the product's price, was used in many printer models, and was probably outsourced to Asia in order to get a lower price—a good example of localized cost-world thinking.

Unsynchronized flow caused overproduction of models that were not immediately needed (workers must be kept busy producing) and shortages of products that customers were demanding. Not only did customers not get their products on time, but the congestion on the shop floor also used up valuable floor space, probably damaged some semifinished products, and created a variety of administrative headaches. A characteristic of A networks, when they are traditionally managed, is the presence of high work-in-process inventories coupled with constant expediting efforts.

I have been in companies that have had an "expediting" department, with an entire hierarchy structure that included a supervisor, lead expeditors, expeditors, and so forth. Expediting is a costly and non-value-added process that often creates more problems than it solves. We've often thought that the direct and ancillary costs of these efforts should be assigned directly the senior managers who insist on the systems and measurements that cause them.

The solution lies in defining an appropriate TOS for an A network. It begins with the selection of a control point. This control point serves two major functions. It is the mechanism, or valve, for pulling and synchronizing the flow of work. It is used to determine when and how much material should be purchased and when it should arrive. It's also the driver for releasing work into the network based on when it is needed, not when there is unused capacity to process it. The control point is also the mechanism for establishing production priorities.

In A networks the control point is usually the buffer of items needed for the next several assemblies. As an example, all the items needed to assemble the next several products should be in the buffer and ready to be assembled. Items that are missing are called "holes" in the buffer; they need to be given first priority regardless of where they are in the network. First priority always goes to the first scheduled assembly; second priority goes to items needed for the second scheduled assembly, and so on.

The second function of the control point is to create a connection to the marketplace so we better understand how the demand for our products is changing. Ideally, this connection should be with the market need for our products and not necessarily the orders we are receiving from our customers.

In order to make such a management system work, a new, more global system of measurement is needed. Such a system should focus on increasing T, while proportionately reducing I and OE. In our experience, a visual picture of the company's A network should be widely promulgated. This pictorial view should be accompanied by an explanation of the objective—smoother, faster, more synchronized flow—and how actions will be measured in order to achieve this objective. This explanation should begin with how and why the current local measurement system directly causes unsynchronized flow. The old measurement mantra of people producing all the time is to be replaced by material moving all the time. Sometimes it is better for people not to be producing than it is for material not to be moving. Such a shift in measurement will immediately create apprehension in the workforce and needs to be dealt with by management's assurances that this change will not result in layoffs and will produce a more profitable company and a better place to work. Despite the sincerity of such assurances, they will only partly assuage the fears of the workers, but they are a necessary first step.

The new system for managing each of the four networks should produce the following:

- An increase in T

- Increases in T/OE—we should be generating more T in proportion to the money we spend

- Increases in T/I—we should be generating more T in proportion to the monies tied up in inventories and fixed assets

- Improvements in delivery performance

Variations of these measurements at a local level are often helpful in aligning local actions with the global objective.

The control point (buffers of the parts needed for the next assemblies) are used to "pull" work into the system, both from vendors and into and through operations. "Holes" in the control point buffer are also the driving mechanism for our TLS efforts. The causes of these holes are the disruptions that most threaten throughput and should be the area where we need to use our best TLS tools. It is here that improvements will both impact the long lever of throughput and help speed and smooth the flow of work. It is important to recognize that we should be focusing on balancing the flow of work, rather than trying to balance the use of the capacity available to process it. Current systems have great imbalances in capacity that we try to mask by releasing work into the system much earlier than it is needed, thereby creating great imbalances in the flow. As we apply TLS to the biggest disruptions, we will systematically smooth the flow and move toward more balanced capacities. However, an organization can operate with perfectly balanced capacities only when all disruptions or variations have been removed, a lofty but probably unattainable goal.

As disruptions are reduced by the elimination of waste (Lean) and reduction in variation (Six Sigma), additional capacity will be exposed. Instead of cutting labor costs, a very short lever, we should be using the additional capacity and space gained to sell and produce more. Remember, at this stage you have a great competitive advantage—you can produce additional product at about the cost of the purchased materials.

V NETWORKS

V networks, or V river flows, may look like upside-down As, but they have quite different characteristics. They usually start with one major input, which after a number of processing steps results in a large number of outputs. Oil refineries and slaughterhouses are good examples of V networks. In the first case, crude oil is used to produce a variety of products (gasoline, jet fuel, heating oil, etc.) often sold in a variety of containers. In a slaughterhouse, an animal is converted into many end products. It has been claimed that in hog slaughterhouses only the squeal isn't used.

V networks are characterized by many fork points at which a common material can be converted into different products (production operations) or sent to different locations (distribution systems). The fork points are also referred to as divergent points, because the item can go in various directions at that point. Refineries are an example of V networks where the same equipment is focused on gasoline production in the summer and heating oil in the winter. A slaughterhouse can produce different amounts of bacon and sausage from the same pig, depending on market demand. Making the right decisions at the fork points is critical in effectively managing V networks. Poor decisions result in both missed throughput and excess inventories.

Triage operations in the medical field are classic Vs. At the first step, someone decides which patient should be processed first (i.e., which case is most urgent) and the appropriate next step for that patient (a test, an X-ray, or another procedure). The results of these procedures often lead to additional fork points.

Another example of a V river flow is the logistics of overhaul and repair operations. When a unit arrives at the repair center, the first step is to gather failure information. The result of this analysis acts as the fork, or decision point, for the next actions or diagnosis. This process can continue through a number of diagnostic troubleshooting steps and repair steps.

A pick-pack-ship warehouse is yet another example of a V network. In the first step, a truckload of products consolidated onto fewer than a hundred pallets is unloaded. The contents of the pallets are then separated into hundreds of distinct products. Products that have been damaged are moved to the materials review board area (MRB) for disposition. Products lacking the proper identification need to be researched and are moved to a separate area. Varying quantities of the remaining products are then staged for distribution to thousands of different customers based on their orders. A graphical picture of a V river system is shown in Figure 7.2.

Distribution systems are often V networks. In a distribution system, a decision at a fork point changes the location of a product, not its nature. For example, if a product is sent to the Midwest warehouse rather than one on the East Coast, the product is unchanged but its location is now different. These regional warehouses are additional fork points for distribution to many retailers. A final fork point occurs in the retail outlet, where the same product may be purchased by many customers.

Ideally, a V river system will be driven by consumer demand or, even better, by consumer consumption of the products. Products should be delivered to

Processes	Product distribution process receive—unpack—pick and ship to customers	Number of separate products produced at each stage

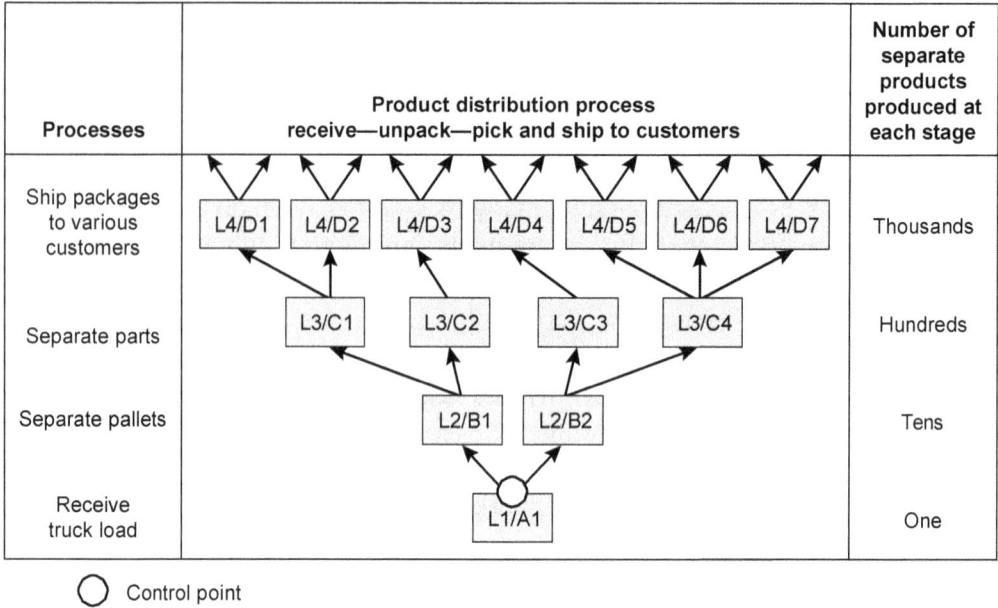

Figure 7.2 V river flow operation network—a pick-pack-ship warehouse.

customers or consumers just in time, or shortly before they need them. Knowing that there are inevitable variations in both supply and demand, it is useful to have a small buffer, or dam, of inventory available to customers/consumers. When this inventory of products is purchased, it should trigger a quick replenishment at every level of our V network. Essentially, each level would replenish what had been consumed by the next upper level. Envision the process as a real river system: Once water is released from the various dams or buffers prior to the customers, water is released at each of the fork points on the preceding levels to refill these buffers/dam. As a result, the dam feeding customers is quickly replenished. The replenishment of products that have been sold flow should flow in a similar manner. Lest the reader believe such a system is not possible, I worked with a consumer products company that both produced and delivered their products through V networks. Initially, they had about three months of finished products in their system; that is, on the average when the consumer purchased a product it was about 13 weeks old. The company was able to implement a very smooth-flowing river system with its major customer and reduced the average born-on date of these products to about 8 days.

If this is how a V network should operate, how does the prevalent cost-accounting thinking impact its operation? The impact is somewhat different in production and distribution networks. The driving forces for both networks are customer orders, forecasts, or, most likely, a combination of the two. Production operations are driven by the need for high efficiencies. Fork points in production operations often involve packaging activities. The same material is often packaged in many different-sized containers. Changing equipment over to produce a different size is usually not a trivial operation—production must be halted, the line needs to be cleaned of material and cleared of the existing containers, and new containers need to be brought in and adjustments made to the equipment. Typically, cost-accounting measurements penalize operating managers for the time lost in line changeovers. What type of behavior do these measures engender—longer runs, bigger production batches? When a poor decision is made at a fork point, too much is produced of one product and not enough of another, which results in both excess inventory and unneeded expediting.

Similar problems are created in distribution systems because of the current measurement system. It is often considered to be more cost efficient to ship truckloads of a few items rather a mixture of many products. The result is waves rather than a smooth replenishment of products. In addition, because regional warehouse managers are primarily evaluated on how often they can't completely fill retailer orders, they have an incentive to over-order products, often creating shortages at other regional warehouses.

If a decision at a fork is wrong and there are multiple levels of fork points, the risk of producing and distributing the wrong products at the wrong time increases significantly. For example, if there are three levels of fork points, each having only two options and a 50% probability of a bad decision, the probability of taking the wrong path grows to 87.5% after the third step. As the number of forks or divergent points in a V network increases, the magnification of an error increases significantly (see Figure 7.3).

$$\text{Probability of success:} (0.5 \times 0.5 \times 0.5 = 0.125)$$

Probability of failure: $1 - 0.125 = 0.875$, or 87.5%

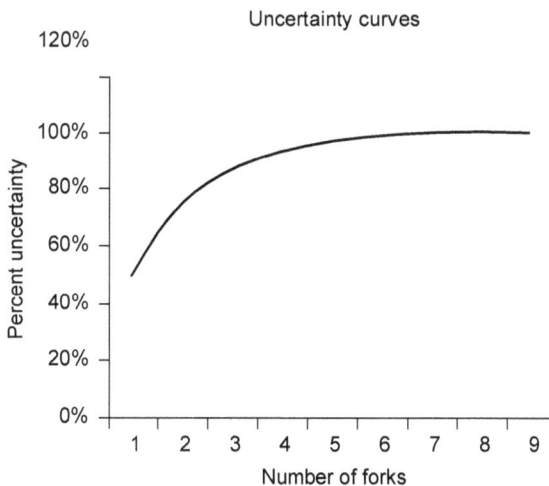

Figure 7.3 Relationship of increased uncertainty with the levels of two-headed forks.

In a V distribution system, the most important place to hold inventory is at the base of the V (a central warehouse) and then produce and/or replenish frequently and quickly the amounts that are used at the next higher level. Because most retailers now scan products at the cash register, daily sales information is often available in electronic form and can readily be transmitted to producers and distributors.

In an effective V distribution system, the products sold yesterday would be replenished today and the retailer would need only enough inventory to cover the expected maximum sales for a day.

If a V plant is producing products sold through such a distribution system, the plant would ideally produce and ship to its warehouses the next day the amount sold at the retail stores it serves. I once worked with a major producer of consumer products that had five plants that serviced a number of warehouses and had not missed a replenishment shipment in over six years.

Unfortunately, most V networks do not operate in this fashion. Products are usually pushed through the plants and out to regional warehouses and often to the retailers based on forecasts (which are always too high or too low) rather than on actual sales. In an ideal V river system, products flow, or are pulled, through the production and distribution steps based on actual sales.

Trying to forecast the daily sales of individual products at many retail locations is mission impossible, yet that is how most of these river systems still work. In order for them to function, they must have a great deal of "not needed now" inventory spread throughout their systems. Even with a great deal of excess inventory they still incur shortages. They have enough inventories in total; they're just in the wrong location.

Before the consumer products company mentioned earlier improved its river system, the average born-on dates for the same products averaged 14–16 weeks, and they still had frequent stock-outs at the retail level. Stock-outs meant lost throughput today and potentially lost throughput in the future. A customer who can't find a product may try another vendor and find out they like it better.

The obvious question is why most companies operate in the latter rather than the former fashion. The answer lies in the common approach of trying to manage a system by managing the pieces of it. We try to optimize or manage closely the performance of the various pieces of the system, assuming that as a result the total system will be well managed. Unfortunately, the opposite is true.

Maybe some specifics will help. V networks in production environments are often characterized by heavy capital requirements, particularly at the early operations. Because we want to maximize the use of these investments, there is a tendency to produce more than the market is consuming. Additionally, if this equipment produces more than one product (almost the nature of Vs), we would prefer to make long runs to avoid the cost of many changeovers. In most organizations, management pushes for efficiencies at the local level, not taking the entire organization or global view in consideration. There is a tendency for department supervisors to view their departments as separate entities. This silo view of operations sub optimizes global effectiveness.

Each supervisor, in order to make his or her efficiency numbers, wants to run as large batches as possible. This approach unintentionally steals materials or capacity from other products that use the same material or rely on the same equipment. As a result, a particular department may look very good from an efficiency standpoint, but the organization may not be able to efficiently serve its customers. The impact of this behavior can devastate the organization's bottom line, and the organization may not realize what is happening because its metrics are not detecting the root cause problem. It is not uncommon to see interdepartmental conflicts when such operations are managed by local optimization.

The results are periodic production surges of some products followed by no production of other products—not exactly a smooth-flowing river system. This problem of production surges and no production is magnified when there are multiple fork points in the flow. It's even worse if the producing plant does not have a central warehouse and is forced to push its output to multiple regional warehouses. The focus on being efficient at each production operation, misallocating production at the fork points, and prematurely pushing products into the distribution system, driving the entire process based on an erroneous forecast rather than actual sales, results in a dysfunctional river system and subpar financial results.

How did the consumer products company make such a dramatic important improvement, and how long did it take? The transition to a short, fast-flowing river system requires two types of changes. The first and most important changes were changes in policies and measurements, which can occur quickly or seem to take forever.

The second requires physical changes and other actions, which take more time. These actions typically include:

- Dramatic reductions in the time to change over equipment by application of SMED techniques

- An improvement in the reliability of the equipment by applying preventive maintenance (PM) and autonomous maintenance (AM)

- Reductions in wasted or scrapped product by understanding the source of variability and scrap and by removing process errors

- All the things that disrupt a fast flow of saleable product

- Building central warehouses at the producing plants while eliminating or reducing the size of regional warehouses

- Pulling to the demand

- Reliable information technology and valid pull signals

TNETWORKS

Companies that have T networks are characterized by the flow of a number of items to an assembly point where there is a virtual explosion into a large number of end items. The U.S. automobile industry is prime example of a T structure. A few thousand components, such as paint, fabric, wheel covers, and audio systems, combined differently can result in millions of unique automobiles. Vaccines and other chemical/drug products also are often produced in T structures.

The logical control point location for a T network is the buffer of components just ahead of final assembly. The control point should be used to pull material into the system and synchronize its flow. Ideally, the release process must be carefully scheduled to make sure that component batch sizes are small and lead times are short so that work can be pulled based on demand rather than forecast. It is critical to assemble only those items needed by customers *now* and not products needed at a future date. The premature allocation of components to assemblies causes unnecessary shortages of parts for other assemblies. By closely managing the use of these finished components, a company can ensure nearly 100% delivery performance, despite offering a very broad range of end items.

Contrary to the thinking of Ford and Ohno, sometimes inventory should be placed strategically. The shape of the networks and whether capacity exceeds demand, or vice versa, need to be assessed in deciding where to strategically use

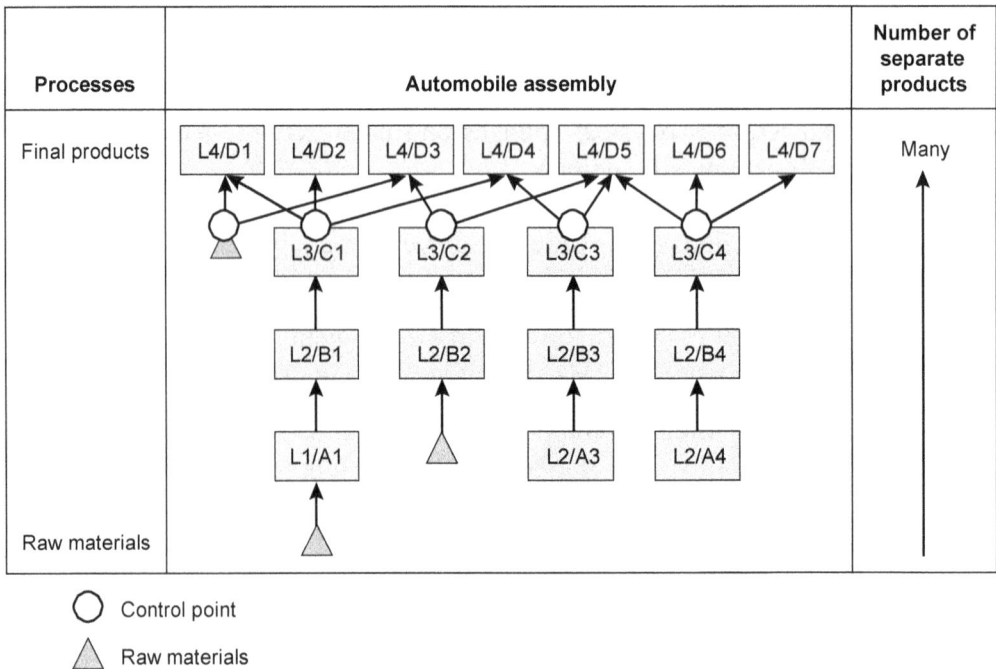

Figure 7.4   T river flow operation network—automobile assembly.

inventory. In this model, the strategic buffers should be the control point. It is important to note that the buffers should be time buffers able to absorb most of the disruptions and variations in the demand for products and supply of the components. The fewer the disruptions in flow and variations in demand, the smaller the assembly buffer needed.

In T networks, the impact of cost-world thinking creates a number of problems. The first and most significant is the misallocation of components at assembly. The driving force behind this misallocation is the need to meet end-of-the-month/quarter shipping targets. Every operations manager knows the intense pressure to meet these targets. In fact, this pressure and the reactions to it have a name—the end-of-the-month syndrome. This syndrome is the classic example of the ongoing struggle between cost-world and throughput-world thinking. In the first portion of the reporting period, cost-world thinking dominates and the focus is on minimizing setups, high efficiencies, limited overtime, and the like. In the latter part of the reporting period, reality sets in and we realize we are far short of the shipment target. Now we intuitively switch to a throughput-world focus. It's all hands on deck in order to get more shipped. Do whatever it takes to increase shipments—work tons of overtime, break setups, and forget about efficiencies. This behavior is particularly prevalent in A, T, and I networks. However, in T networks another cost-world factor dominates management behavior. Because not all the components are usually available to assemble the products that customers want shipped this month, why don't we assemble some products due to be shipped next month? If we can find enough of these opportunities, we'll meet our goal for this month.

In T networks, this cycle repeats month in and month out. It is common for T networks managed from a cost-world perspective to ship about 40% of their products as promised, 30% late, and 30% early. The constant stealing of components to ship products early in order to meet targets is the primary cause of why other products are consistently shipped late. The only reason why companies with such abysmal delivery performance survive is that their competitors are driven by the same cost-world thinking and have similar delivery performance records.

The existence of constant and shifting shortages at assembly causes a host of other problems. Components are now short at assembly. Planners and production supervisors push to increase lot sizes and lead times, which, in the end, simply compound the shortage problem and creates more waves in the flow of work and magnifies the problem. These frequent shortages eventually cause excessive expediting, which create scheduling nightmares, missed deliveries, and unhappy customers. Excessive expediting also promotes creation of even larger batch sizes. The larger batches create temporary and floating bottlenecks, which cause more assembly shortages.

I know a company with a T-shaped network that developed a robust TOS and switched its management model from a cost to a throughput focus. Its delivery performance improved so much that it made an unusual market offer, one that significantly increased sales and throughput. It offered to reduce the price of every invoice by 1% for every day a shipment was late. This offer was made in an industry in which companies (including this one) typically shipped 30–40% of their orders late.

Not only was it able to keep its commitment, with very few penalties, but within six months it also had reduced its total inventory by 50%. Over the next year, as it further reduced the disruptions in the flow of components, it lowered inventory further and continued to grow its business.

Essentially, the company designed and operated its river system so that components were almost always available regardless of the products customers ordered. When components are available, products can be assembled and shipped in a few days. In addition, the company slashed component lead times by reducing lot sizes and lead times in order to better balance and more quickly replenish component inventories.

A successful throughput operating system coupled with a TLS in T networks typically results in:

- Delivery performance 98%+

- Inventory reduction >50%

- Productivity (T/OE) up 20%+

- Sales growth due to increased delivery reliability and market offers

- Finding significant amount of hidden capacity >50%

The implementation a TOS/TLS effort in a T network typically entails:

- A switch from forecast-driven schedules to pull signals based on actual demands

- More frequent replenishment of component inventories

- Reducing batch sizes by at least 50%

- Using TLS efforts to break temporary bottlenecks and reduce disruptions in the flow

I NETWORK

An I network is the simplest form of a network (Figure 7.5). Companies that have I networks are characterized by the flow of essentially a single item through a number of operations, often a large number of operations, to produce a single end item.

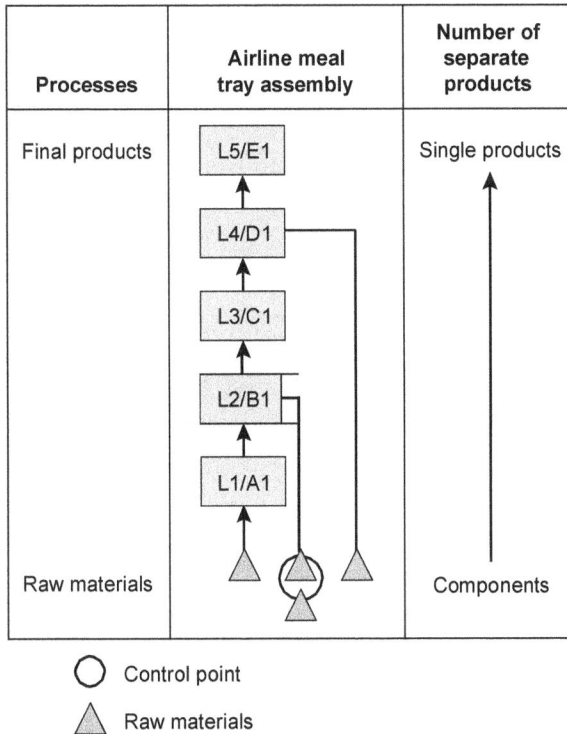

Figure 7.5 I network—airline meal tray assembly operation.

In an I network, although items may be fed into the flow at various points, the focus is on the linear flow of a raw material. Ideally, the rate of flow in an I network and the amount of throughput generated will be determined by the weakest link, or constraint, in the network. Unfortunately, this is rarely the case, because the weakest link or control point is seldom identified and used to manage the flow. The results are floating bottlenecks, less throughput, poorer delivery performance, and generally unneeded chaos.

The bigger question is which operation should be selected as the control point. Unlike the other three networks, the shape of the network does not help us. One of the two factors to consider in selecting the control point is the amount of investment required at the various operations—the higher the investment, the more we want to squeeze the most out of it. Squeezing the most out of an operation can be done by processing more through it. The other factor to consider is the operation that yields the highest octane for the products it processes. Octane is essentially the amount of throughput that is generated compared to the time of the control point takes to produce it.

Measurements that help us manage these networks from a global perspective are T, I, and OE. The overall productivity of the network can effectively be measured by T/OE. Inventory and investment utilization can be measured by T/I, which illustrates how fast investments and inventories are converted to throughput. Operations that are managed with close control of locally focused budgets often sub optimize global profitability and profits. It is not uncommon for managers to transfer their costly processes or expenses to other departments to hide them. This would probably make those managers departments look good at the local operations level and on budget perhaps, but in the global sense the company has incurred those expenses, which will be deducted from the overall net profits.

A traditional focus to managing this type of operation is to maximize line efficiencies. This approach can undermine quality and the focus of CPI efforts. Often an MRP system determines what to buy based on forecasts and pushes the schedule for production. Large batch sizes are preferred to mask quality, rework, or process issues. Large batch sizes create large work-in-process inventories that could be vulnerable to change notices becoming obsolete or requiring rework. Process cycle times tend to be longer due to large batch sizes, putting on-time deliveries at risk. To guard against these problems, additional finished goods inventories are kept, but that also has a risk of excess and obsolescence.

The I river system is simple, but if mismanaged it can become an ineffective operation and unresponsive to customer requirements. An example of an I network in transactional operations could be a signature route to approve a request. Certainly there are processes that do require close scrutiny and require multiple checks and verifications, but there are also processes that in fact go through a series of signature loop without individuals actually adding value to the paperwork or process. In reality, they could become multiple bottlenecks stopping the flow of process and create significant pockets of work-in-process inventories. Frequently, these processes are designed not based on actual process requirements, but based on some sort of legacy protocol or policy without a clear justification for the hierarchical travel. An approval process for release of funds to an insured individual in an insurance company could become a serious bottleneck, particularly when there is a significant phenomenon, such as a natural disaster like Hurricane Katrina. In reality, the individuals on the signature route may not have the time or resources to review, read, analyze, or question a fraction of the documents while the client is in dire need of funds to attend to its urgent needs. A process for employees' company expenses approval could be another example.

These types of situations can be temporarily solved by adding additional resources to process the work. Or, iTLS could be applied, recognizing that this is a policy constraint issue. What makes sense would be to question why reviews are necessary. Could the causes of inaccuracies and variability be removed without disrupting the overall process?

To best manage an I network, it is critical to ensure that quality is managed at every process step, with close monitoring of the first-pass yield to address the root causes of any quality or flow problem immediately. Application of 5S, preventive maintenance, and visual factory are essential to maintain continuous flow of this river system. System scheduling should be based on actual demand and kanbans used to signal what material to pull from previous stations and the raw materials purchases. With application of iTLS, the focus will be on what needs improvement and finding the root cause of the bottlenecks in the process. Then, systematically, processes become lean and free of wasted efforts. By controlling the process variability, smooth flow of this river system could be achieved. Also see application of the iTLS-O tool in the case study.

BETTER UNDERSTAND YOUR PROCESSES

Ford and Ohno developed incredibly efficient A-shaped river systems for two high-volume automotive companies. Is it possible to devise similar systems in companies regardless of the shapes of the river systems and the volume of their output? Not only can such systems be devised, but when we couple them with the iTLS process similar results can be achieved more rapidly than Ford and Ohno were able to accomplish. By understanding the shape of our networks and selecting the control points, we immediately gain insight in where to focus improvement efforts. As a result, powerful improvement tools and techniques are used where they provide the greatest benefit. The value of this focus on the systems and networks that organizations use to produce throughput can be described as Archimedes's long levers.

8

"MOST" iTLS Project Management

LEADERSHIP RESPONSIBILITIES

How many times have you been faced with project teams struggling to close their projects or project deadlines that have extended well over an intended time line? Whether you've used TOC, Lean, or Six Sigma continuous improvement methodologies, you probably have heard a variety of teams' responses regarding questions as to why projects have not closed on time or have failed to be completed at all. Often, the blame is placed on the project leadership.

The reasons offered for why continuous improvement programs lose traction despite their potential for improvement are numerous. Dusharme (2004) surveyed team leaders in order to understand the reasons why continuous improvement projects have often not delivered the intended results. Respondents cited the following reasons:

- Lack of management support
- Lack of resources
- Lack of management alignment and understanding
- Unreasonable expectations
- Misunderstanding of what the continuous improvement approach is

What can leaders do to ensure that critical initiatives come to fruition rapidly? In order to survive, organizations need competitive leadership and agility. How can we achieve this leadership? Here are some suggestions that could significantly help you to improve a team's ability to complete a project. One suggestion is to apply the Mobilize, Organize, Speed up, Tie up loose ends (MOST) principle of leadership to bring discipline, order, and agility to your continuous improvement project management (Pirasteh, 2005). MOST is a simple process that organizes project management and ensures proper attention is given to your project efforts. Here is how MOST works.

Mobilize

Mobilize to link your organization's strategy to the continuous improvement project efforts. Ward and Poling (2005) stated that "many projects are launched without a tie to the company's strategic goals." To avoid confusion and establish a direct link between the continuous improvement projects and the organization's strategic goals, it is helpful to use the company's balanced scorecard. If your organization does not have a balanced scorecard, you have an opportunity to take a leadership role in establishing this critical document. Balanced scorecards should be applied as a framework to create relevant "line of sight" for:

- Improvement targets

- Stretch goals

- Appropriate measures

The absence of these critical components can result in unfocused projects that increase the costs without an assurance of a significant return on the efforts. To mobilize continuous improvement projects, it is imperative to have a balanced scorecard (see Figure 8.1). In order to develop a balanced scorecard, you need to:

1. Clearly identify your customer requirements.

2. Identify the key processes that need to be measured and controlled.

3. Develop the appropriate metrics for the key processes identified in step 2.

4. Determine the process performance drivers. You may use a cause- and-

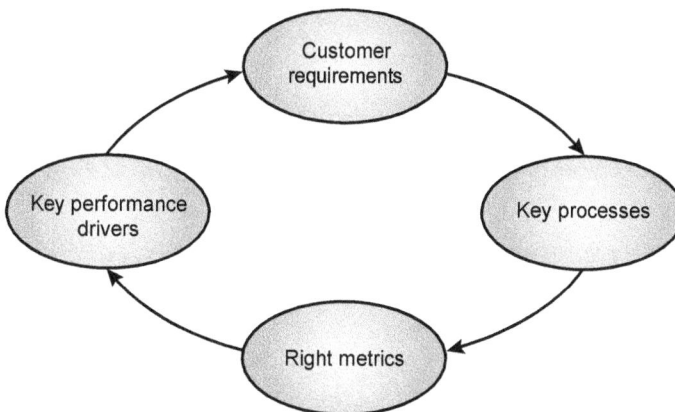

Figure 8.1 High-level process of developing a balanced scorecard.

are causing the symptoms, the performance gaps, but that may not be). These are the factors that need to be prioritized by failure mode effect analysis (FMEA) and brought under statistical control.

Your balanced scorecard will be the tool to provide the line of sight from your organization's vision to the individual goals.

Leadership needs to articulate its vision, mission, goals, and targets and clearly define the gaps that exist. These gaps then become focusing targets for improvement by the project teams. These gaps should address:

- Direct links to strategic business goals

- Direct impacts to key business objectives

- Contributions to bottom-line performance

- Benefits to key customers

- Direct benefits to the entire organization

Any closing of these gaps should be evident in the balanced scorecard, which, in turn, is directly linked to the organization's health (financial, quality, processes, people, and so forth).

The balanced scorecard is a living document and reflects the dynamic requirements of your business world. Thus, you need to review this document periodically to ensure a direct relevance between continuous improvement projects and the balanced score card metrics (also see

Organize

After mobilizing, you will have determined the organization's performance gaps and prioritized which areas need the most improvement. Then you must actively organize and empower the organization and facilitate implementation of the improvement projects. You should assemble a steering team composed of cross-functionally affected department heads. Typically, continuous improvement steering teams are made up of customer services/program management, finance, operations, materials, human resources, quality, and engineering (Figure 8.2).

This team would act as the enabling body to remove barriers that could impede project completion. The steering team should also review the project's status regularly. It is critical for the team to maintain its discipline in meeting regularly with the project team leaders to ensure that teams are focused on their missions and detect any signs of trouble early on. Because the steering team selects the project team leaders, it should be best positioned to support them, as they would be most likely to have the buy-in with their efforts. All projects that are selected should have:

- Clear charters

- Measurable success criteria

- Regularly scheduled reviews

Your teams should be well trained on a continuous improvement approach to be able to deliver the optimal results. If you want maximum impact from your training, actual projects should be incorporated into this activity.

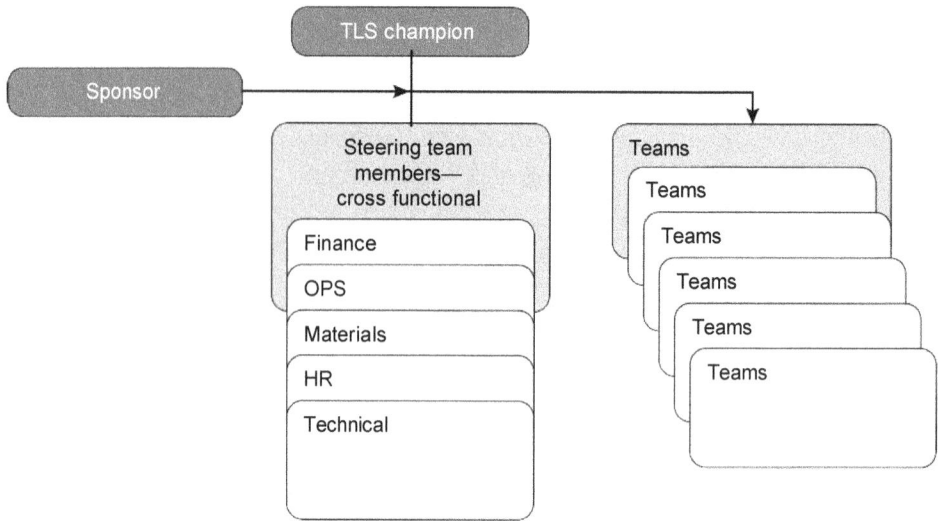

Figure 8.2 Continuous improvement steering team configuration model.

The teams should pursue their projects during the training to get hands-on experience. This ap- proach will ensure rapid implementation and maximum effectiveness. This is an effective strategy when teams have specific projects to deliver and then receive training on a continuous improvement approach. It is vital that you review teams' performances regularly with the steering team's involvement.

Speed-up

As projects begin, teams may be delayed or slowed down for a variety of reasons. Some of these reasons could be:

- Distraction by other activities
- Distraction by routine job responsibilities
- Lack of clarity
- Constraints (policy, political, material, physical)
- Lack of attention and review
- Negative team dynamics
- Lack of manager/supervisor support

If your teams are experiencing a slowdown, it is the steering team's responsibility to understand which constraints are the culprits and ensure that the team leaders are involved in the resolution of these bottlenecks. It is important to keep a log of issues and lessons learned to ensure that the lessons learned are applied to existing and future opportunities. Your overall goal is to ensure that projects are deployed rapidly, managed for timely execution, and that targeted results are delivered. Our recommendation is to use critical chain project management (CCPM) when you are scheduling multiple CPI projects. CCPM is a strong tool that applies TOC and JIT concepts in managing and scheduling your resources.

Tie Loose Ends

It is possible for a project to linger due to unresolved issues. It is a leadership responsibility to be aware of these circumstances and facilitate or negotiate closure for these lingering issues. You must:

- Show visible sponsorship.

- Provide training.

- Rigorously review projects.

- Provide ongoing knowledge sharing and proactive communications to the teams.

- Apply lessons learned.

Applying MOST steps should significantly increase the likelihood of successful continuous improvement project management and implementation. Early detection and resolution of issues are key enablers of this process, resulting in reduced rework (non-value-added activities) and cycle time.

Real-World Application

A global manufacturing organization has successfully deployed the iTLS (Pirasteh & Farah, 2006) methodology as its primary continuous improvement tool for over three years. One of the key project management tools used for effective project implementation was close adherence to application of MOST. Project managers discovered that application of MOST ensured timely project completion and an organized and disciplined focus on targeted issues. By using this approach, they had clarity in project management.

The steering team was active in the project-review and barrier-removal processes. J. A., the global quality systems manager and project manager for one of the plants using this approach, explains his experience with application of MOST. His project teams have been able to significantly contribute to bottom-line productivity and quality improvements. The following is an excerpt of an interview with J. A.

Question: Why do you think MOST has been effective in your continuous improvement project implementation process?

Answer: "MOST is a technique that aids projects from the beginning to the end. It ensures that projects are aligned with high-priority issues as defined by management, ensuring their support. It is a simple technique that helps projects to be completed quickly and effectively. The process takes little time but produces quick results."

Question: What did MOST do for your project team?

Answer: "MOST gave confidence to the team that the project was a high priority for the entire facility. The team was assisted through weekly meetings attended by management in order to immediately break down roadblocks. Projects were kept on track and completed ideas generated for next projects. The team enjoyed completing projects and seeing actual change takes place."

Question: How did you apply MOST principles?

Answer: "First, we trained the site management on MOST principles to provide leadership and direction for the rest of the facility. After reviewing monthly performance indicators, we performed root cause analysis using a cause-and-effect diagram ranked by priority using an FMEA. This allowed us to employ our resources on the highest contributors. Next, we selected team members who were knowledgeable about the most important projects and were supported by a trained leader. The steering committee provided the encouragement necessary to keep the teams on track. Presentations were made at the completion of projects to provide closure and a time to enjoy the successes."

Question: Would you continue using MOST? How do you plan on using MOST principles in your future projects?

Answer: "Yes, MOST is the normal way of doing business for us now. It produces results that are seen on the bottom line."

User Feedback

One of our CPI project manager users from Israel shares his experience with   CPI project implementation:

We at Lod plant started implementation last year. After going through the training we had some troubles in the implementation phase, [Did not use the MOST approach.] After an experience of one year we sat down and explored how to improve the implementation.

We found some key elements that we should take into consideration. We have established a steering committee to review the projects weekly, and monthly we gather the top management to discuss the annual plan for implementation. . . . We set a quarterly target for opening new projects and closing active projects.

One of the biggest problems we had at the beginning of the implementation was how to estimate and verify the project's savings. We understood that this was the one of the most important things that we needed to have the ability to control. So we now have the plant controller participating in the weekly meeting and he is a member in some of our teams that have difficulties in estimating savings. He is key to helping the teams focus on the right things.

Another improvement we made was in establishing a time table with milestones and ensuring that the teams stick to their plans. . . . The existence of the weekly meeting and review is very helpful.

To summarize the above, I think that in order to be able to implement the iTLS tool successfully the following key elements should be taken into consideration:

1. Steering committee established

2. Weekly project review

3. Presence of the plant controller in the steering committee

4. Project selection process

5. Tight time table for the projects

Notes:

9
Real-World Application of iTLS Approach

It is our belief that any process-driven operation can significantly benefit from the implementation of iTLS. The following are some examples of various organizations and business environments that have successfully applied iTLS.

STUDY—INVENTORY MANAGEMENT

Abstract

It is clear that for most for-profit enterprises there is a direct and significant benefit in minimizing their financial investment tied up in inventories. Excess inventories increase operating expenses (OE) and raise the potential for excess and obsolescence, thus reducing shareholder value. However, not having the right materials available at the right time also poses serious consequences, such as reworking production plans, lost throughput, failure to meet delivery milestones, and an increased risk of quality defects due to rushed conditions. In addition, there is the risk of losing existing customers and jeopardizing future sales.

The iTLS approach to continuous process improvement (CPI) and problem solving offers numerous benefits in optimizing processes including, as outlined in this case study, the costs associated with inventories. iTLS is a synergetic approach to CPI and problem-solving that combines the theory of constraints (TOC), Lean, and Six Sigma concepts to globally optimize processes, assure focus on the process constraint, remove non-value-added activities, and minimize undesirable variations and errors from the processes (Pirasteh, 2006). Imagine the iTLS approach of using TOC, Lean, and Six Sigma as playing the role of an orchestra conductor who organizes, engages, and emphasizes numerous instruments to create harmonious and pleasant music. Applying the iTLS approach to inventory optimization can significantly reduce the amount of inventory required by using diverse tools and analyses to establish appropriate caps or limits or thresholds on what needs to be inventoried in what quantities and when.

An iTLS optimization (iTLS-O) model was used in the following case study. This application resulted in a 50% ($14 million) reduction in inventory in less than six months without jeopardizing customer serviceability or production capabilities.

iTLS-O Model

This section explains the iTLS-O model (Figure 9.1) in detail for your use and experimentation. This model is designed to optimize inventory levels by specifically establishing feasible min/max thresholds and reorder points (ROP). Setting up a min/max system is not very difficult when you have precise records of historical and daily material usages data available. It is more difficult when the data is incomplete or inaccurate.

When setting up an inventory control or procurement min/max system some of the following considerations should be taken into account:

- Item costs

- Lead times

- Delivery costs

- Usage rate

- Holding costs

- Inventory investment costs

Ignoring any of these elements could increase the likelihood of shortages and/ or overages. In the best of both worlds, you would want to maintain a minimum amount of inventories coupled with maximum flexibility from your suppliers to deliver what you need when you need it without incurring additional costs. This is one of the objectives of just-in-time (JIT). In real life, however, there is almost always at least one condition, or "constraint," that needs to be examined and buffered in order to allow for smooth materials flow.

The iTLS-O model incorporates methodologies and tools from TOC to maintain the optimization objectives and also accommodate real-world constraints. iTLS-O provides simple enhancement to a min/max system for setting up feasible thresholds for the materials pull process. This process takes into consideration a single or multiple constraints and then estimates valid reorder points (ROP) for a Lean materials management process.

The beauty of this model is that it can also easily be used to aid in the design of JIT systems by setting up kanban levels. The model simply applies the desired confidence intervals for guarding against stock-outs by minimizing variability and errors.

Order period 1

	Optimal sum	Maximum sum	Difference
I	$4,969,255	$6,064,945	$1,095,690
A items	Optimal sum $3,855,170	Maximum sum $4,748,748	Difference $893,578
B items	Optimal sum $885,265	Maximum sum $1,057,021	Difference $171,756
C items	Optimal sum $228,820	Maximum sum $259,176	Difference $30,356

	AVG lead	History of delivery	Range	Std dev	95%conf	MOQ qty	MOQ days	MOQ/Lead	Daily Consumption	CAP	Item cost	Optimal investment	Max inv CAP	Max inv $	ABC
12345	3	2-4	2	1	3.00	60	0.17	3.0	360.0	1080	$851.00	$ 919,080.00	1440.0	$1,225,440.00	A 80% of value
23455	3	2-4	2	1	5.00	60	0.24	5.0	246.0	1230	$690.00	$ 848,700.00	1476.0	$1,018,440.00	
34567	3	2-4	2	1	5.00	60	0.45	5.0	134.0	670	$1,172.00	$ 785,240.00	804.0	$942,288.00	
3456	3	2-4	2	1	5.00	60	0.54	5.0	112.0	560	$690.00	$ 386,400.00	672.0	$463,680.00	
6543	3	2-4	2	1	5.00	60	0.42	5.0	143.0	715	$455.00	$ 325,325.00	858.0	$390,390.00	
344565	3	2-4	2	1	5.00	60	2.86	5.0	21.0	105	$3,157.00	$ 331,485.00	126.0	$397,782.00	
4567898	3	2-4	2	1	5.00	60	1.36	5.0	44.0	220	$1,177.00	$ 258,940.00	264.0	$310,728.00	
38L6175	3	2-4	2	1	5.00	60	0.85	5.0	71.0	355	$690.00	$ 244,950.00	426.0	$293,940.00	
43987	3	2-4	2	1	5.00	60	4.29	4.3	14.0	60	$2,622.00	$ 157,320.00	74.0	$194,028.00	B 15% of value
98766	3	2-4	2	1	5.00	60	0.58	5.0	104.0	520	$316.00	$ 164,320.00	624.0	$197,184.00	
9876	3	2-4	2	1	5.00	60	6.67	6.7	9.0	60	$1,980.00	$ 118,800.00	69.0	$136,620.00	
89754	3	2-4	2	1	5.00	60	4.29	4.3	14.0	60	$1,177.00	$ 70,620.00	74.0	$87,098.00	
67483	3	2-4	2	1	5.00	60	8.57	8.6	7.0	60	$1,391.00	$ 83,460.00	67.0	$93,197.00	
27654	3	2-4	2	1	5.00	60	1.40	5.0	43.0	215	$213.00	$ 45,795.00	258.0	$54,954.00	
98765	3	2-4	2	1	5.00	60	3.75	3.8	16.0	60	$455.00	$ 27,300.00	76.0	$34,580.00	C 5% of value
989076	3	2-4	2	1	5.00	60	3.00	5.0	20.0	100	$256.00	$ 25,600.00	120.0	$30,720.00	
5410938	3	2-4	2	1	5.00	60	6.00	6.0	10.0	60	$519.00	$ 31,140.00	70.0	$36,330.00	
1111111	3	2-4	2	1	5.00	60	15.00	15.0	4.0	60	$856.00	$ 51,360.00	64.0	$54,784.00	
322222	3	2-4	2	1	5.00	60	10.00	10.0	6.0	60	$519.00	$ 31,140.00	66.0	$34,254.00	
333333	3	2-4	2	1	5.00	60	10.00	10.0	6.0	60	$519.00	$ 31,140.00	66.0	$34,254.00	
444444	3	2-4	2	1	5.00	60	10.00	10.0	6.0	60	$519.00	$ 31,140.00	66.0	$34,254.00	

Kanban singal

$4,969,255.00 $6,064,945.00

Figure 9.1 Inventory optimization model using TLS.

Examples of Real-Life Constraints

JIT is ultimately the most desirable setup for the users, because it provides them with maximum inventory economy and agility. JIT implementation in its pure form, however, is not always attainable. Following are some typical situations (constraints) that pose challenges, and often prevent full JIT implementation:

- An organization's allowable inventory investment, as dictated by strategic objectives, policies, or budgets, as well as space, labor, and technical resource limitations, do not accommodate holding excess inventory on-hand to facilitate JIT.

- Suppliers' willingness or unwillingness to hold inventory of (their) finished goods to support the organization's demand pulls.

- Suppliers that have an established minimum order quantity (MOQ) for each ROP that is greater than the organization's required quantity. To support a JIT program, suppliers will often charge additional amounts to offset things such as setup, teardown, expediting, lower order volumes, and increased transportation.

- Supply line lead times that are significantly longer than the organization's manufacturing cycle times, making it impractical to pull JIT without adequate strategic buffers.

- Service agreements with the organization's customers do not allow for stock-outs and require high serviceability rates and may even have penalty causes.

Despite these common constraints, companies still want to minimize inventory investments and pull to demand as much as possible.

The iTLS-O model attempts to provide a balanced solution by estimating the ROP and taking into account the significant constraints and serviceability level requirements. Furthermore, the model allows you to examine the outcome of your decisions based on the process constraint assumptions and fine-tune decision elements based on cost and/or serviceability priorities.

CASE STUDY—ELECTRONIC MANUFACTURING COMPANY

Initial Condition

Inventory levels at a kitting plant grew significantly, from $15 million to $28 million, over a seven-month period after a new product was introduced into the plant. This 86% increase in inventory would cost the plant an additional $3 million each year in costs-of-capital plus other inventory management costs. These increased inventories became a prime concern to the division management and triggered efforts to understand the reasons behind the increase and identify actions to reduce them.

A preliminary study found a correlation between inventory increases and the production of the new product (Figure 9.2). It was initially assumed that since ordering practices were in line with the customer-provided forecast and the plant's purchasing policy, that operations did not have enough capacity to meet the customer's forecast. Management believed that the increased inventories resulted from production bottlenecks. As a result, they began pressuring production to increase capacity and produce more products. Unfortunately, the increased production was not being matched by customer pulls and resulted in even more inventory, much of which was now in finished goods.

An iTLS team was formed to uncover the true root cause(s) of the inventory surge and deploy corrective actions and preventive strategies to reduce and control inventory levels and costs.

iTLS in Action and Findings

The TLS team was assembled from members of diverse disciplines, all of whom were intimately familiar with the issue at hand. Their mission was to address the issue through the application of the iTLS seven-step process (Figure 9.3):

1. Identify the constraint.

2. Decide how to exploit the constraint. Specifically, how will you get the most out of the existing situation and resources without adding any additional capacity?

3. Eliminate sources of waste in the constraint.

4. Control process variability and error in the constraint.

5. Subordinate feeder activities to the constraint.

6. Elevate the constraint. Break the constraint so it is no longer a bottleneck or prevents the system throughput.

7. Reevaluate system performance and go after the next constraint.

Step 1—Mobilize and Focus

The iTLS team first defined the problem statement and mapped out the process using value-stream mapping (VSM) Lean tools. While analyzing the data, they discovered that the changes in inventory levels were more of a step function

Chapter 9: Real-World Application of iTLS Approach

Inventory behavior

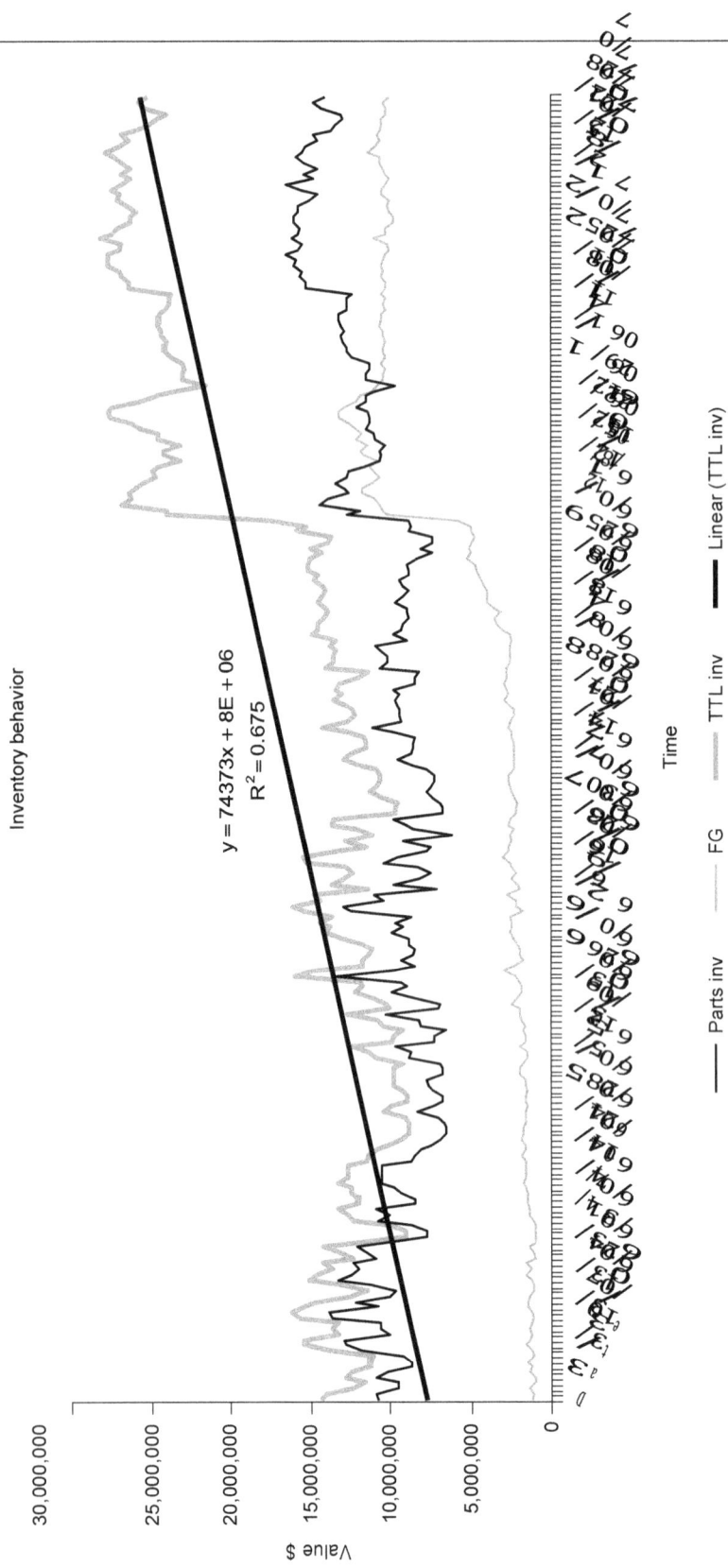

$y = 74373x + 8E + 06$
$R^2 = 0.675$

Parts inv   FG   TTL inv   Linear (TTL inv)

Time

Value $

Figure 9.2   Inventory initial analysis.

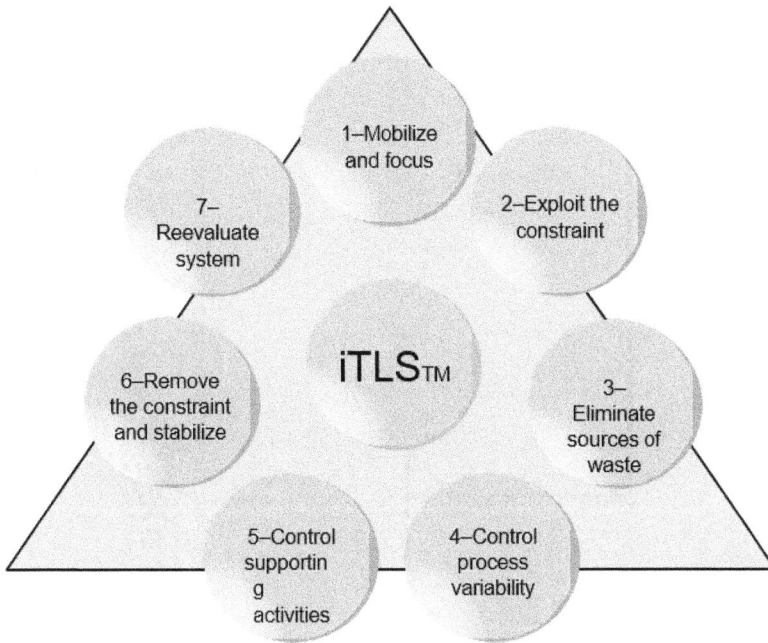

Figure 9.3 iTLS seven-step process.

of a shift in the process' statistical mean. Further investigation revealed the existence of two separate processes, with the shift occurring as shown in Figure 9.4. This discovery revealed that the second process had the undesirable effect of significantly raising inventory levels and acted as a constraint to profitability and throughput.

Further investigation found the nature of this constraint was a change in inventory management policy (policy constraint). Prior to the introduction of product X, parts were procured on a 13-week demand signal. When product X was introduced into the process, the customer began providing a 26-week forecast. The change in the forecast horizon was intended to give operations a wider "heads up" so they could better manage material pulls (Figure 9.5).

Unfortunately, operations did not realize that the 26-week forecast would be used for pull signal requirements. The buyers concluded that the "new" forecast horizon constituted "better" planning data and, in effect, a revised purchasing horizon. This conclusion was neither validated nor challenged, and the buyers changed their ordering policy from the existing 13-week horizon to a 26-week horizon. In addition, there was no review of the existing standard operating procedures (SOP) to see if there needed to be any adjustments given their change in the purchasing horizon. To top it off, weak checks and balances allowed this

Inventory behavior

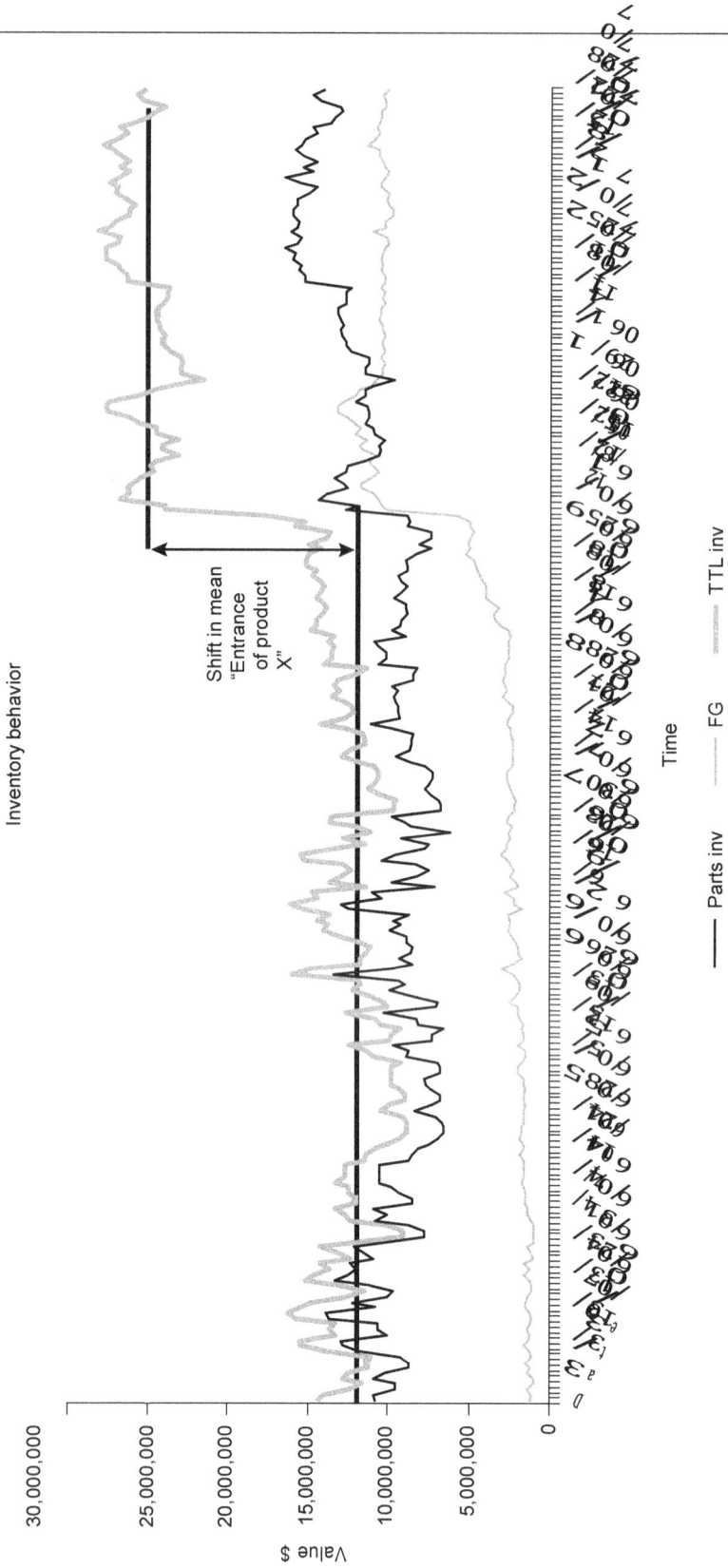

Figure 9.4 Inventory analysis discovering step function.

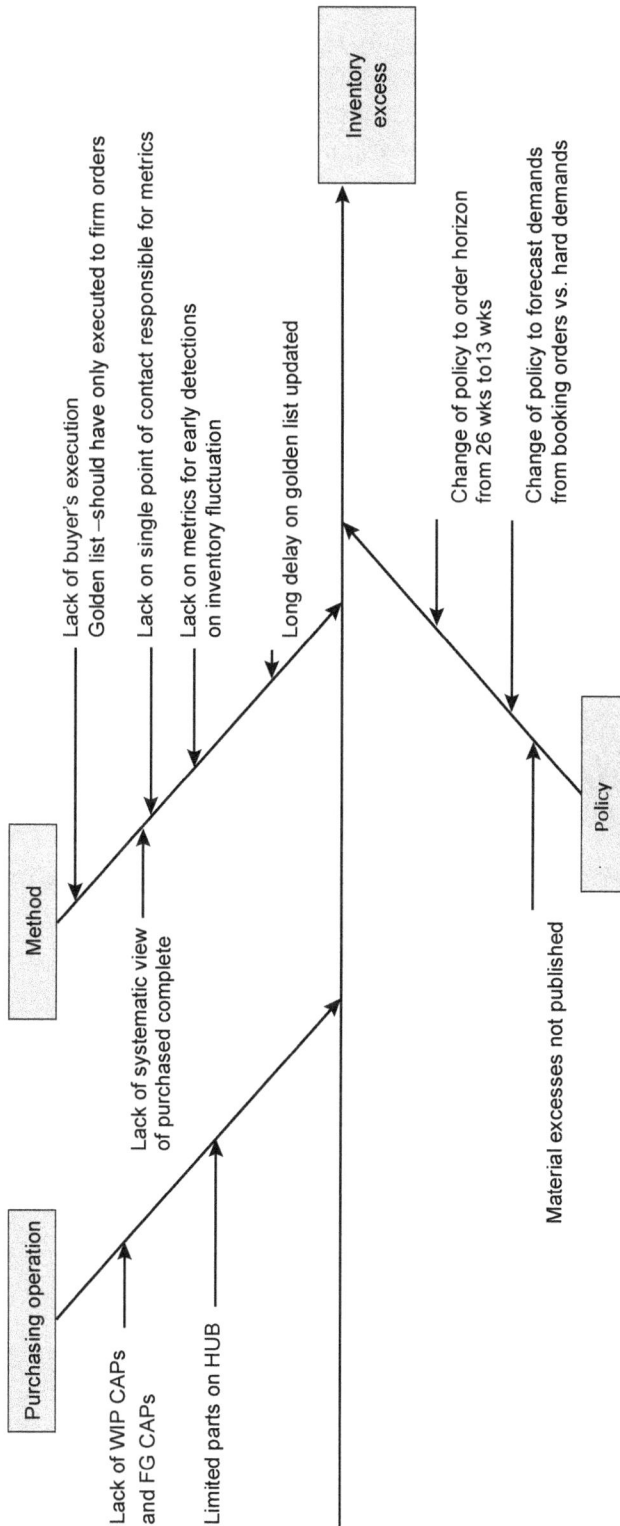

Figure 9.5 Using a cause and effect diagram to identify key factors.

change to be implemented virtually unnoticed. In the end, poor communication and implementation of an inadequately defined SOP created a process that was generating waste in the form of unnecessary inventories.

The iTLS approach realizes that the actual nature of system constraints is often camouflaged. Real-world constraints come in various forms and can only be discovered by challenging existing assumptions. Typical constraints could be:

- Policy

- Political

- Physical

- Capacity

- Materials

It is most often assumed that process constraints must be physical. This assumption, however, is rarely true. As shown in this case study, the root causes were the communication and buying policies, not the introduction of product X or a lack of production capacity.

Steps 2 and 3—Decide How to Exploit the Constraint and Eliminate Sources of Waste in the Constraint

The iTLS team applied the measure, analyze, and implement phases of DMAIC protocol to exploit the constraint by implementing necessary changes to elevate it. Specific actions included:

- Revising the purchasing trigger policy with a more specific SOP.

- Integrating fail-safe checklists into the SOP to ensure that critical items were identified, appropriately understood, and deployed.

- Trimming the purchasing horizon, not the forecast horizon, to 13 weeks.

- Training the procurement teams on the revised processes, SOPs, protocols, and control measurements.

These decisions and actions were based on cause and effect analysis and CNX factor characterization process to determine the X factors (see Chapter 6) and use of FMEA to prioritize which items to address first. The X factors that were identified and addressed were:

- Policies

  - The purchasing trigger (min/max) policy was inappropriate

- Processes

  - Training process not well understood

  - Controls

  - Well-defined SOPs were not in place

- No fail-safe checklists integrated / deployed

- Purchasing horizon corrections (Lead time policy)

Step 4—Control Process Variability and Error in the Constraint

Additionally, an inventory-level control model, iTLS-O, was applied. This tool sets out to minimize process variability and control the process within the "normal" limits by ensuring that buy triggers are demand driven. The expectations were to reduce inventory levels, increase inventory turns, and prevent excess inventories. iTLS-O proved to be reasonably robust in dealing with imperfect data. The tool functioned well and became more precise as more accurate data points became available and used. An audit was also scheduled to ensure that iTLS-O system was working and using the most updated information and assumptions.

Step 5—Control Supporting Activities to the Constraint

After the iTLS team identified the constraints, the team had to ensure the critical activities that were feeding the constraint were controlled in order to keep the constraint elevated. This step essentially required the subordination of feeder activities. Further, metrics and measurements had to be established to ensure that these processes were statistically controlled and their variability was within acceptable limits so as to not adversely impact the constraint. In this case, the constraint was a poor policy that was deployed without understanding its impact. The activities that directly impacted the constraint were:

- SOP based on "out-of-date" parameters and a lack of fail-safe checklists

- Procurement rules

- Min/max system to ensure inventory levels are properly maintained and provide flags where upper or lower limits are violated

Step 6—Remove the Constraint and Stabilize

The iTLS team was able to identify the nature of the constraint and its feeder activities which allowed them to properly throttle the procurement and inventory

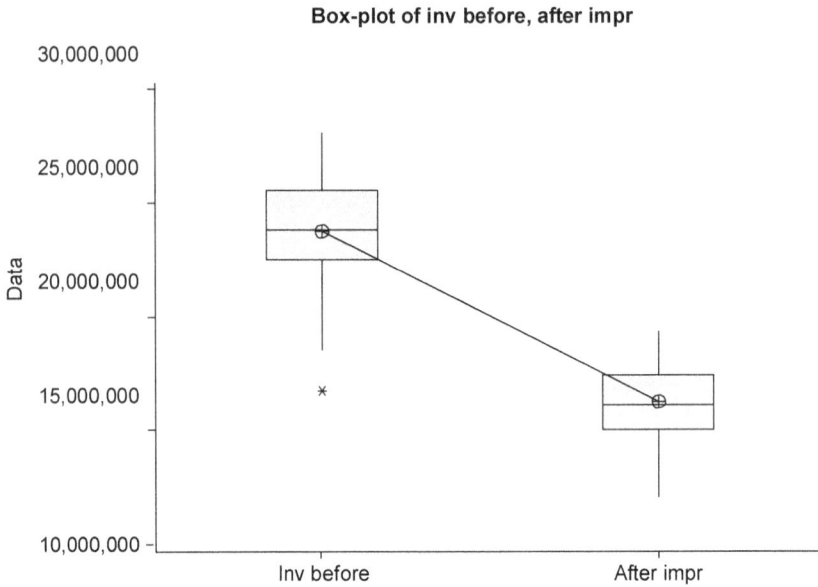

Figure 9.6 Box plot of inventory before and after iTLS implementation.

control processes. The procurement team was trained on and implemented the revised SOP and fail-safe processes, along with the appropriate buying horizons. Thus, the constraint was broken. Additionally, to ensure early detection of warning signals, a control chart was developed to monitor inventory fluctuation behavior, particularly looking for mean shifts, outliers, or any unusual trends (Figure 9.6 and Table 9.1).

The Two-Sample T-Test (Table 9.1) clearly indicates the significant differences between the initial condition (before) and improved condition (after), with a P-value of 0.0000. A P-value of 0.0000 indicates that the significant difference from

Table 9.1 ANOVA indicating reduction significance.

Two-sample T-test and CI: inv before and after improvements

Two-sample T for inventory before vs. after improvement

N Mean StDev SE Mean

Inventory before 182 23813166 2266168 167980

After impr 52 16306094 1543055 213983

Difference = mu (inv before) – mu (after impr)

Estimate for difference: 7507072

95% CI for difference: (6968451, 8045693)

T-test of difference = 0 (vs not =): T-value = 27.60 P-value = 0.000 DF = 120 "before" to "after" could not have been due to random process variability, therefore rejecting the hypothesis that both processes (before and after) are the same.

Step 7—Reevaluate System Performance and Go after the Next Constraint

Figure 9.7 shows that inventories were significantly reduced as a result of these changes. This is clear indication that the procurement rules are effective and the iTLS-O tool is properly guiding the team as what to purchase and when to choke the procurements to prevent waste. The inventory levels were reduced by 50% in addition to the reduction of about $3 million in cost of capital.

Inventory control and management requires continual improvement through systems that constantly strive to reduce the capital investments tied up in inventories. The TLS team was able to break the policy and communication constraints and improve inventory conditions, resulting in cost savings and waste elimination. After this significant achievement, the next step in the iTLS process is to recognize that it is essential to remap and reanalyze the entire process. It is important to avoid process improvement complacency. Once a constraint is removed, it is not uncommon for another constraint to emerge. If another constraint is discovered, it is necessary to go to step 1 of the TLS process and repeat the cycle.

Going Forward

Effective inventory control and management requires continual improvement through systems that embrace and address real-world constraints beyond not just

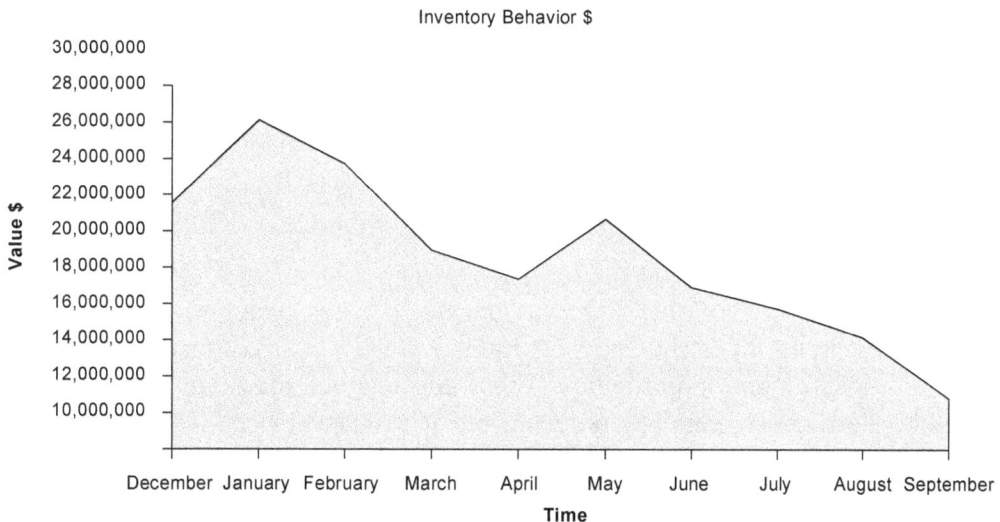

Figure 9.7 Inventory position after implementation of the iTLS.

those that are physical or resource-capacity based. We must adjust to internal and external changes, such as market dynamics, changing organizational structures, and evolving communication protocols. These systems must also constantly strive to reduce unnecessary capital investments tied up in inventories. iTLS is an effective methodology to continuously challenge existing assumptions and effectively eliminate waste and error from processes.

If you are interested in applying the iTLS-O model to your applications, the following procedure may assist you in its development.

Summary

- The iTLS approach is an effective continuous process improvement and problem-solving tool in inventory management as well as in manufacturing.

- Application of iTLS in proper sequence yielded over 50% in inventory reduction.

- The iTLS-O model can be an effective tool in controlling procurement, resulting in significant financial savings on the inventory cost of capital.

CASE STUDY—VALVE ASSEMBLY

Initial Conditions

The 300MM Slit Valve is a subassembly that can be sold as a spare part or used as part of integrated 300MM assembly. The assembly lead time for the 300MM Slit Valve was unpredictable, and its flow in the assembly area was convoluted. The time required to complete a 300MM Slit Valve was 35 minutes for a skilled technician and 60 minutes for an unskilled one. The engineering team used iTLS approach to improve this situation.

Background

The Slit Valve assembly line was unable to meet customer demands. Dawn Ulbricht, an industrial engineer trained in iTLS was charged with finding improvement opportunities. The entire engineering team knew that assembly lead times could be reduced, but it had never been a high priority. The industrial engineer solicited the help of three others: a manufacturing engineer with knowledge of clean rooms and skills at creating change, a clean room assembly technician to -

represent manufacturing, and the Slit Valve planner who was familiar with the customer and his needs. Each team member was a stakeholder and would benefit from any reduction in lead time and increase in capacity.

Step 1—Mobilize and Focus

The following problem statement and project goals were determined after initial process mapping and analysis to find the constraint:

Problem Statement:

Slit Valve production is not meeting the customer's demand. The time required for the complete assembly of a Slit Valve is 35 min for a skilled technician and 60 min for an unskilled technician. The assembly process is inconsistent; therefore, it creates an unpredictable schedule.

Goals:

• Reduce the cycle time by 40%.

• Reconfigure the assembly line/process flow.

• Develop concise SOP.

• Redefine the components in kanban.

• Implement 5S.

Figure 9.8 illustrates the improvement goals for both skilled and unskilled technicians.

Step 2—Decide How to Exploit the Constraint

In order to reduce the cycle for the Slit Valve subassembly, the team mapped its flow through the assembly department. Figure 9.9 shows the current layout of the assembly area and the flow of material. The analysis clearly indicated a spaghetti flow. Each assembly technician built a complete work order at one station while sharing original equipment manufacturer parts, documentation, and tooling with other assemblers. In addition, the test fixture for leak-checking the units was located on the opposite side of the room from where the assembly work was done.

The assembly cycle time was selected as the key process output variable (KPOV) for establishing a baseline measurement and tracking improvements. A time study verified that cycle time to build 1 unit was 60 minutes for an unskilled technician and 35 minutes for a skilled one.

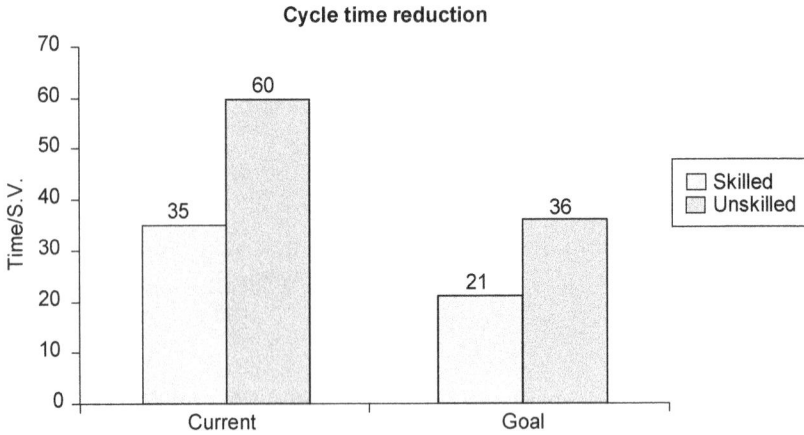

Figure 9.8 Goals.

Step 3—Eliminate Sources of Waste

It was determined through CE-CNX analysis that the following major factors were affecting the unit cycle time (Figure 9.10); consequently the X factors were identified as:

- Cumbersome work environment

- Unclear SOP

- 5S

Although the priority of the improvement activities was defined by the FMEA, there were direct links between the major factors and the minor factors, with both contributing to a long cycle time. Given this, the majority of the failure modes shown on the FMEA dissolved once improvement activities began (Figure 9.11).

After analyzing the value-stream map of the processes and focusing on X-factors, non-value-added activities were identified and removed from the process. The result was a smooth linear flow of material through the work center (Figure 9.12).

Step 4—Control Process Variability

In order to track and sustain the greatly reduced cycle time, a takt board was put in place to record the data. The assembly technician recorded this information

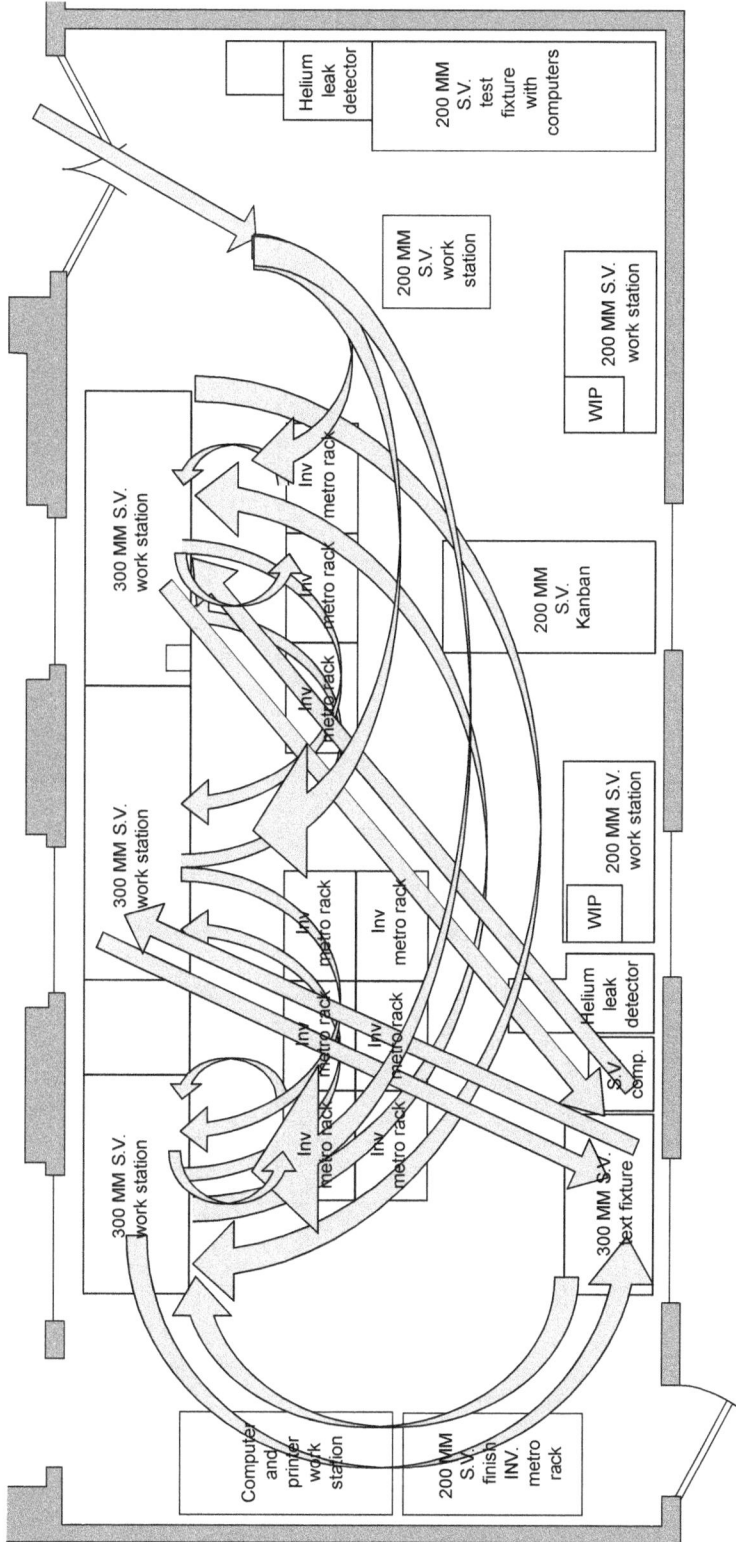

Figure 9.9 Spaghetti flow of the current layout.

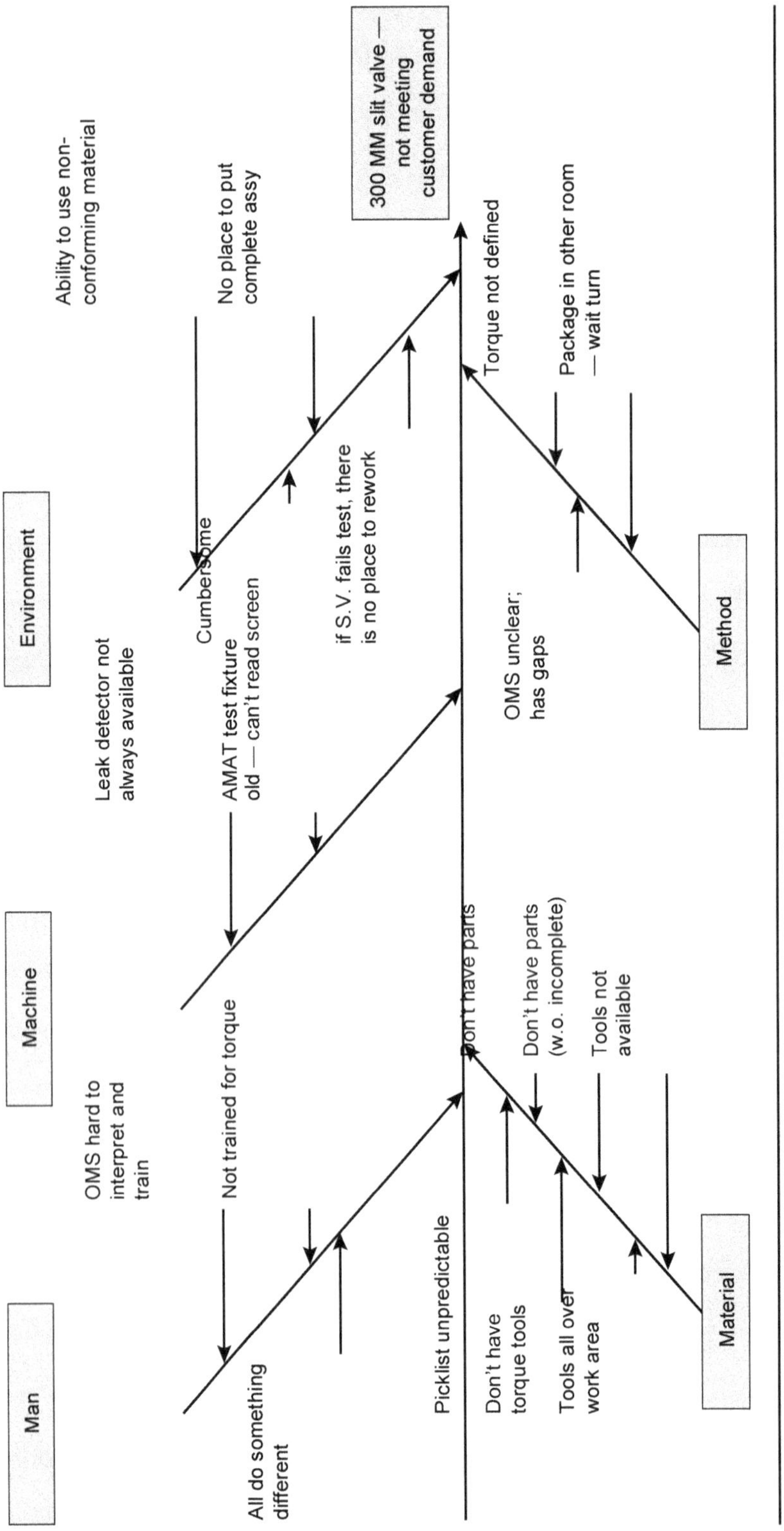

Figure 9.10 Cause and effect analysis.

Potential failure mode	Potential consequences of fault	Severity	Potential reasons for fault	Occurrence	Current process controls	Detection	RPN	Recommended corrective action
No place to put complete assembly	Damaged components	2.00	Process map	4.00	None	1.00	8.00	Create WIP location
Packaging done in different area than where built	Damaged components	2.00	Process map	4.00	None	1.00	8.00	Create packaging area
Cumbersome environment	Increased cycle time	3.00	Process map	5.00	None	1.00	15.00	Linear flow
Parts all over area	Increased cycle time	3.00	Process map	5.00	None	1.00	15.00	5S
Tools all over area	Increased cycle time	3.00	Process map	5.00	None	1.00	15.00	5S
All technicians assemble differently	Much variation in assembly process	5.00	Undefined requirements	4.00	Basic SOP	2.00	40.00	Well defined SOP
Ability to use non-conforming material	Non-conformant material shipping to customer	5.00	Process map	3.00	Redtag process	3.00	45.00	Create redtag station
Don't have torque tools	Non-conformant material shipping to customer	5.00	Undefined requirements	5.00	None	4.00	100.00	5S
Tools not available	Non-conformant material shipping to customer	5.00	Multiple builds at once	5.00	None	1.00	25.00	5S
If S.V. fails, no place to rework assembly	Possibility shipping failed assembly to customer	5.00	Process map	3.00	None	2.00	30.00	Create rework area
OMS hard to interpret and train to	Technician not building assembly correctly—non-conformant	5.00	Incomplete SOP	5.00	None	1.00	25.00	Well defined SOP
OMS unclear and does not encompass all assemblies	Technician not building assembly correctly—non-conformant	5.00	Incomplete SOP	5.00	None	1.00	25.00	Well defined SOP

Figure 9.11 FMEA.

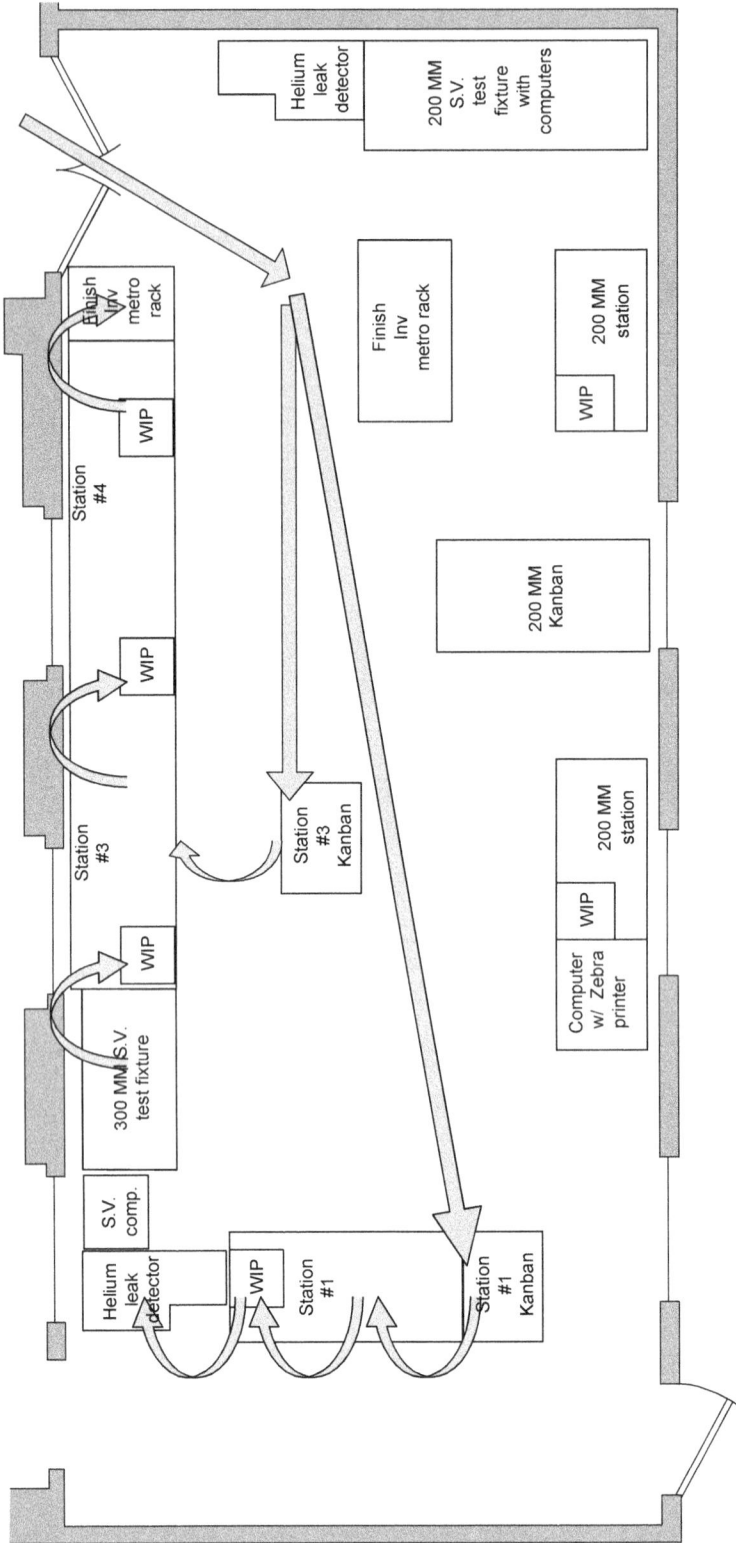

Figure 9.12 New process flow after implementation of improvements.

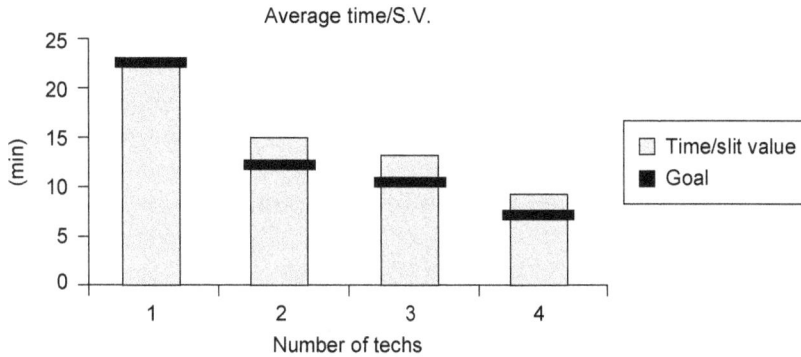

Figure 9.13 Process time reduction monitoring.

for each work order. This tool allowed operations to monitor the cycle time and ensure that the new process did not trend out of control (Figure 9.13).

Step 5—Control Supporting Activities to the Constraint

Production commenced and the assembly technicians were allowed a few days to familiarize themselves with the new flow of material. The team leaders and a well-defined SOP aided in this effort.

Once the assembly technicians felt comfortable with their new surroundings, another time study was done to determine if any adjustments needed to be made. Through subordination activities, the following improvements took place:

- Created space for packaging area for both Slit Valves and doors

- Added red tag cart to immediately pull nonconforming material off the line

- Linear work center layout

- Dedicated tooling

- Added a rework area to reduce the "backward" flow of material

- Station-specific SOP

- Implemented kanban

Step 6—Remove the Constraint and Stabilize the Process

The cycle time was reevaluated based on the changes to the assembly area. One of the key benefits of the linear flow line configuration was its flexibility with resource availability. The line lead now had the ability, based on the demand requirements, to allocate one to four assembly technicians to the line at any given time. These process improvements produced the following results:

- Reduced the likelihood of using nonconforming material—higher quality online

- 71.8% average reduction in assembly cycle time

- 50% reduction in work order picking time

- "Flexible" line configuration

- All-inclusive SOP

- Well-organized work area

- Elimination of muda

System throughput significantly increased by 600%. Essentially six times as many units were produced with the same amount of resources. It is important to note that despite the existence of direct labor savings for this project, it paled when compared to the six-fold gains in throughput.

Step 7—Reevaluate the System

Although there were individuals from the assembly group involved in every aspect of this improvement project, resistance to change was apparent. Going forward, we concluded that it would be beneficial to spend more time on step 1 to ensure total buy-in from all team members. The team reassessed the balanced scorecard to determine where to focus their improvement efforts next.

CASE STUDY—OF MINING OPERATIONS
IN BRAZIL (By Celso Calia)

Introduction

For-profit enterprises that produce products strive to achieve their targeted revenues by effectively using their available capacities. Unreliable and below-target production levels lead to low revenues, high inventories, and high operating expenses. Such results jeopardize profit and ROI, creates an enormous amount of stress and frustration on the organization's resources, and potentially jeopardize future revenue opportunities. In this case study, the iTLS approach synchronized production with available capacity levels while providing process stability. This was achieved with simple application of iTLS and implemented through involvement and participation of the organization's people and their powerful commitment for success.

Our Model

iTLS integrates (synchronizes and harmonizes) three powerful ingredients (Figure 9.14):

- Focus on the few, yet critical, elements that limit the global performance by applying TOC tools

- Elimination of waste in the "hidden factory" through application of Lean tools

- Reduction in undesirable variability to ensure process stability by applying Six Sigma tools

The application of iTLS to production in a continuous process environment, ensured that the invested capacity and resources were converted into stable production flow.

The case study that follows is a summary of the application of iTLS in a Brazilian conglomerate. It encompassed mining plants, ore concentrating plants, and metallurgical production plants. In every instance, the application of iTLS resulted in increased throughput within three to four months. In another three to four months, the processes were stabilized, and the strategic target production levels attained. Production exceeded previous thresholds without adding capacity. The results included increased revenues, more profits, and a higher ROI.

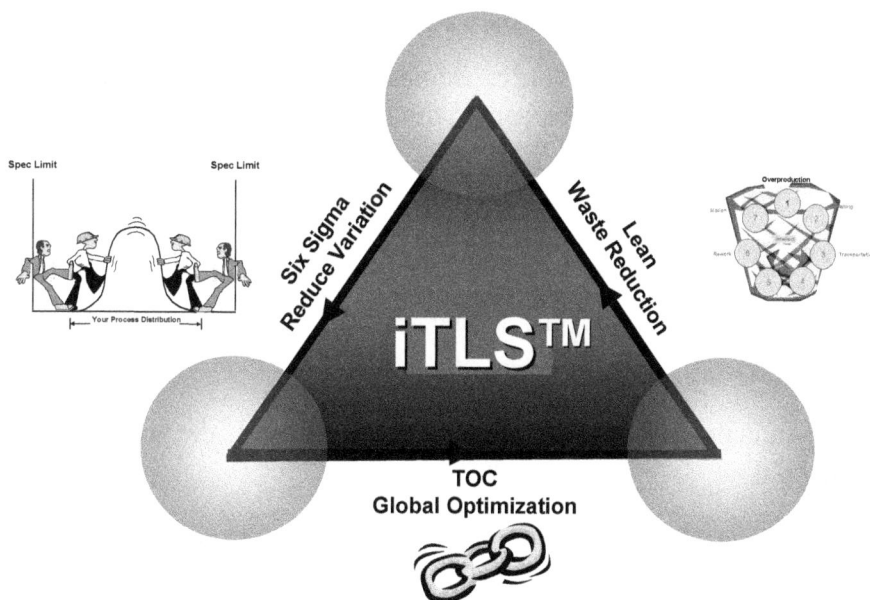

Figure 9.14   iTLS model applied.

The iTLS model that was implemented in these plants is depicted in Figure 9.15. The iTLS model ensured stable and protected process flow to the marketplace and consisted of the following basic elements:

- A drum that sets the production pull tempo and establishes the delivery takt of the plant's products to the market

- Buffers (kanban) that respond to the process drum and protect the vulnerable processes and shipment schedules

- A rope that creates a material-release (pull) discipline synchronized with the pace of the drum

- Implementation of Lean tools to identify waste and eliminate them from the processes

- Application of Six Sigma tools to make improvements sustainable and under statistical control

When implementing a new production model, a series of considerations need to be taken into account. Some of these are:

- Process flow—sequence of operations

- Higher capital investment operations (alternatives)

- Current process variability of the various operations

- Current gap between available capacities, production targets, and actual production levels compared with customer requirements

- Throughput (sales minus direct material costs) losses with current gaps

- Fixed costs

- Inventory investments, levels, number of turns

- Roles and responsibilities

- Policies and procedures that influence the outcome of the plants' throughput

There is a direct correlation between the stability of an operation's drum and the amount of financial gains achieved. Once the process drum was identified, we worked to ensure that its takt set the pace for material releases (rope) and shipments (deliveries). These two activities need to be protected against variability caused by feeding and interdependent operations in order to ensure that its entire capacity is being converted to shipments to the market. In continuous process

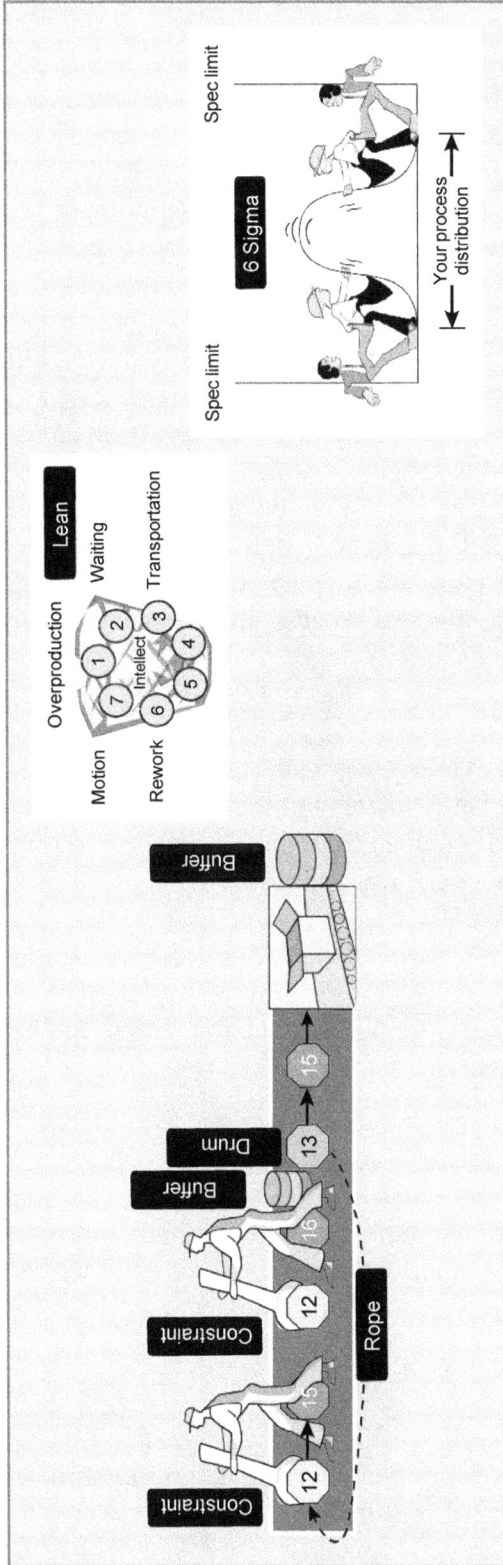

Figure 9.15 The DBR model → D = drum, B = buffer, R = rope.

environments, protecting the drum and shipments is done by creating buffers prior to these two operations, to ensure a continuous flow of throughput to the marketplace. Once buffers are adequately sized and implemented, they will insulate the drum and shipments from the process variability that exists in feeding operations. It is important to note that variability in the feeding operations results a reduction in level of the buffers, which somehow must be recouped. This is possible only if all other operations have some extra capacity—protective capacity—so they can operate at a higher pace (~10%) than the drum and shipment's pace. Any operation with a capacity below 110% of the capacity of the drum is tagged as a constraint, because it could potentially have a global adverse effect and jeopardize throughput. The work teams focus on increasing the capacity of these operations by reducing waste and variability. Lean and Six Sigma have the ideal tools to satisfy both needs.

This model is optimized by making decisions based on the status of the buffers over time. Buffers tell the story by letting us know what is going on in the entire flow and allowing us to anticipate potential disruptions, identify causes, and derive actions for continuous process improvement (CPI).

The Votorantim Cases

Votorantim is the fourth-largest private Brazilian group and operates in several countries in various market segments in the mining and metal industries. Five facilities have adopted and benefited from the iTLS approach for production. Two of these plants were mining operations and three were metallurgical plants.

Initial Condition

- All plants were unable to meet production targets and had a sporadic production performance, leading to lost revenues.

- A new technology was introduced into the Três Marias Zinc Plant—autoclaves for silicate. This technology treats silicate at high temperatures and pressures in order to eliminate the calcination of zinc crude concentrate in the rotatory kiln operations in the Vazante and Milling and Magnesium Treatment sectors of the Três Marias plant. The undesirable conditions included:

  - Targets were not met.

  - The subsequent areas, like filtration, were operating badly.

  - A huge quantity of problem-solving actions (attempts to improve everything, everywhere) emerged.

- People were frustrated. Their perception was, "The more we do, the less we achieve."

- Finger-pointing attitude- "It was not me!"; trying to portray that "I am not part of the problem" was commonplace, creating an environment of noncooperation and covering one's back.

- Preventive maintenance was not always done, because they were not meeting production targets.

CE, reality trees, and other process tools were used to brainstorm about the situation and to achieve consensus about the root problem. A partial diagram is shown in Figure 9.16.

The thinking-tool diagram should be read bottom-up, along the arrows, with "IF Cause THEN Effect," or "IF [tail of the arrow] THEN [tip of the arrow]." When more than one arrow exists, it becomes a summation and should read "IF [tail of the arrow 1] AND [tail of the arrow 2] AND . . . , THEN [tip of the arrows]."

Step by Step

The iTLS framework gave us the sequence for implementation:

1. Mobilize and focus.

2. Exploit the drum.

3. Eliminate sources of waste.

4. Control process variability.

5. Control supporting activities to the drum.

6. If necessary and viable, enhance the pace of the drum or change it.

7. Reevaluate the system and go after the next drum.

Step 1 — Mobilize and Focus

- Organize people in cross-functional focused teams (Figure 9.17), achieve consensus on the root problem, and educate about the new paradigms.

- Get consensus about what operation should be the drum and what should be its pace. The drum's pace coincides with what the whole plant ships to the market.

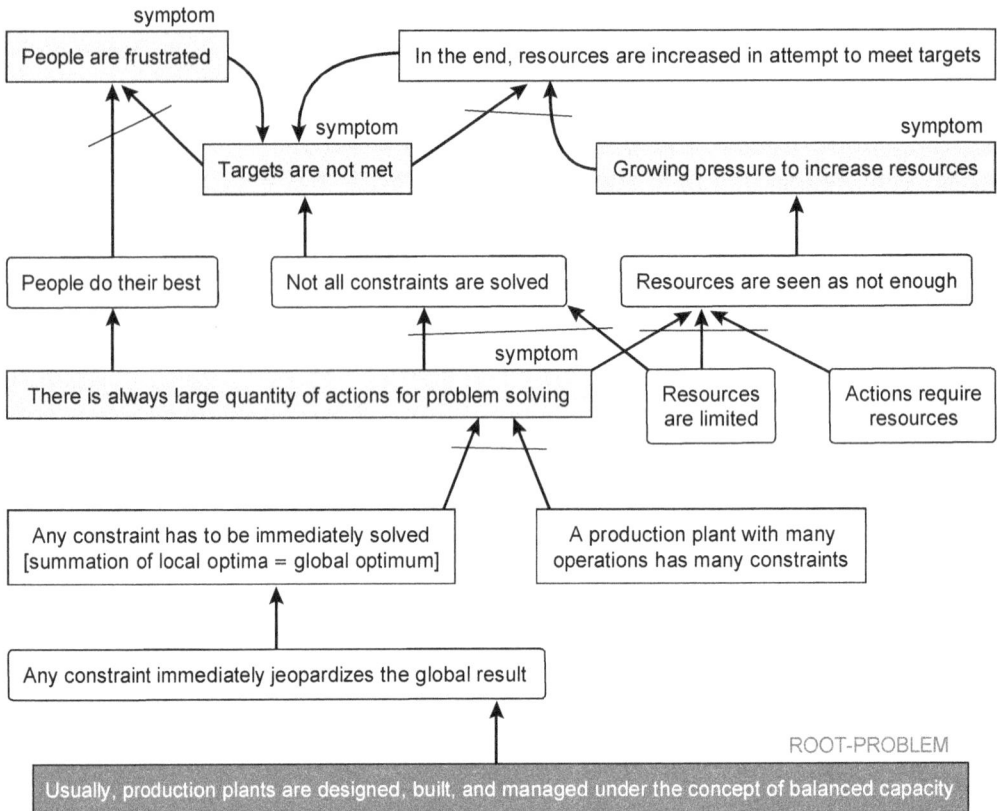

Figure 9.16 Thinking tool applied for cause-and-effect determination.

Step 2—Identify and Exploit the Constraint (Drum)

- Provide protection to maintain the pace of the drum and shipments—create buffers before them.

- Implement a kanban management routine with rules to interpret buffer status and determine the causes and improvement action needed to eliminate them (Figure 9.18).

Step 3—Eliminate Sources of Waste

- Identify the constraints as operations whose average current capacity is less than 110% of the drum's capacity. Buffer management can be very helpful in this process (Figure 9.18).

- Establish kaizen teams to eliminate waste at each constraint and discover "hidden capacity" by applying SPC, cause-effect techniques, Pareto, and so forth (Figure 9.19).

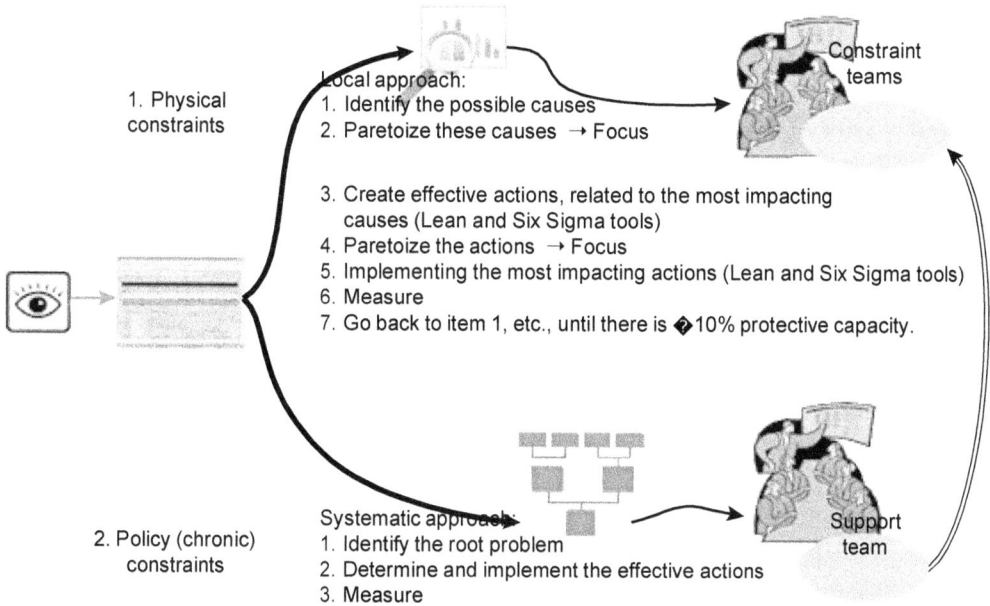

1. Physical constraints

Local approach:
1. Identify the possible causes
2. Paretoize these causes → Focus

3. Create effective actions, related to the most impacting causes (Lean and Six Sigma tools)
4. Paretoize the actions → Focus
5. Implementing the most impacting actions (Lean and Six Sigma tools)
6. Measure
7. Go back to item 1, etc., until there is ◆10% protective capacity.

2. Policy (chronic) constraints

Systematic approach:
1. Identify the root problem
2. Determine and implement the effective actions
3. Measure

Constraint teams

Support team

Figure 9.17 Mobilize work teams.

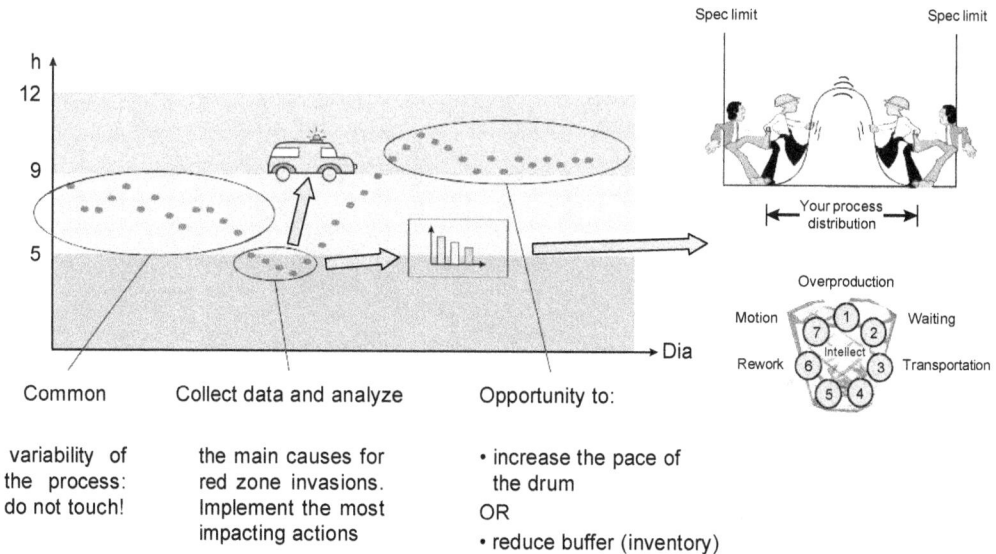

Common

variability of the process: do not touch!

Collect data and analyze

the main causes for red zone invasions. Implement the most impacting actions

Opportunity to:

• increase the pace of the drum
OR
• reduce buffer (inventory)

Figure 9.18 Buffer management.

Step 4—Control Process Variability

- After eliminating these constraints, reduce the process variability of these operations by applying simple Six Sigma techniques.

Step 5—Control Supporting Activities to the Drum

- Control material release to ensure that materials are released at the pace of the drum (Figure 9.20). Apply I river configuration setup control parameters (see TOS, Chapter 7).

Step 6—Control Supporting Activities

- Stable processes and increases in throughput capabilities allow the plants to reduce cycle times, expand production, and increase revenues and ROI (Figure 9.21).

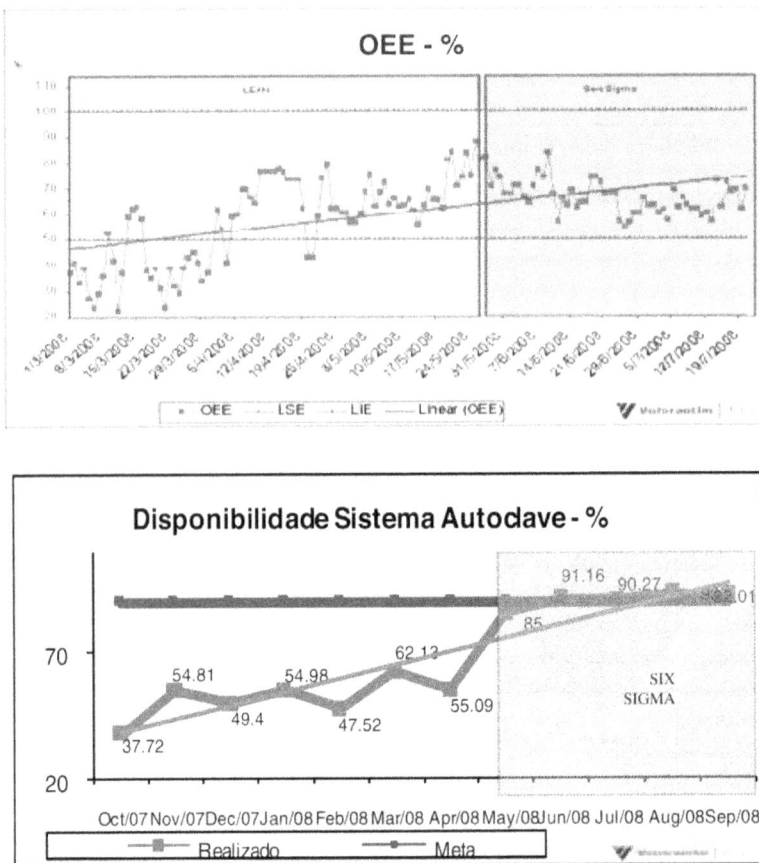

Figure 9.19   Application of SPC, Lean, and Six Sigma tools and techniques.

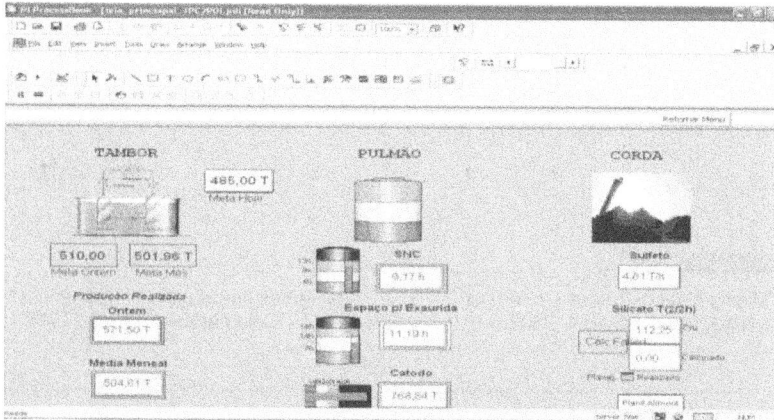

Figure 9.20   Buffer performance and status dashboard in real time.

The repeatability of results achieved with iTLS implementations was quite consistent, as can be seen in Figure 9.22a, b, c, d.

Step 7—Reevaluate the System and Go after the Next Drum

- Go back to step 1.

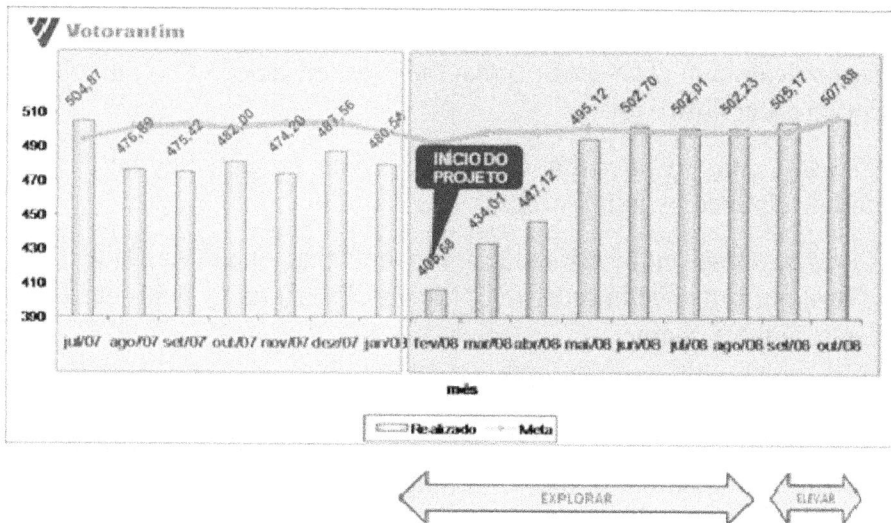

Figure 9.21   Metallurgical plant expansion.

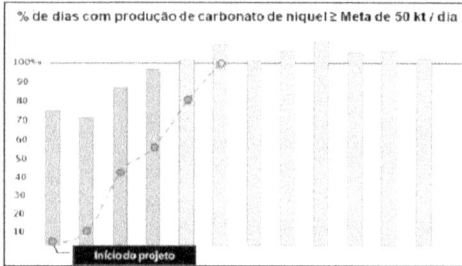

a). Mining plant of Votorantim Metais
Niquelândia – Brasil / 2002.

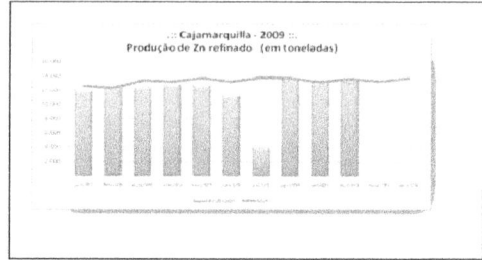

b). Metallurgical plant of Votorantim Metais
Cajamarquilla – Peru / 2009.

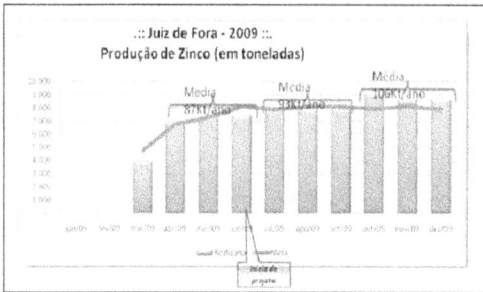

c). Metallurgical plant of Votorantim Metais
Juiz de Fora – Brasil / 2009.

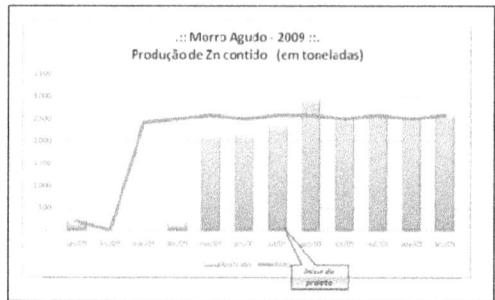

d). Mining plant of Votorantim Metais
Morro Agudo – Brasil / 2009.

Figure 9.22a, b, c, d   Examples of four plants' performances applying iTLS.

Summary

The application of iTLS ensures that the invested capacity is converted into a stable production flow with:

- *Constant delivery pace* that is demand driven, protected by buffers, and disciplined by a pull process.

- *Constant focus* on the critical few elements that tend to limit the global performance in order to optimize CPI efforts by applying TOC, Lean, and Six Sigma.

- *Constant buffer management* that highlights when a new constraint is emerging.

- *Constant elimination of waste,* turning "hidden capacity" into productive and protective capacity.

- *Constant reduction of variability* that ensures stability and sustainability of results.

- *The Autoclave Project met the targets,* like volume processed, OEE, and magnesium removal. The global zinc recovery at Três Marias Zinc Plant was increased from 93% to 95%. The project, which was initially a problem, was recognized as a 2009 Best Practice in the Votorantim Group.

- *The Zinc Recovery at Vazante Mining and Concentration was improved* from 86% to 90.5% when iTLS was applied, because it focused efforts on solving the flotation problems of willemita mineral.

NOTES:

10
Closing

We began this book by suggesting that TOC, Lean, and Six Sigma practitioners could significantly benefit by embracing the iTLS integrated knowledge approach. Throughout the book we attempted to make this point clear by addressing two significant interest groups:

- Leaders of organizations who are interested in taking their organization's profitability and performance to the next level

- The change agents and the practitioners who physically facilitate such a transformation process

We believe that by addressing these two groups simultaneously, it will improve communication, cooperation, and understanding between these two groups.

We have also attempted to recognize the favorite CPI knowledge areas (Lean, Six Sigma, TOC) and their contributions to improving our business environments. We have further demonstrated the powerful interaction effect that results from combining these methodologies in an appropriate sequence. Finally, we have shown that in a controlled experiment the outcome of these combinations boosts results by over 400%. Subsequent results with a refined iTLS process coupled with a TOS have consistently delivered another 50% increase in benefits.

Now the choice is yours: liberate your organization by going beyond your existing knowledge and achieve higher profitability and greater effectiveness, or remain trapped by your current knowledge and paradigm.

To close this, it may be fitting to share a story told by a Zen master. A young widower returned home one day to find his house burned to the ground and his five-year-old son lost. Near the ruins of his house, he found the charred corpse of a child that he believed to be his own son. In his enormous grief, he placed the child's ashes in a container and carried it with him everywhere.

Actually, his son was not lost in the fire but had been carried off by bandits. One day the son escaped and found where his father was living. The boy arrived at midnight as his father, still carrying the ashes, was preparing to sleep. The son knocked on the door. "Who are you?" asked the father. "I am your son" replied the boy. "You are lying. My son died more than three months ago," the father said. The father refused to open the door and persisted in his belief and knowledge. The story ends with the boy having to leave and the poor father losing his son forever!

Clinging to what we believe as absolute knowledge may prevent us from opening the door to new opportunities, even if they are knocking at our door.

References

Anderson, M. J., & Whitcomb P. J. (2000). *DOE Simplifi ed.* New York: Productivity.

Bakerjian, R., ed. (1993). *Tool and Manufacturing Engineers Handbook: Volume 7, Continuous Improvement.* Dearborn, MI: Society of Manufacturing Engineers.

Ballis, J. P., Sr. (1996). *TQMIII: An Alternative to Re-engineering.* Dallas: Brown Books.

Ballis, J. P., Sr. (2001). *Managing Flow: Achieving Lean in the New Millennium to the Gold.* Dallas: Brown Books.

Benbow, D., & Kubiak, T. M. (2005). *The Certifi ed Six Sigma Black Belt Handbook.* Milwaukee: American Society for Quality Press.

Bluman, A. G. (1997). *Elementary Statistics.* New York: McGraw-Hill.

Breyfogle, F. W., III. (2003). *Implementing Six Sigma* (2nd ed.). Hoboken: John Wiley & Sons.

Breyfogle, F. W., III, Cupello, J. M., & Meadows, B. (2001). *Managing* York: John Wiley & Sons.

Brue, G. (2003). *Design for Six Sigma.* New York: McGraw-Hill.

Brussee, W. (2004). *Statistics for Six Sigma Made Easy.* New York: McGraw-Hill.

Chase, R. B., Jacobs, R. F., & Aquilano, N. J. (2004). *Operations Management for Competitive Advantage* (10th ed.). New York: McGraw-Hill.

Creveling, C. M. (2002). *Design for Six Sigma.* Upper Saddle River, NJ: Prentice Hall PTR.

Crosby, P. B. (1984). *Quality without Tears: The Art of Hassle Free Management.* New York: McGraw-Hill.

De Feo, J. A., & Barnard, W. W. (2003). *Juran's Six Sigma: Breakthrough and Beyond.* New York: McGraw-Hill.

Deming, E. W. (1989). *Out of the Crisis* (7th ed.). Cambridge: Massachusetts Institute of Technology.

Dusharme, D. (2004). Got Six Sigma on the Brain? *Quality Digest 24*(11), 25–32.

Fisher, R. A. (1925). Applications of 'Student's' Distribution. *Metron 5,* 3–17.

Ford, H., & Crowther, S. (1922). *My Life and Work.* New York: Doubleday, Page.

George, M. L. (2002). *Lean Six Sigma: Combining Six Sigma Quality with Lean Speed.* New York: McGraw-Hill.

Goldratt, E. M., & Cox, J. (1992). *The Goal* (2nd ed.). Great Barrington, MA: North River Press.

Goldratt, E. M., & Fox, R. E. (1986). *The Race.* Croton-on-Hudson, NY: North River Press.

Goldratt, E. M., Schragenheim, E., & Ptak, C. (2000). *Necessary but Not Sufficient.* Great Barrington, MA: North River Press.

Goldratt, E. M. (1990). *The Haystack Syndrome.* Great Barrington, MA: North River Press.

Goldratt, E. M. (1990). *Theory of Constraints and How Should It Be Implemented.* Great Barrington: North River Press.

Goldratt, E. M. (1994). *It's Not Luck.* Great Barrington, MA: North River Press.

Goldratt, E. M. (1996). *Production the TOC Way.* New Haven, CT: Avraham Y. Goldratt Institute.

Goldratt, E. M. (1997). *Critical Chain.* Great Barrington, MA: North River Press.

Gooch, J., George, M., & Montgomery, D. (1987). *America Can Compete.* Dallas: George Group.

Gryna, F. M. (2001). *Quality Planning and Analysis* (4th ed.). New York: McGraw-Hill.

Hammer, M., & Champy, J. (1993). *Reengineering the Corporation.* New York: Harper Business.

Harrington, J. (2005). Six Sigma: Quality's Viagra? *Quality Digest 25*(8), 14.

Hobbs, D. (2004). *Lean Manufacturing Implementation.* Boca Raton, FL: J. Ross Publishing.

Hoffherr, G. D., Moran, J. W., & Nadler, G. (1994). *Breakthrough Thinking in Total Quality Management.* Englewood Cliffs, NJ: Prentice Hall.

Imai, M. (1986). *Kaizen: The Key to Japan's Competitive Success.* New York: Random House Business Division.

Inamori, K. (1995). *A Passion for Success: Practical, Inspirational, and Spiritual Insight from Japan's Leading Entrepreneur.* New York: McGraw-Hill.

Juran. J. M., & Godfrey, B. A. (1998). *Juran's Quality Control Handbook* (5th ed.), New York: McGraw-Hill.

LaMarch, J. (2005). The People Behind the Process. *America Production & Inventory Control Society 15*(5), 26–28.

Levinson, W. A., & Rerick, R. A. (2002). *Kaizen: The Key to Japan's Competitive Success.* Milwaukee: ASQ Quality Press.

Mann, D. (2005). *Creating a Lean Culture.* New York: Productivity Press.

McClave, J. T., Benson, G. P., & Sincich, T. (2004). *Statistics for Business & Economics* (9th ed.). New York: Prentice Hall.

Mills, C., Carnell, M., & Wheat, B. (2001). *Leaning into Six Sigma: The Path to Integration of Lean Enterprise and Six Sigma.* Cambridge, MA: Publishing Partners.

Nadler, G., & Hibino, S. (1990). *Breakthrough Thinking.* Rocklin: Prima Publishing.

Ohno, T. (1988). *Toyota Production System.* Portland, OR: Productivity Press.

Omdahl, T. P. (1997). *Quality Dictionary.* West Terre Haute: Quality Council of Indiana.

Pande, P., Neuman, R., & Cavanagh, R. (2000). *The Six Sigma Way.* New York: McGraw-Hill.

Pearson K. (1976). *Biometrika Tables for Statisticians.* New York: Lubrecht & Cramer.

Pirasteh, R. M. (2005). *Effects of Combined Approach of Theory of Constraints, Lean and Six Sigma on Process Improvement*, PhD dissertation.

Pirasteh, R. M., & Farah, K. (2006). Continuous Improvement Trio: The Top Element of TOC, Lean, and Six Sigma Make Music Together. *APICS* 16(5), 31–33.

Pirasteh, R. M., and Farah, K. (2006). Squeezing the MOST from Continuous Improvement: Key Leadership Principles Make the Difference. *APICS* 16(9) 28–31.

Pirasteh, R. M., and Horn, S. (2009). The Many Sides of TLS: Using the Theory of Constraints, Lean, and Six Sigma for Multidimensional Results. *APICS* 19(3) 40–43.

Pirasteh, R. M., and Calia, C. G. (2010). ntegration of Lean, Six Sigma & TOC Improves Performance. *IndustryWeek.* http://www.industryweek.com/articles/integration_of_lean_six_sigma__toc_improves_performance_21537.aspx

Pirasteh, R. M., and Kannappan, S. (2013). The Synergy of Continuous Process Improvement: Integration Lean, Six Sigma and Theory of Constraints Can Multiply their benefits. IIE 45(6) 41-45

Calia, S, Hibiz, E, Kannappan, S., Luiz, J, Plaza V. (2014). A continuous Process Improvement Case Study. APICS 24(2)42-45.

Salvendy, G. (1992). *Handbook of Industrial Engineering* (2nd ed.). New York: Wiley & Sons.

Schmidt, S. R., & Launsby, R. G. (1988). *Understanding Industrial Designed Experimentation* (4th ed.). Colorado Springs, CO: CQG Ltd Printing.

Schonoberger, R. J. (1982). *Japanese Manufacturing Techniques: Nine Hidden Lessons in Simplicity.* New York: The Free Press.

Sekine, K., & Arai, K. (1998). *TPM for the Lean Factory.* Portland, OR: Productivity Press.

Sharma, A., & Moody, P. E. (2001). *The Perfect Engine: How to Win in the New Demand Economy by Building to Order with Fewer Resources.* New York: Free Press

Taguchi, G., Chowdhury, S., & Wu, Y. (2005). *Taguchi's Quality Engineering Handbook.* Hoboken, NJ: Wiley & Sons.

Triola, M. F. (2000). *Elementary Statistics* (8th ed.). New York: Addison-Wesley.

Triola, M. F. (2004). *Elementary Statistics* (9th ed.). New York: Addison-Wesley.

Umble, M. M., & Srikanth, M. L. (1995). *The Principals of Synchronous Management* (Vol. 2). Guilford, CT: Spectrum Publishing.

Umble, M. M., & Srikanth, M. L. (1997). *Synchronous Management* (Vol. 2). Guilford, CT: Spectrum Publishing.

Wantuck, K. A. (1998). *Just in Time for America* (10th ed.). Key Largo, FL KWA Media.

Way, M. (2005). Lean Thinking for Knowledge Work. *Quality Progress 38*(6), 27–32.

Welch, J., & Welch S. (2005). *Winning.* New York: HarperCollins Publishing.

Wheat, B., Mills, C., & Carnell, M. (2003). *Leaning into Six Sigma.* New York: McGraw-Hill.

Womack, J. P., Jones, D. T., & Roos, D. (1991). *The Machine That Changed the World.* New York: Harper Perennial.

Womack, J. P., & Jones, D. T. (2003). *Lean Thinking.* New York: Free Press.

Womack, J. P., & Jones, D. T. (2005). *Lean Solutions.* New York: Free Press.

Yang, K., & EI-Haik, B. S. (2003). *The Six Sigma Handbook.* New York: McGraw-Hill.

Glossary

A

analysis of variance—A way of presenting the calculations for the significance of a particular factor's effect, especially for data in which the influence of several factors is being considered simultaneously. Analysis of variance de- composes the sum of squared residuals from the mean into non-negative components attributable to each factor or combination of factor interactions. Usually it is used to distinguish between fixed and random effects. In the case of only random effects, the term *variance components* is often preferred.

assignable cause—A synonym for special cause.

B

bias—The difference between the average or expected value of a distribution and the true value. In metrology, the difference between precision and accuracy is that measures of precision are not affected by bias, whereas accuracy mea- sures degrade as bias increases.

blocking—The practice of partitioning an experiment into subgroups, each of which is restricted in size, time, and/or space. Good experimental design practice has all factors changing within blocks, unit assignment within blocks randomized, and block order and assignment randomized.

box plot—A univariate graphical display of a distribution designed to facilitate the comparison of several groups, especially when each group has a substantial number of observations. Each group is represented by a box; the ends of the box denote the 25th and 75th percentiles; a midline denotes the median. In ad- dition, from the ends of the box outward are two lines drawn to either (a) the largest and smallest values of the distribution or (b) the largest and smallest values that are not considered outliers. By the latter convention, individual val- ues that are considered outliers are plotted as

C

calibration—In metrology, the process or method for comparing actual readings to their known values and of making suitable adjustments so that the agreement between the two is improved.

constraint—In either an experiment or a production process, a limitation in the range of a factor or combination of factors that is either physically not possible or greatly undesirable to execute.

capability—The natural variation of a process due to common causes.

capability index (C_{pk})—A measure of the natural variation of a stable process compared to the closeness of the specification limit(s). When the process is both stable and normally distributed, it is possible to estimate from C_{pk} the fraction of product out of specification. Let LSL denote the lower specification limit and let USL denote the upper specification limit. Let AVG denote the mean or similar typical value of a distribution, and let SIGMA denote an estimate of the total common cause variation. Then C_{pk} is defined as the smaller of [AVG—LSL]/3*SIGMA and [USL—AVG]/3*SIGMA. Sometimes only a lower or only an upper specification is appropriate. For a lower limit, the one-sided capability index, C_{pl}, defined as [AVG— LSL]/ 3*SIGMA, can be used instead. For an upper limit, C_{pu}, is defined as [USL —AVG]/3*SIGMA. Because of their similarity, C_{pk} is sometimes used as a general term to include the cases of both one- and two-sided specifications.

capability study—Any study of the common cause variability of a process.

capable process

1. A process in which there is sufficient tolerance in the specification range that, in principle, one can detect out-of-control situations and take corrective action without placing production material in jeopardy

2. A process for which the capability index C_{pk} exceeds 1.0. (Other criteria for C_{pk} are sometimes promoted. Among these are 1.33, 1.5, and 2.0, but these latter values are usually reserved for the label *manufacturable*.)

cause-and-effect diagram—Also called a CE diagram, an Ishikawa diagram, or a fishbone diagram. First presented by Kaoru Ishikawa, a picture describing the various causes and sources of variation on a particular quality of interest. The quality of interest is usually placed at the right, at the tip of a horizontal arrow. Major categories of causes branch off this main arrow in a manner of the bones of a splayed fish. Other coding conventions draw boxes around cause labels when the influence of a cause is quantified and underline labels when such causes are believed to be important but the effect is not yet quantified.

centerpoint—In an experiment with quantitative factors, the experimental condition corresponding to all factors being set to the midpoint between their high and low values. Centerpoints, which serve to test for the presence of curva ture, give information about quadratic effects. When repeated, centerpoints also provide estimates of the magnitude of the experimental error.

characteristic—A distinguishing feature of a process or its output on which vari- ables or attributes data can be collected. The response of a process.

characterization—Any description of a process or its measurable output that aids in the prediction of its performance.

checklist—A method of data recording, or of data analysis, in which the scale of the measurement is broken into distinct lines. On observing a value that falls in a particular interval, one records a vertical stroke. Each fifth stroke is drawn horizontally across the preceding four.

common cause—A source of natural variation that affects all of the individual values of the process output being studied. Typically, common causes are nu- merous, individually contribute little to the total variation (although the total variation can still be substantial), and are difficult to eliminate.

confidence interval

1. Any statement that an unknown parameter is between two values with a certain probability. For example, if one says that the 95% confidence interval for theta is 1.1 to 10.3, this corresponds to the probability statement that $Pr\{1.1 <= theta <= 10.3\}$.

2. Based on the observation of a certain set of data, the range of plausible values of an unknown parameter that are consistent with observing that data. For example, if one says the 95% confidence interval for theta is 1.1 to 10.3, then this is equivalent to saying that based on the data observed there is a 95% chance that theta is between 1.1 and 10.3.

control—A corrective action based on feedback. *control chart*—A graphical representation of a process characteristic. A time- sequence chart showing plotted values of a statistic or individual measurement, including a central line and one or more statistically derived control limits. Some typical examples of control charts are X-R charts, batch averages ("individuals") control charts, within-wafer range and standard deviation charts, wafer-to-wafer range and standard deviation charts, cumsum charts, exponentially weighted moving average control charts, analysis of means control charts, and cumulative count control charts.

control factor—Especially in an experiment, a factor or process input that is easy to control, has a strong effect on the typical value of a response, and little effect on the magnitude of its variability. Usually distinguished from noise factors.

control group—The set of observations in an experiment or prospective study that do not receive the experimental treatment(s). These observations serve (a) as a comparison point to evaluate the magnitude and significance of each experimental treatment, (b) as a reality check to compare the current observations with previous observation history, and (c) as a source of data for establishing the natural experimental error.

control limits—The maximum allowable variation of a process characteristic due to common causes alone. Variation beyond a control limit is evidence that special causes may be affecting the process. Control limits are calculated from process data.

COPQ—The cost of poor quality.

correlation—A measure of the strength of the (usually linear) relationship between two variables. The usual correlation coefficient, called the Pearson correlation coefficient, ranges from –1 to 1. A value of +1 corresponds to the case where the two variables are related perfectly by an increasing relationship; a value of –1 corresponds to a perfect but decreasing relationship. In the case of the Pearson correlation coefficient, a value of +1 (–1) implies the relationship is linear and increasing (decreasing).

critical parameters or characteristic—A critical parameter is a measurable characteristic of a material, process, equipment, measurement instrument, facility, or product that is directly or indirectly related to the fitness for use of a product, process, or service.

critical to quality—CTQs are the key measurable characteristics of a product or process whose performance standards or specification limits must be met in order to satisfy the customer. They align improvement or design efforts with customer requirements. CTQs represent the product or service characteristics that are defined by the customer (internal or external). They may include the upper and lower specification limits or any other factors related to the product or service. A CTQ usually must be interpreted from a qualitative customer statement to an actionable, quantitative business specification.

customers—Organizations that use the products, information, or services of an operation.

D

data-driven—The property of requiring data and facts, but not requiring subjec- tive opinions. As opposed to opinion-driven.

distribution—A representation of the frequency of occurrence of values of a variable, especially of a response.

dot plot—A form of a histogram for which an observation with a value within a certain range is plotted as a dot a fixed interval above the previous dot in that same range. Useful for small numbers of observations.

defects per unit (DPU)—A measure of how many defects are found per unit.

defects per million (DPM)—A measure similar to PPM indicating defects per million incidents.

E

effect—The change in the average or expected value of a given response due to the change of a given factor. The change of the given factor is usually from the lowest to the highest value of those tried experimentally, and the units of the effect are usually in the same units as the response.

evolutionary operation (*EVOP*)—An EVOP is a special type of online experi ment with several distinguishing features:

1. The experimental material is production material intended to be delivered to customers.
2. In each experimental cycle, the standard production recipe is changed.
3. The experimental factor levels are less extreme than in conventional offline experiments.
4. The experiment is run over a longer term, with more material than in conventional offline experiments.

F

factor—The input variable of a process, and especially of an experiment. Experimental factors are those variables that are deliberately manipulated during the experiment. Experimental factors can be divided further into control factors and noise factors. Control factors are those factors that are easy to control and usually have a strong influence on the response. (A classic example is the time involved for a deposition process.) Noise factors are factors that are either dif- ficult or inconvenient to control. A difficult-to-control noise factor might be the ambient air flow around a furnace tube. An inconvenient-to-control noise factor might be the recent use history of a wet clean sink.

factor level—In experimental design, the value that an input variable or factor takes on.

factor range—In experimental design, and especially for a quantitative factor, the difference between the highest value that the factor takes on and the lowest.

factorial experiment—An experiment in which the values of each factor are used in combination with all the values of all other factors. A fractional experiment takes a judicious subset of all combinations, with the following objectives in mind:

1. The total number of experiments is small.
2. The experimental space is well covered.
3. For subsets of factors (say of size 2, 3, or 4), the total number of experimental combinations is kept large.

focus groups—A method of interviewing people not individually but in small groups. This method is often favored as a preliminary tactic to formal, questionnaire-based surveys. The groups are usually composed to be comparable in some way (income, age, etc.). Disadvantages include small sam- ple sizes relative to the effort expended, potential biases from hearing other respondent views, and a lack of structure for synthesizing results.

G

goodness-of-fit

1. As a fuzzy concept, the opposite of lack of fit.
2. Any measure of how close a probability model reproduces the frequencies of an observed distribution.
3. A measure, such as R-squared, of how close a statistical model predicts observed values.

H

histogram—A graphical display of a statistical distribution; a form of bar chart. One axis (usually x) is the scale of the values observed, the second (usually y) is the frequency that observations occur with (approximately) that value.

I

in control—The opposite of being out of control.
individuals chart

1. A control chart for variables data in which the rational subgroup size is one. A synonym for X chart.
2. The algorithm for a variables data control chart in which the multiple readings of the rational subgroup are reduced to some single number, usually the average, and then limits are calculated as if the rational subgroup size were one.

inspection—The measurement of a characteristic and its comparison to a standard.

interaction—A property of a physical process (or a model describing such a process) wherein the average (or predicted average) change in the response from changing a particular input factor depends on the values of other input factors.

K

kanban—Japanese word for card. The card is the production system's order for more raw materials or parts. A card is a signal to build, how much to build, and when to build.

L

linearity—In metrology, the difference in bias throughout the range of the measured instrument. This definition is best understood if one views the relation between measured result on the y-axis and the true value on the x-axis. Ideal linearity is a line with slope 1.0. (Pure bias would correspond to the intercept = 0.0.) Linearity is a little bit of a misnomer, because it refers to any difference from a line with slope of 1.0, and this can happen both by having a nonlinear relationship and by having a linear relationship with a

M

model—A mathematical statement of the relation(s) among variables. Models can be of two basic types, or have two basic parts: statistical models, which predict a measured quantity, and probability models, which predict the relative frequency of different random outcomes.

muda—Japanese word for friction, describing the waste in processes. It also is synonymous with non-value-add (NVA).

N

noise factor—Especially in an experiment, a factor or process input that can be either difficult or inconvenient to control. Noise factors also include product-use conditions (the temperature, test conditions, environment). Usually distinguished from control factors.

noise-to-signal ratio—The ratio of the measurement system's precision to the average measurement value; the reciprocal of the signal-to-noise ratio.

The noise-to-signal ratio allows one to express the magnitude of measurement precision on a percentage scale.

normal distribution—A symmetric distribution, with one high point or mode, sometimes called the bell curve. The average is one of many statistical calculations that, even for only a moderate amount of data, tend to have a distribution that resembles the normal curve. In industry, there are four important properties of the normal distribution:

1. It is symmetric.
2. Within plus and minus one standard deviation, about 68% of the distribution is enclosed.
3. Within plus and minus two standard deviations, 95%.
4. Within plus and minus three standard deviations, 99.7%.

O

orthogonal array—A table consisting of rows and columns with the property that for any pair of columns (factors) all combinations of values (levels) occur and, further, all combinations occur the same number of times.

outliers—Observations whose value is so extreme that they appear not to be consistent with the rest of the dataset. In a process monitor, outliers indicate that assignable or special causes are present. The deletion of a particular outlier from a data analysis is easiest to justify when such an unusual cause has been identified.

out of control—A process is out of control when a statistic such as an average or a range exceeds control limits or when, although within the control limits, a significant trend or pattern in this statistic emerges. Being out of control defines a time-bounded state, not an intrinsic property of a process. By analogy, at any given time a driver may be involved in an accident (out of control) or not. The intrinsic property of the process is whether the driver is a safe driver (whether the frequency of out-of-control conditions is excessive). Determining the latter, the intrinsic safety (stability), typically requires observation over a sustained period of time.

P

parts per million (PPM)—A measurement of number of defects per million incidents.

Pareto analysis—A problem-solving technique in which all potential problem areas or sources of variation are ranked according to their contribution.

population—The entire set of potential observations (wafers, people, etc.) about whose properties we would like to learn. As opposed to sample.

precision

1. In metrology, the variability of a measurement process around its average value. Precision is usually distinguished from accuracy, the variability of a measurement process around the true value. Precision, in turn, can be decomposed further into short-term variation or repeatability and long-term variation or reproducibility.
2. A fuzzy concept term for the general notion that one knows more or has shorter confidence intervals if one has more data; that is, more data gives greater precision in answers and decisions.

prevention—The class of process monitors and corrective actions taken before production material is placed in jeopardy.

probability plot—A plot designed to assess whether an observed distribution has a shape consistent with a theoretical distribution, especially with the normal distribution. The values observed are plotted against the expected order sta tistics from the theoretical distribution. When a straight line is apparent, the observed and theoretical distributions are said to have the same shape. Prob ability plots are especially good when the observed distribution consists of many observations and for comparing at most only a few groups.

process—A combination of people, procedures, machinery, material, measure- ment equipment, and environmental conditions for specific work activities. A repeatable sequence of activities with measurable inputs and outputs.

process capability study—A study that quantifies the common cause variability of a process. See also capability study.

process potential C_p—A comparison of the voice of the customer (specification band) divided by the voice of the process ($6<$). This would be a theoretical capability of a process meeting the customer requirements/specifications.

R

randomization—Scientific.

1. The assignment of experimental material to treatments and treatment order through the use of random number tables.
2. The selection of observational units through the use of random number tables. Scientific randomization is to be distinguished from arbitrary assignments and selection and from systematic assignments (e.g., wafers 1–12 receive treatment A, 13–24 treatment B).

range—For a given set of observations, the difference between the highest and lowest values.

rational subgroups—Multiple readings taken to monitor a process, including the magnitude of short-term variation. Rational subgroups of size 2 to 6 most common. Well–constituted rational subgroups are the basis of SPC's most sensitive Shewhart charts, the X-bar-R (X-bar-S) chart.

R chart—A control chart that plots ranges. Like S charts, R charts are typically used to monitor process uniformity and measurement precision. Constant sample sizes for the rational subgroups are strongly recommended. When the rational subgroup size is greater than 9, S charts are preferred to R charts for reasons of efficiency.

repeatability—In metrology, the component of measurement precision that is the variability in the short term and that occurs under highly controlled situations (e.g., same metrology instrument, same operator, same setup, or same ambi- ent environment).

reproducibility—In metrology, the total measurement precision, especially in- cluding the components of variability that occur in the long term, occurring from one measurement instrument to another, one laboratory to another, and so on.

residual—The difference between the actual value observed and the predic- tion or fitted value derived from a model. Residuals give information about the model's lack of fit and about experimental error of the measurement process.

resolution

1. In experimental design, especially for two-level designs, the length of the word of the shortest confounding relationship. Geometrically, design resolution corresponds to the 1 plus the strength.

2. In metrology, the number of significant digits of a measurement system that can be meaningfully interpreted.

response—The measured output of a process or experiment. Responses usually depend on the choice of metrology tool. In planning experiments, several re- sponses are usually of interest, and their selection is tied closely to the overall purpose of the study.

response surface model (RSM)—A polynomial model of several factors, es pecially one including terms for linear, quadratic, and second-order cross products.

R-squared—A statistic for a predictive model's lack of fit using the data from which the model was derived.

1. R-squared is a measure of significance in linear equations. The RSquared value ranges from 0 to 1. As this value approaches 1, the indication of significance in correlation becomes stronger.

2. The latter definition is flawed by giving more credit to complicated models than is appropriate. To achieve an average value of zero when the model has no merit, R-squared-adjusted is often proposed.

S

sample

1. The set of observational units (wafers, people, etc.) whose properties our study is to observe. When we select a sample by scientific randomization, we are more easily able to generalize our conclusions to the population of interest. As opposed to population.
2. For a given characteristic, the collection of measurements that are actually observed.

sample size—The number of observations in, or planned to be in, a study or other investigation. Key considerations in selecting a particular sample size are

1. Value associated with any particular level of precision
2. The costs of obtaining observations
3. Available resources

Some generic advice on sample sizes is

1. 16, to estimate the center of a distribution by its average
2. 20, to estimate the correlation between two measurements
3. 32 per group, to estimate average difference between two groups
4. 50, to estimate the standard deviation of a distribution

sampling error—In surveys, the error that results when the selection of respondents (the sample) is biased in a way so that the population about which one wishes to make conclusions is not accurately represented.

scatter plot—A graph of a pair of variables that plots the first variable along the x-axis and the second variable along the y-axis. In a scatter plot, the points of successive pairs are not connected.

S chart—A control chart that plots standard deviations. Like R charts, S charts are typically used to monitor process uniformity and measurement precision. Constant sample sizes for the rational subgroups are strongly recommended. S charts are preferred to R charts for reasons of efficiency regardless of rational subgroup size, but this becomes especially important for sizes greater than 9.

sigma level—A measure of how many standard deviations a random variable is away from the mean. Same as the Z-score.

special cause—A source of variation that is large, intermittent, or unpredictable, affecting only some of the individual values of the process output being stud ied. Also called an assignable cause.

specification limits—The numerical values defining the interval of acceptability for a particular characteristic.

stability—The degree to which observations of a process can be represented by a single random "white noise" distribution, in which the prediction of the next value is not improved by knowing the process history.

stable process—A process that is in a state of statistical control.

standard deviation—A measure of spread or dispersion of a distribution.
It esti- mates the square root of the average squared deviation from the distribution average, sometimes called the root-mean-square. Among all measures of dis- persion, the standard deviation is the most efficient for normally distributed data. Also, unlike the range, it converges to a single value as more data from the distribution is gathered.

standard error—The standard deviation for a statistic's sampling distribution. Because many have sampling distributions that are approximately normal, plus and minus 2 standard errors is usually an approximate 95% confidence interval.

statistic—A value calculated from sample data. *statistical control*—The state of a process that is influenced by common causes
alone. See *in control*.

statistical design of experiments (SDE)—Also called design of experiments (DOE, DOX).

1. The theory of experimental design emphasizing factorial and fractional factorial designs, response surface modeling, and analysis of variance methods.
2. A particular experiment based on this theory.
3. The scientific principles, experimental design strategies, and model building and evaluation techniques that lead to the efficient and thorough characterization and/or optimization of products and processes.

statistical process control (SPC)—The conversion of data to information using statistical techniques to document, correct, and improve process performance.

stratification

1. In SPC sampling, the property by which samples are more systematically broad than would be expected by chance.
2. In surveys, a systematic property of the sample by which one or more demographics have an association with the response.
3. Same property as in 2 except that the property is associated with the sample frame (i.e., population).

survey—A method of data collection that involves asking a fixed set of questions of selected individuals. Key issues involve questionnaire development, (ideally random) sample selection, and nonresponse management.

T

takt—A German word for pulse. Takt time is the rate of production of any activity.

target value—The ideal value of a parameter or characteristic.

theory of constraints (TOC)—A management philosophy developed by Elliyahu M. Goldratt. This methodology uses a five-step approach to constraint management. The constraint is viewed and resolved considering global optimiza- tion of the system.

two-level designs—A category of experimental designs in which the input fac- tors take only two distinct values (two distinct levels).

V

value—Defined in Lean principles with three dimensions: value added (VA), the proportion of the effort that customers pay for; business value added (BVA), the proportion of efforts necessary to maintain an operation's health; and non-value-added (NVA), or waste in the processes.

value stream—The map of the process that identifies every action required to design, order, and make a specific product.

variance components—Estimates of contributions to total common cause varia- tion that are attributable to distinct causal or sampling parameters. One ex- ample is to describe total thickness variation as the sum of contributions from variation in gases, temperature, power, and so forth. Another example is to describe the total variation in an electrical parameter in terms of the sum of contributions from lot-to-lot variation, wafer-to-wafer variation, within wafer variation, and measurement error.

variation—The difference among individual outputs of a process. The causes of variation can be grouped into two major classes: common causes and special causes. The common cause variation can often be decomposed into variance components.

X

X-bar-R chart—Any pair of control charts that plots both the average (the X-bar)and the range of a rational subgroup. By convention, the plot of averages is above the plot of ranges, with the two X-axes denoting rational subgroup sequence order, aligned. See also X-bar-S chart.

X-bar-S chart—A control chart that plots both the average (the X-bar) and the standard deviation of a rational subgroup. X-bar-S charts are completely analogous to X-bar-R charts, except that the role of the ranges has been replaced by standard deviations. As with R charts compared to S charts, X-bar-S charts are more efficient than X-bar-R charts.

X chart—A synonym for an individual's chart.

Y

yield—The number of units that pass some inspection criteria divided by the number submitted.

Index

About the Authors

Dr. Reza (Russ) M. Pirasteh is founder of iTLS-ISO Group®. He has held executive, staff,and line positions and has 40 years of solid experience in implementation of continuous improvement systems in manufacturing and transactional environments. He has earned a Ph.D. in Engineering, an MBA in Industrial Management, a BS in Industrial Engineering, and a PMP (PMI).He is also a Certified Lean Six Sigma Master Black Belt and a Certified Lean Master Sensei. Hehas formulated iTLS™® to fill the gaps among CPI methodologies he has experienced. He Authored the series: *Profitability With No Boundaries: Optimizing TOC, Lean, Six Sigma Results,*and in the same series authored: the *Executive Edition and Leadership Summary.* Reza has published numerous articles and conducted lectures for APICS, IIE, TOCICO, Weber State University, UTA, OSU, and *Industry Week.* He is a member of APICS, ASQ, IIE, and PMI.

Robert E. Fox is a founder of The Goldratt Institute, The TOC Center, Inc., and Viable Vision LLC. He earned an MS in Industrial Administration from Carnegie Mellon and a BS in Engineering from the University of Notre Dame. His has extensive industrial and consulting experience and has served as Vice President of Booz & Co. and President of Tyndale, Inc. He authored *The Race* and *The Theory of Constraints Journal*. In honor of his 50 years ofcontribution to organizational improvement, the Fox Award was established to honor organizationsand individuals who have demonstrated excellence. Steven Covey and Peter Senge have been recipients of a lifetime Fox Award.

Other Books from these authors*:*

1. Profitability with No Boundaries: Optimizing TOC, Lean, Six Sigma Results
2. Profitability with No Boundaries: Optimizing TOC, Lean, Six Sigma Results – TheExecutive Edition and Leadership Summary
3. Profitability with No Boundaries: Optimizing TOC, Lean, Six Sigma Results – theiTLSBOK: Body Of Knowledge – Practitioner Guide
4. Profitability with No Boundaries: Optimizing TOC, Lean, Six Sigma Results – theiTLSBOK: Body Of Knowledge – Practitioner Guide (Third Edition)

www.ingramcontent.com/pod-product-compliance
Lightning Source LLC
Chambersburg PA
CBHW081807200326
41597CB00023B/4172